15—

Library of
Davidson College

# ADMINISTRATION OF LORD ELGIN
IN INDIA, 1894-99

# Administration of Lord Elgin in India, 1894-99

P.L. MALHOTRA

Exclusive Distributor
for USA and CANADA
**Advent Books, Inc.**
141 East 44th Street
New York, NY 10017

**VIKAS PUBLISHING HOUSE PVT LTD**
New Delhi Bombay Bangalore Calcutta Kanpur

VIKAS PUBLISHING HOUSE PVT LTD
5 Ansari Road, New Delhi 110002
Savoy Chambers, 5 Wallace Street, Bombay 400001
10 First Main Road, Gandhi Nagar, Bangalore 560009
8/1-B Chowringhee Lane, Calcutta 700016
80 Canning Road, Kanpur 208004

COPYRIGHT © P.L. MALHOTRA, 1979

ISBN 0 7069 0747 7

1V02M6301

954.03
M249a

81-3592

Printed at Dhawan Printing Works, 26-A Mayapuri, New Delhi 110064

*To the memory of my father Amir Chand Malhotra
and my son Nonu Malhotra*

# CONTENTS

*Preface* ix

*Introduction* xiii

I  The Currency Question   1

II  Cotton Duties   33

III  Railways   68

IV  The Famine of 1896-97   106

V  Plague and Sedition   145

VI  Conclusion   187

*Bibliography* 194

*Index* 211

# CONTENTS

SECTION

I. The Chancery Practitioner

II. Certain Clerks ... ... ... ... ... ... 23

III. Pleaders ... ... ... ... ... ... ... 93

IV. The Canons of 1295-97 ... ... ... ... 105

V. Private Instructors ... ... ... ... ... 119

VI. Conclusion ... ... ... ... ... ... 121

III. Canons ... ... ... ... ... ... ... 131

Index ... ... ... ... ... ... ... ... 145

# PREFACE

This work deals primarily with the economic and political issues of the administration of Lord Elgin II. His period is of immense significance though, unfortunately, relatively neglected. So far, no comprehensive study of Elgin's administration in India has been published, nor has Elgin found a biographer.

The period provided a strong and meaningful link between the Lansdowne administration in India and the Curzonian period, and threw up new, emerging forces in India's economic and political life. It was during this period that the British attitude towards India hardened, politically speaking. This was because England was facing stiff competition on the economic and industrial fronts from the United States and Germany and, consequently, the British dependence on India became more pronounced. This aspect has been fully discussed in this study on the basis of statistical data.

The response to this attitude of the British Indian Government on the part of Indian nationalists like Dadabhai Naoroji, D.E. Wacha and Bal Gangadhar Tilak also showed a shift—they took more articulate and vociferous positions on various important social, economic and political issues.

The problems faced by the administration of Lord Elgin were mainly financial and economic. In 1893, the entire currency system of India was changed, imposing heavy indirect taxes on poor Indian peasants, in order to give financial benefits to the Home Government and to meet expenditure on military expeditions. The Indian Government also imposed duties, including those on cotton goods and, in order to safeguard the Manchester cotton interests, it imposed countervailing excise duties on Indian cotton goods. This gave rise to a serious controversy, and clearly showed how Indian economic interests were being blatantly sacrificed to maintain British imperial interests.

The outbreak of famine and plague added to the economic

problems of the administration. Owing particularly to the drastic anti-plague measures taken by the Government, the social and religious prejudices of the people were roused and this resulted in widespread riots and murders of a few British officials in western India. As a consequence, the government was disposed to regard educated Indians and the press with suspicion and as being largely responsible for creating political troubles. In order to deal with them effectively, the government changed the sedition laws and armed the executive with immense judicial powers, showing how a dexterous executive could manoeuvre things in a direction favourable to its interests.

The period also saw the first trial of Tilak, and with that the emergence of extremist politics in the Indian National Congress, and the first frontal attack launched against "British pride and self complacency." Though Elgin's administration was plagued with immense economic and social problems, Elgin found time to introduce some reforms in the field of railways and formulated a policy for their rapid expansion.

This work is largely based on my Ph.D. research completed at the School of Oriental and African Studies, University of London, in 1966. The book has been long in the making as I could work on it only at intervals, as and when I could take some time off from my heavy administrative and academic duties.

The incitement to publish this work I owe principally to Dr B.N. Pandey, Chairman, Centre of South-Asian Studies, at the London School of Oriental and African Studies, who also supervised my Ph.D. research, to Sir Cyril Philips, former Vice-Chancellor of London University, and to my esteemed friend and mentor, Professor V.V. John. I wish to record that the stimulating atmosphere of scholarship and ideas which pervades at the School of Oriental and African Studies is ideal for creative research work. I am grateful to the British Council for having awarded me a short-term visitorship this year which enabled me to collect fresh materials at the India Office Library and the British Museum. I express my gratitude to the staff of the India Office Library, particularly Martin Moir, for their kind courtesy and helpfulness. My thanks are due to Lord Bruce for granting me the use of papers in the possession of the family. My sincere appreciation is due to Samuel Israel for editing this work and making valuable suggestions. I G.S. Jolly, the Librarian of the

College of Vocational Studies, deserves my sincere thanks in preparing the Index of the book. The task of typing fell to B.L. Bhatia, my Personal Assistant, who showed great diligence and deserves my sincere thanks. A special mention to my two children, Anu and Rishi who suffered my neglect patiently and good-naturedly. I owe a very great debt to my wife, Renu Malhotra, but for whose assistance, inspiration and encouragement, this book would never have been written.

*College of Vocational Studies,*                      P.L. MALHOTRA
*University of Delhi,*
*Delhi*

# INTRODUCTION

Victor Alexander Bruce, Ninth Earl of Elgin and Thirteenth Earl of Kincardine, was the eldest son of James Bruce, the Eigth Earl, by his second wife, Lady Mary Louisa Lambton. He was born on 16 May 1849 at Monklands near Montreal, when his father was the Governor-General of Canada. Alexander Bruce was only fourteen years old when his father, who was then Viceroy of India, died in October 1863 at Dharamsala.[1] This was a grievous loss to young Elgin.[2] After Eton and Balliol, he proceeded to take an active interest in the liberal politics of Scotland. By 1886, he became the chairman of the Scottish Liberal Party.[3] As a supporter of Gladstone at the time of the Home Rule split, he served in the short-lived Liberal Government of 1886, first as the Treasurer of the Household and then as the First Commissioner of Works.[4]

When Gladstone formed his fourth Cabinet in 1892, he had soon to appoint a new Viceroy of India as Lord Lansdowne was due to retire by the end of 1893. The first two choices of the Cabinet were Lord Spencer, the First Lord of the Admiralty, Lord Herschell, the Lord Chancellor. However, both preferred their Cabinet posts.[5] On 9 August 1893, the name of Sir Henry Norman, a Member of the Viceroy's Executive Council from 1870-7 and then the Governor of Queensland, was proposed. His candidature was strongly supported by Arthur Godley, the Permanent Under Secretary of State for India, and other members of the India Council.[6] Lord Elgin's name was suggested by Campbell-Bannerman, Secretary of State for War in Gladstone's Cabinet, and Lord Rosebery.[7] Gladstone and Kimberley, Secretary of State for India, preferred Lord Elgin, but Queen Victoria did not think him well-suited for this important post. She felt he was too reserved and lacked experience.[8] Unfortunately, both Norman and Elgin declined, the former on grounds of own health and the latter due to that of his wife's.[9]

In the meantime, Kimberley decided to ask Lansdowne to continue for another six months or so. By September, the invitation was again extended to both Norman and Elgin. The majority of the Cabinet preferred to send a non-military man and thus the choice fell on Elgin.[10] Lord Rosebery personally persuaded Elgin to accept the call of duty and, in October 1893, Elgin accepted the appointment.[11]

There appeared to be some misunderstanding regarding Elgin's initial refusal and his subsequent acceptance. He did not refuse, as is alleged by some, on account of his own modest estimate of himself. Nor was he offered the Viceroyalty merely because his father once occupied that coveted office.[12] James Robert Rose,[13] biographer of Lord Rosebery, quotes his letter to Queen Victoria out of context, in which he maligns Elgin as an unfit and unaspiring man. Actually, the letter in question, written by Rosebery to the Queen, makes no reference to Elgin and reads as follows: "Lord Rosebery knows nothing of the new Viceroy Sir Henery Norman who is obviously too old to undertake the post. ... It seems positively sad to Lord Rosebery that more fit and aspiring men should not be found for this splendid position."[14] Elgin had refused Viceroyalty for the first time on account of two reasons. First, he was more keen to remain in England and had set his heart on the Secretaryship for Scotland. His desire for that office was understandable because of his keen interest in the Scottish Liberal Party. Though Rosebery knew about Elgin's preference, it was not possible at that time to offer that post to him. Secondly, Elgin was worried about his wife's indifferent health[15] and about the education of his ten children. His mother too was sick and ageing.[16] It was only after a good deal of persuasion by Rosebery that he finally accepted the appointment.

Elgin had no experience in practical politics but in his political thinking Elgin was a *Whig* and in his economic thinking he was a firm believer in free trade and private enterprise. He was guided by these principles in the formulation of major policies.

It is gratifying that there have recently been indications that the neglect by historians of the period of Elgin's Viceroyalty is coming to an end. L. Harris[17] has devoted a good deal of attention to British activities on the North Western Frontier, the Chitral expedition of 1895 and the Tribal rising of 1897. These aspects of Elgin's administration have therefore been deliberately omitted from the scope of this study, which deals essentially with his internal administration, with special reference to economic and political policies. Although some other scholars[18] have studies certain aspects of these policies, a systematic and interpretative study has not so far been attempted.

The most pressing problem faced by Elgin on his assuming office was financial. The budgets of the Government of India had been showing continuous deficits since 1892. The gold liabilities of the Government, like "home charges," had been increasing since the 1870s because of the fall in the value of the rupee. For example, in 1871, the exchange value of the rupee was 2s.; in 1892, it was 14d. The fall in the gold value of the rupee also discouraged foreign investment in the country and caused dislocation in India's foreign trade. In an attempt to meet this situation, the Government decided in June 1893 to abandon the automatic silver standard. To achieve the desired financial benefit, the Government fixed an artificial rate of exchange at 1s. 4d. to a rupee, which was much above the market rate current at that time. It was planned that, when the ratio of 1s. 4d. was achieved after contracting the supply of currency, India would be placed on the gold standard. As was to be expected, this drastic change had an adverse effect on the economic condition of the common people.

Growth of population and trade generally necessitates an increase in the volume of currency, and when this is not forthcoming, business and trade starve. A sound currency is the economic life-blood of a country. Over-circulation of currency in the market is as bad as its relative shortage. Similarly, the currency must adequately serve the requirements of both internal trade and other economic activities as well as foreign trade. Did the Government consider all these questions while announcing the change, or was the Government motivated only by narrow considerations of improving only its own financial condition? Was the closure of mints and the fixing of so high an exchange ratio the only means left to the Government to overcome its financial difficulties? Did the Government realise its objective and how did it react to the adverse impact of the steps it took? These are some questions which would obviously arise when dealing with complicated problems of monetary policy. As the impact of the change was manifested fully during Elgin's administration, the circumstances under which the change in India's currency system was undertaken by his predecessor have been treated as an essential part of this work.

Elgin, on his arrival in India, found himself face to face with an experimental and controversial currency system and a considerable financial deficit. Throughout his viceroyalty, the Indian Government was faced with one or another form of financial and curreney crisis. The period also witnessed a great deal of debate and even clashes with the Home Government on the question of introducing the gold standard.

Another problem faced by Elgin concerned cotton duties. There was a budget deficit of Rs 35 million in 1894-95. The only avenue open for raising the revenue was the imposition of import duties, including those on the cotton goods which accounted for nearly half of the total import trade. The question arose as to whether the imposition of import duty would be against the principles of free trade. If the financial situation was serious and imposition of duty on the cotton goods was essential, what possible steps could be taken to safeguard Manchester's interests? Would the imposition be against the imperial tariff policy which had been inaugurated during the Salisbury-Lytton period? Was there any real threat to British economic interests from the growing Indian textile industry? Could the imposition of a countervailing excise on Indian cloth satisfy the Home interests? And would the imposition of an excise on Indian made goods be justified, taking into consideration the general economic and political attitude of the British towards India? Such were the questions involved in the cotton duty controversy which had a profound impact on the Indian administration in general and on Elgin in particular.

In 1896, a very widespread famine broke out in India. The Government was called upon to put into practice the famine policy (formulated by 1880) of providing effective relief to the starving millions. Government had also to decide how best to meet the food needs of the public. Should Government intervene and regulate the supply of food or leave it in the hands of the private trade? What should the general strategy be to meet the challenge of famine?

To make matters worse, an epidemic plague broke out, compelling the Government to take certain stern measures which caused widespread resentment. Famine and plague coming together created an extremely difficult situation and led to extensive social and political unrest and upheavals. The Government responded to the public criticism in a negative way and amended the Indian Penal Code and the Criminal Procedure Code to restrict "dangerous and seditious" utterances of the public and the press.

Thus, Elgin was confronted with one problem after another and had no time to initiate reforms, except in the field of railway development, to which he devoted particular attention, both in the formulation of policy and railway organisation. Elgin realised that, for the economic development of the country, it was most essential to open up as much of the interior as possible. Unfortunately, on account of the falling rate of exchange, the Government failed to attract foreign investors who demanded firm guarantees that the value of their investments and their returns would be protected. Elgin recognised the need for providing such guarantees and reformed the railway administration in such a way that would lead to its rapid expansion.

These were the main economic, social and political problems which absorbed the attention of Lord Elgin from January 1894 to January 1899.

## NOTES

[1] There are two excellent biographies of the Eigth Earl of Elgin: Theodore Walrond, *Life of Earl of Elgin*, London, 1872 and J.L. Morrison, *The Eigth Earl of Eigin*, London, 1928.

[2] There are several very personal letters in the family collections which reflect the immense loss to the family at Lord Elgin's death.

[3] See James G. Kellas, "The Liberal Party in Scotland 1876-1895," *Scottish Historical Review*, vol. XLIV, no. 137, April 1965, pp. 1-17.

[4] *Dictionary of National Biography, 1912-1921*, London, 1927, p. 72.

[5] Kimberley to Gladstone, 2 August 1893, Gladstone Papers, Add. MSS. 44229, Fol. 142.

[6] Kimberley to Gladstone, 9 August 1893, *ibid*.

[7] Kimberley to Gladstone, 11 August 1893, *ibid*.

[8] Queen Victoria to Gladstone, 12 August 1893, George Earl Buckle, *The Letters of Queen Victoria, 1891-1895*, vol. II, London, 1931, p. 300.

⁹Algernon West, *Private Diaries*, London, 1922, entry of 28 August 1893, p. 192.
¹⁰Kimberley to Gladstone, 21 September 1893, Add. MSS. 44229, Fol. 159ff.
¹¹Rosebery to Gladstone, 2 October 1893, Gladstone Papers, Add. MSS. 44290, Fol. 190.
¹²S. Gopal, *British Policy in India*, p. 180.
¹³*Rosebery*, London, 1963, p. 290n.
¹⁴Rosebery to Queen Victoria, 4 September 1893, Letters of Queen Victoria, *op. cit.*, p. 309.
¹⁵Ripon to Gladstone, 16 August 1893, Gladstone Papers, Add. MSS. 43526, Fol. 161.
¹⁶Elgin's attachment to and concern about his mother is lucidly expressed in this letter of Elgin to his mother dated 9 October 1893: "Need I say that in the step, if we must take it, I see plainly enough that the call on you is the most severe of all. But once again you know me by your example how duty is to be faced—bravely, without a murmur or thought of self—and nothing could bring back to me remembrance (if that were needful) the example of my father's life more forcibly than the way in which you are sending me forth—encouraging me to believe that you consider me to be following the course he would have chosen." Family Papers.
¹⁷L. Harris, *British Policy on the North West Frontier, 1889-1901*, Ph.D. thesis, London University, 1960.
¹⁸H.L. Singh, *Problems and Policies of the British in India, 1885-1898*, Bombay, 1963. S. Gopal, *British Policy in India, 1858-1905*, Cambridge, 1965. J.R. Mclane, *Indian Nationalism and the Early Congress*, Princeton, 1977.

CHAPTER I

# THE CURRENCY QUESTION

On 26 June 1893, with a view to introducing the gold standard in India, Lord Lansdowne's administration discontinued the free coinage of silver in Indian mints. This marked the beginning of a radical change in Indian currency policy. It also sparked off a controversy, the brunt of which was borne by the administration of Lord Elgin. There was hardly any branch of administration which was not affected by the change. To fully appreciate its consequence, a study of the background and the reasons that induced the Government to abandon the free and automatic standard is essential.

It was the East India Company which made the first British attempt to introduce into India both gold and silver coins with a definite legal ratio, weight and fineness. Immediately before that, there existed in India 994 coins of varying weight and fineness.[1] But the real currency policy of British India was not laid down till 1835. Act XVII of 1835 declared one uniform silver rupee as the standard coin for the whole of British India. During 1835-93, the period of open mints, the value of the rupee was natural, and was determined by the market price of silver. The value of the rupee against gold or commodities was, therefore, equal to the value of the silver contained in it. The expansion and contraction of rupee circulation was perfectly automatic and was regulated by the conditions of trade and commerce, internal as well as external.

In 1873, a change took place in the relationship between silver and gold. The gold price of silver, which had till then remained stationary, began to fall. India's exchange relationship with gold standard countries naturally followed the market price of silver in terms of gold. The rupee, which was freely mintable in exchange for silver, began to depreciate in relation to the currency of Great Britain. While in 1880, the Indian rupee was worth 20.3/8d, it exchanged for 14.5/8d in 1892.[2]

The rapid exchange fluctuations of this period evoked serious criticism in several quarters. The adverse effects were felt most by the Government of India, which had the largest sterling liabilities in terms of "Home Charges." The position was all the more embarrassing since the Government collected its revenue in silver and, with the decline of the gold value of silver, the obligations of the Indian Government, in terms of silver rupees, increased. For example, in 1894-5, the sterling value of the Home Charges was £15,770,533. The rupee equivalent actually paid by the Indian Government was Rupees 28.9 crores, while at the rate prevailing in 1872-3, it would have been only Rupees 16.6 crores. The gap could be imagined by the fact that the difference, Rupees 12.3 crores, was more than half the amount of the net land revenue collected that year.[3] The total loss on account of exchange fluctuations during 1875-98 was about Rupees 154 crores, an average of Rupees 6.4 crores per year.[4] Besides the loss to the Government, exchange vagaries had made it almost impossible to draw up reasonably accurate budget estimates. Commenting on these uncertainties, David Barbour, Finance Member in Lansdowne's Council, aptly stated that a fall in the exchange rate by a penny might increase the deficit by more than Rupees 3 crores and a rise by a penny might produce a surplus. The Indian budget had become a "gamble in exchange."[5]

The destabilisation of the exchange rate was also affecting India's foreign trade adversely. Those engaged in trade between India and the United Kingdom or other gold standard countries, complained that fluctuations in exchange rates were transforming legitimate foreign trade into sheer speculation and even a gamble. The mercantile classes, particularly importers, argued that the falling exchange value of the rupee depressed the import trade, in as much as it increased the price in rupees of goods imported from the gold standard countries. They further pointed out that it conferred an unfair advantage on the exporter from India in as much as it enabled him to receive a higher silver price in respect of the same gold price.[6]

British officials in India also protested against the falling rate of exchange. Every fall in the sterling value of the rupee imposed a burden on them since while their incomes were in silver (rupees), part of their expenditure was in gold (sterling).

It was also pointed out that the instability and fall in the exchange value of the rupee would retard the rate of investment of British capital in India. India stood to lose because she would have to pay a higher price for imported capital; British investors would lose because India would not, at this high rate, take as much capital as she otherwise would have.[7] This, it was maintained, was hindering the extension of the railway system in India. Lord Lansdowne was of the opinion that the only way to financial solvency for the Government lay in closing the mints.[8]

This view of the Indian Government was supported by the newly founded Indian Currency Association, (which represented the interests of importers) led by J.L. Mackay (later Lord Inchcape), a then leading British commercial figure in India. In addition, the whole of the European official community, obviously because of their self-interest, supported the move. The Indian Government and the mercantile group were primarily interested in obtaining international agreement to check exchange fluctuations by fixing the price ratio between gold and silver. Failing this they urged that India should adopt the gold standard.[9]

In 1892, at the initiative of the Indian government, the British government accepted an invitation from the U S. Government to attend the International Monetary Conference to be held in Brussels that year.[10] The purpose of the Conference was to secure the introduction of a system of international bimetallism. But the failure of the Conference seemed inevitable from the very beginning; England, the largest trading country, refused to adopt the system of double legal tender in spite of the fact that this would have suited her varied imperial interests. The final blow to bimetallism was struck by Kimberley, Secretary of State for India, in September 1892, when he categorically stated that it had been a mistake on the part of the previous Conservative government to have agreed to participate in the Brussels Conference.[11]

Anticipating the failure of the Brussels Conference, Lansdowne asked David Barbour to prepare a scheme for the introduction of the gold standard in India. It was clear to Lansdowne that no political party in Britain would readily agree to place India on the gold standard to India in view of the guarded opposition of Lombard Street (which represented the gold assets of England) to any such scheme, as the gold interests in England were fearful of losing their gold to India. They believed that if the Indian mints were closed and the gold standard introduced in India, their gold would be attracted to and accumulate in India. The result could be an "appreciation in the value of gold" and hence a lowering of prices in England where manufacturers were already suffering because of low prices.[12]

But Lansdowne argued desperately that the Government of India was going bankrupt, that Indian commerce was intolerably dislocated, and that there was no means of raising further revenues without arousing public indignation, other than closing the mints, contracting the currency and ultimately introducing the gold standard in India. In suggesting this, the Viceroy claimed the popular support of the public and complete unanimity in his executive council. Why it was argued, if the gold standard was good for England and Europe, it would not be good for India?[13]

The scheme of the Indian Government was set out by David Barbour in his famous Minute of 21 June 1892.[14] He recommended that, as a preliminary to the introduction of the gold standard, mints be closed to the free coinage of silver, rupee currency be reduced and gold coins be made legal tender at a fixed ratio. On 30 September 1892, Kimberley agreed to appoint a Committee under the Chairmanship of Lord Herschell, the Lord Chancellor, to investigate the Indian currency question.

With a few modifications, the Herschell Committee accepted, in principle, the main plea of the Indian Government. It recommended that the closure of the mints should be accompanied by an announcement that "though closed to the public, they will be used by the Government for the coinage of rupees in exchange for gold at a ratio to be then fixed, say 1s. 4d. per rupee; and that at the Government treasuries gold will be received in satisfaction of public dues at the same ratio."[15]

The major recommendation of the Herschell Committee was that money issued by private bankers against the silver standard be banned and that the issue of currency should be a Government monopoly. The value of the rupee was to be completely divorced from its silver content and enhanced by reducing the quantity of money in circulation. The rupee was to lose its natural value and acquire an artificial value. The purchasing power of the rupee would thus increase and prices would fall.

On 26 June 1893, an Act was passed as an emergency measure

## The Currency Question

putting these proposals into effect. Three separate notifications were also issued to the effect that gold coins and gold bullion were to be received at the mints in exchange for rupees at the rate of 7.53344 grains troy of fine gold for one rupee; and that sovereigns and half sovereigns were to be received in payment of "public dues" at Rupees 15 and Rupees 7-8 annas respectively. The notifications also provided for the issue of currency notes in exchange for gold coins or bullion at the same rate till "further notice."[16]

To appreciate fully, the implications of the change and its impact on the administration, it is necessary to examine certain factors which then were not publicly discussed.

One of these factors related to the decline in the price of silver. Though the silver standard was given up, it was nowhere stated that the price of silver had fallen more than the price of the gold had risen. On the contrary, in all Government despatches and private correspondence, the words "decline in the price of silver" was conspicuously absent.[17] On examining the Herschell Committee Report thoroughly, one is struck by the obvious and deliberate avoidance of the expression, "depreciation of silver." It occurs only once, in paragraph 134. In a separate note, L. Courtney (one of the members of 1893 Currency Committee), points out that the Commissioners had not examined the preliminary question whether there was a rise in the price of gold or a fall in that of silver. But he was himself of the opinion that the divergence between gold and silver had been "to a large extent due to an appreciation of gold."[18] Yet the Herschell Committee tacitly assumed that a fall existed and thereby adopted a scheme for contraction of the currency. It may, therefore, be assumed that the silver standard was given up, not because it had failed to serve as a standard of value, or was redundant or stringent, but because of the inconveniences it caused to Government and importers. Commenting on the Indian Government scheme, Kimberley aptly remarked:

> Every interest must be affected more or less, and, apart from hardship of the civil servants, and embarrassment caused to your finances, it is not shown that the population as a whole is injured by the fall in the silver.... I quite admit the force of your argument that stability would be a great gain, but this

does not cover the whole ground.[19]

Another factor relates to the exchange ratio. By suggesting 1s. 4d. as an exchange ratio, the Herschell Committee decisively enlarged the gap between silver bullion and the rupee. If the purpose of the Commission was to check exchange fluctuations, it was not essential to fix the ratio above the existing market rate which at that time was 14d. From the private correspondence of Lansdowne we can infer the difference between what the Government intended and what it actually accomplished. Lansdowne had said, "If we were to close the mints to the free coinage of silver, and to endeavour to fix the value of the rupee in terms of gold, we should, I have no doubt, have to fix it somewhere near its present gold value." He had added, "If it would be steadied, even at a low rate, we should know where we were, and be able to get along, while capitalists would not be discouraged, as they now are, from investing their money in Indian enterprises."[20] In another letter, Lansdowne sounded more positive and stated that he was not in favour of raising the gold value of the rupee. He said that "the rate adopted should, in the first instance, approximate to that obtaining at the time of the change. It has always seemed to me, that what we suffered from was, not a low rate of exchange, but an uncertain rate. . . ."[21] Kimberley was also of the same opinion and he inclined to agree with the observations of Currie, a member of the Currency Committee, that mints should first have been closed and the ratio fixed sometime later.[22] Even the Manchester Chamber of Commerce considered 1s. 4d. to be too high a rate.

A third aspect that was not discussed at the time was the fact that the currency changes were undertaken primarily to disguise an increase in direct and indirect taxation. The whole purpose of the exercise was to evolve a system of raising taxation without letting this be known. More than once, reference to this fact was made in Lansdowne's private correspondence. He repeatedly threatened that, if the mints were not closed, recourse to additional taxation would have to be taken; implying thereby that a closure of the mints and the raising of the artificial value of the rupee would be equivalent to an increase in taxation.[23] When the ratio of 1s. 4d. was announced, Lansdowne remarked that this would save the Government from resorting to additional taxation.[24] A little later the Indian Government in their despatch alluded to this very point and stated that the 1s. 4d. ratio was selected because "it was considered that a lower rate would not relieve the Government from its financial difficulties."[25] As early as August 1892, Kimberley had written to Lansdowne that the proposal to fix so high a ratio might reduce the burden of home charges and could be a source of benefit to persons who remitted money from India to discharge their gold obligations and debts, but the "amount of charge so avoided will have to be borne by some other persons (the mass of the Indian people)."[26]

Not many Indians understood the intricacies of these currency problems and the Indian Government was not keen to examine the real significance in the light of the socio-economic habits of the people. Both Cross and Kimberley had repeatedly asked the Indian Government about the impact of their scheme on the Indians, but this particular aspect was discreetly ignored for a long time. Ultimately, at the insistence of Kimberley, Lansdowne yielded and wrote a very revealing letter stating:

> Native mind is always a somewhat obscure factor in any circulation. I should be inclined to answer that in all probability the great mass of the Natives will know very little, or, at all events, care very little, about the change. It would probably never occur to the owners of the uncoined silver in the shape of ornaments, etc. that their bangles and necklaces had become less valuable than they were. . . . The owners of the coined silver will of course, if anything, gain by the change, should it lead to a fall in prices. As for the producers of the commodities and earners of wages, they ought no doubt, if the question is regarded from a strictly economical standpoint, to be losers, because a rise in gold value of the rupee ought, properly speaking, to diminish their receipt.[27]

To rationalise his point, Lansdowne further added in the same letter that "the people of this country (India) are so used to fluctuations of prices, that it will be impossible for them to distinguish between a fall of prices due to alteration in the standard of value, and a fall of prices due to an abundant harvest, or to diminished exportation." It is quite clear that Government intended to take and took advantage of the ignorance and the illiteracy of the people.

Yet, on the other hand, the Government of Lansdowne, under the pressure of military and civil officials, committed themselves to increase expenditure far beyond available resources. They agreed, for example, to increase military expenditure for the year 1893-4 and granted Exchange Compensation Allowance to civil and military officials at a privileged rate of 1s. 6d. to a rupee. Objections to such policies were raised both within the Viceroy's Executive Council and outside. David Barbour, in his confidential minute, very forcefully protested against the allocation of Rs 5,450,000 more than that of the previous year. He was equally assertive concerning the grant of Rs 1,100,000 as compensation of the officers and to the increase in the already existing deficit from Rs 1,600,000 to Rs 2,700,000.[28] David Barbour frankly admitted that the immediate cause for the financial difficulties might be a fall in the exchange rate of the rupee, "but there are contributory causes, increased military expenditure of all kinds, the annexation of Upper Burma, a decline in the revenue of opium, and additional expenditure in connection with the North Western and Eastern frontier." He insisted that military expenditure be reduced and concessions to European officials be postponed. Strangely, the Herschell Committee had avoided discussing this question. The financial difficulties of the Government were thus not due to the currency problem alone but also to certain extravagant expenditure.

It was, therefore, natural that the Act of 1893 was not well received by the Indian National Congress.[29] Dadabhai Naoroji condemned it as "dishonourable";[30] R.C. Dutt very strongly deprecated the idea of "artificial currency"; and D.E. Wacha, who was the most ardent of the Congress spokesman on currency problems, vigorously criticised it as "indirect taxation of burdensome and indefinite character," which according to him meant that Government officials and usurers would "fatten" at the expense of the poor peasants.[31]

The Indian Press was almost as unanimous in protesting against the 1893 Act as the Indian National Congress. It asserted that the currency legislation would act as a deterrent to both the agriculturists and the manufacturers. The *Mahratha* of 2 July 1893, wrote: "He (the peasant) will get fewer rupees for the produce of his field, while he will have to pay the same number of rupees for assessment." The Act was variously described as "mischievous," "hasty," and likely to breed discontent. On his arrival, Elgin found for himself that Indian public opinion, "with a reasonable unanimity," was opposed to the currency policy.[32] He confessed to the new Secretary of State, Fowler, that his main interest was completely "swallowed up in the matters of finance."[33]

The immediate impact of the change was a sudden rise in the sterling/rupee exchange rate. On 27 June 1893, it touched 1s. 4d. This sudden rise completely paralysed the export trade for some time. Importers made rapid gains and imports into India rose by 18 per cent, while the export of cotton yarns declined by 23 per cent. The revenue from opium fell by 13.2 per cent. J.E. O'Conor, then Director General of Statistics and Trade to the Indian Government, attributed the decline of the export trade to the closure of the mints.[34] The rise in the exchange rate being speculative, it did not continue for long and soon there was a setback. By December 1893, the exchange rate fell to $15\frac{1}{3}$d. and by April 1894 it further declined to 13d. In January 1895 it slumped to $12\frac{13}{32}$.

In this period of renewed uncertainties, two interacting factors played a significant role. First, in order to raise the level of exchange, the Indian Government asked the Secretary of State for India never to sell his council bills below the minimum rate of 16d. to a rupee. It was through the sale of council bills that the surplus of exports was transferred into credit for India. When an importer in Europe wanted repee to be paid for his imports from India, he paid sterling to the Secretary of State in London for council bills. These bills were presented at a Government treasury in India, were the holder received rupees drawn from Indian revenues in exchange. It was thus that the Secretary of State obtained most of the money required to pay the "home charges."[35] By banning the sale of bills at rates below 16d. to the rupee, the Government hoped to check the downward trend in the market rate of exchange. In other words, the restriction was expected to lead to a contraction in the supply of money. The Secretary of State was advised to borrow money in sterling to meet his needs. In August 1893, he actually borrowed £5 million because he could not find buyers for bills at the high rate prescribed.[36]

The sale of council bills (through which exporters got cash in rupees at the Indian treasury) was adversely affected by another unexpected development. Along with the closure of the mints, large scale import of silver bullion took place. In the eight months between July 1893 and February 1894, the import of silver was 41 million standard ounces, as against an average of 28 million ounces for the corresponding eight months of the previous five years.[37] Most of the silver imports were of a speculative nature because the Herschell Committee report had leaked out and some importers knew that the mints were soon to be closed down.[38] The Government was forced to accept the silver which was in transit on or about 26 June 1893 and was obliged to inflate the currency by coining silver to the extent of two crores of rupees.[39] The expansion of the currency not only brought down the exchange rate but the importation of silver bullion far in excess of the usual demand competed with the sale of council bills as a means of paying for imports from India. The import of silver into India enabled the Exchange Banks to obtain rupees in India which, in the absence of these imports, would have had to be acquired through the purchase of council bills. A virtual suspension of sale of council bills for an indefinite period could do immense harm to Indian export trade, because most of it was financed by the sale of such bills. Kimberley was personally averse to the fixation of a minimum rate because it was impractical to fix it at a level that was not justified by market conditions; for no one could compel anyone to buy a bill at a price he did not consider worth his while.[40] He emphasised that the market needed to recover its equanimity which had been completely upset by the currency legislation and urged that the situation should not be aggravated further by resorting to further artificial means like the withholding of council bills.[41] Not being able to tolerate this situation any longer, on 13 February 1894, Kimberley abandoned the "minimum" and sold his council bills freely.[42] As a result it became impossible to force exchange to a level that could not be justified by market conditions.

This action of the Secretary of State was vigorously criticised by the Indian Currency Association, which blamed him for letting the exchange rate fall further by his "arbitrary interference."[43] Kimberley was not prepared to revoke the decision. He firmly maintained that it was wrong in the first place to have fixed the "minimum," because it created a gulf between silver and the demand for council bills, and termed the fixing of the "minimum" as "extremely mischievous" and responsible for much disorganisation of trade.[44] But what is probably more significant is that the controversy between the Secretary of State and the Government of India further enhanced the atmosphere of doubt and distrust which shrouded the currency question.

Throughout 1894, uncertainties concerning the exchange rate persisted and "exchange" continued to be "sick." The fall in exchange rate for sterling against the rupee was not checked in spite of the fact that in nine months £9 million were borrowed by the Secretary of State on account of India.[45] The year 1894 recorded a deficit of Rupees 35 million. It therefore became imperative for the Government to impose additional taxation. Lord Elgin was constrained to impose import duties which brought in Rupees 30 million.[46] The increase in taxation and the contraction of currency was like "burning of the financial candle of the population at both ends."[47] This was hardly an auspicious augury for Elgin to start his career as Viceroy.

By October 1895, the exchange rate began to rise and the money market became stringent. This was caused by various factors. The first and foremost reason was the relative contraction of the currency. Secondly, in the absence of a stable rate of exchange, people and traders remitted their money out of the country with every rise in the exchange rate. Foreign capital, instead of being attracted into India, still stayed out. Thirdly, between November 1895 and March 1896, the money position was further aggravated on account of large sale of council bills. This was to be expected as, during these months, India's export trade was usually most active. The heavy demand for remittance from England to India (that is for council bill) naturally affected the Government cash balances which were already in full use for famine relief and extension of railways. It was the mercantile community which needed more money in circulation. There was unfortunately now no automatic means by which the currency could expand in response to the demands of trade.

The stringency of the money market was evinced by the steady rise in the bank rate which rose from 3 per cent in October to 8 per cent in November and nearly 10 per cent in December 1896.[48] Elgin warned Hamilton that there was a definite deficiency in the provision of money in India and a commercial crisis seemed imminent. At this stage the mercantile community which had long been seeking to secure stability of exchange grew restive and demanded immediate relief.[49]

Elgin's administration responded to the crisis in a positive way. The Indian Government realised that the root cause of the trouble lay in the high exchange ratio of 1s. 4d. to a rupee. As a first step towards easing the tension, they proposed to the Secretary of State, on the recommendation of Westland, the Finance Member, to revise the exchange ratio from 16d. to 15d., a rate at which sovereigns could be received in Government Treasuries. Westland believed that ordinary trade would settle at a lower rate earlier. He considered the 1s. 4d. rate too high and injurious to the interests of trade and commerce.[50]

The Government thought that a low sterling: rupee ratio of exchange would remove the element of uncertainty once and for all and would benefit both the traders and the Government. The Government expected that the excess remittances which would be made from England to India would come out in the shape of sovereigns of gold. They would be presented to the Indian treasury, like council bills, in exchange for rupees. So long as the conditions of excess trade demand for remittance from Europe remained in force, gold would continue to come out to India at the rate of 1s. 3d.[51] This could prove conducive to the establishment of the gold standard in India.

Another proposal to help ease the monetary stringency was made by J. Finlay, Finance Secretary to the Government of India. He did not agree with the Westland's proposal to change the gold point, for he believed that it would cast doubt on the Indian Government's adherence to its earlier proposals. Instead, he suggested, that if an emergency arose, the Secretary of State should buy silver and ship it to India where the Government would coin it on its own account and issue it as rupees.[52] However, Lord Elgin, and his executive, preferred the former to the latter course, because, if Finlay's scheme had been accepted, the Government would (in any emergency) have been obliged to open the mints.[53]

The proposal of the Indian Government to issue rupees against gold at 15d. to a rupee was unanimously rejected by the Secretary of State and his Council. It was not considered advisable to interfere with the working of the currency policy as laid down in 1893. The Secretary of State categorically stated that to reduce "your gold point to 15d. is to allow ephemeral causes to obviate the permanent object of your policy."[54] To add strength to his argument, Hamilton informed Elgin that the Chancellor of the Exchequer disapproved of the reduction of the ratio to 15d., particularly when the exchange rate was rising.[55] He finally rejected the Indian scheme with the assertion that he was better placed in London to obtain the advice of financial and economic experts than the Viceroy was in India. Instead, he suggested the utilization of Rupees twenty million from the Currency Reserves.[56]

The Indian Government regretted this decision. As the situation was desperate, Westland agreed to utilize Rupees twenty million from the Currency Reserve through the issue of an ordinance. Finally, the Indian Government dropped the proposal to reduce the gold point. The real reason for this was the threat it posed to the gold interests of England. It was feared that English gold might go out to India. There was a strong group in Lombard Street which was against the introduction of the gold standard in India. Hamilton elucidated the point fully by saying that, if the Bank of England which, to a large extent, regulated the purchase and transmission of gold, found that gold was going out of the country to any appreciable extent "and to relieve your necessities gold must go out in large quantities they (the Bank of England) would raise the rate (of discount) and stop protanto the remission of gold."[57] Finlay, the Finance Secretary to the Government of India, in his note had already forewarned that the Secretary of State would never agree to reduce the ratio. He wrote, "there is almost no prospect that the Secretary of State would accord his sanction to a proposal to lower the rate of 1s. 3d. The object of the proposal and its effect, if successful, would be to attract gold to India. This is not an object which the Secretary of State would be allowed by his colleagues in the Cabinet and his London advisers to advance at a time when the fears of London's financial world already are that gold may be withdrawn from London to a most inconvenient extent."[58]

If the scheme of reduction of the gold point was rejected by the Secretary of State, the scheme to buy silver for coinage in India was rejected by the Indian Government. Westland explained the Government's point of view by saying that, though to buy silver, and coin it, would temporarily relieve money stringency and this would, also be profitable to the Government because of the difference between the value of coined and uncoined silver, such an operation would depress the rate of exchange of the Indian rupee. He believed that any more rupees coined would interfere with the process of gradually raising the exchange value of the rupee. To Westland, the purchase and coinage of silver was harmful and, "from point of view of commerce, it may conceivably come in as a relief, but only as a relief from the consequences of a mistake which it is easy to avoid and far better both for commerce and for ourselves that we should avoid."[59] The primary motive for Westland's suggestion to reduce the gold point was to clear the doubt in the minds of the public regarding the exchange fluctuations and so encourage confidence by a stable exchange.

To sum up, the proposal to reduce the gold point to 1s. 3d. was given up because it did not suit the gold interests of England and the policy of coining more rupees was given up because it was against the established interests of the currency policy of the Indian Government. As usual, business continued to suffer. The bank rate rose still higher. Prices of foodstuffs rose very high and went beyond the reach of the common man. Both Elgin and Hamilton confessed that the soaring of prices was "due to the tightness of money."[60]

In February 1897, the Indian Government made another attempt to take a step towards placing India on the gold standard. It found once again that obstacle to this policy lay in the notification of 26 June 1893, according to which gold coins were to be received by Government treasuries only in payment of sums due to Government.[61] The Indian Government wanted to substitute this by a "free offer" to receive sovereigns and half sovereigns of current weight at their reserve treasuries. By so doing, the Government would provide for a continuous flow of gold into India at a ratio of 16d. to the rupee.

The Government saw no objection to making such an offer. If Government received gold in excess of the amount remitted in sterling towards meeting "Home Charges," there could be, it was contended, other ways of finding relief; like declaring sovereigns and half sovereigns to be legal tender in India. Such a declaration would even avoid any possible embarrassment arising from the Government holding too large a proportion of Government balances in gold, and it would render the gold coin available for Government's ordinary payments. Secondly, the declaration of sovereigns and half sovereigns as legal tender could never harm the public—the creditor or the debtor—as long as Government treasuries were open to receive them at Rupees 15 and Rupees $7\frac{1}{2}$ respectively.[62]

Moreover, the Indian Government felt that such a step would be a step towards the ultimate goal: placing India on the gold standard. "We mention it here only to show that the greater facilities which we propose to give to the importation of gold coin will not produce any result from which we do not ourselves see any issue which is strictly in furtherance of our declared policy." Another advantage urged was that the Exchange Banks could keep spare funds in gold in India (which the Government undertook to accept) and this would prevent sudden scarcity as had happened in earlier years.[63]

Any scheme which was likely to attract gold from England to India (as the purport of this scheme was) could not readily find approval with the British Government. In May 1897, Hamilton put forth two objections against the scheme. First, exchange at 16d. was still not stable and, secondly, government action as suggested would be misconstrued by public as a deliberate measure to raise the exchange rate to 16d., particularly when it was still oscillating around 15d.[64] It may be noted that Hamilton had earlier objected to the Indian Government's proposal of a 15d. ratio under the pretext that 16d. ratio was about to be achieved; now he objected to 16d. because he was not certain that it was going to stay. Behind these objections lay apprehensions concerning the advisability of the gold standard in India.

With no definite solution forthcoming, the financial condition of India deteriorated. Monetary stringency reached breaking point and the measures resorted to solve the currency question did not pass the test of time.[65] The seriousness of the situation was reflected in the Indian Government's failure, in July 1897, to raise a public loan at 3 per cent. Westland asked the Secretary of State to borrow in Sterling on India's account and desperately sought to revise the railway programme by reducing its estimates by Rupees hundred lakhs. He once again suggested reduction of the gold point, this time to $15\frac{1}{2}$d. Another proposal to meet the crisis was made by Babington Smith, Private Secretary to Lord Elgin. He suggested that the Secretary of State should borrow money in London, buy gold and then send that gold out to India. The Indian Government would place that gold in the Currency Reserves and in turn release silver on public demand.[66] This proposal was enthusiastically supported by Westland.

With no concrete counter-proposal to offer, Hamilton agreed to Westland's proposal to curtail railway extension and undertook to raise sterling liabilities to meet the inability of the Indian Government to raise loans.[67] But in no case was he or his council prepared to accept the reduction of the gold point or to send gold to India.

By now it was clear that the British Government was opposed to the introduction of the gold standard in India. At this stage, both France and the United States proposed an agreement on international bimetallism. Hamilton showed great enthusiasm for the proposal and sent it to the Indian Government. It was contemplated that France and the United States would open their mints to the free coinage of silver as well as gold at a legally fixed ratio of $15\frac{1}{2}$ of silver to 1 of gold. This was to be followed by an international agreement. In the meantime, India was to reopen her mints to the free coinage of silver.[68] Arguing on behalf of the proposal the Secretary of State stressed that its implementation would not only enhance the gold value of silver but inaugurate a more stable ratio. The "artificial and arbitrary restriction" of the currency would be removed and would leave the contraction and expansion of the currency to the natural forces of the market.[69]

The Indian Government reacted very swiftly and rejected the offer.[70] In doing so the administration showed a far greater insight into the currency problems than the home government. The rejection was on four counts. First, the adoption of $15\frac{1}{2}$ silver to 1 of gold would involve a sudden rise—say from 15d. a rupee to 23d. a rupee. Such a sudden rise would have a very serious effect on the Indian trade and could "certainly throw some branches of the export trade into the most depressed condition for a time."[71]

Secondly, the Indian Government stated that while, no doubt, the rise in exchange would reduce their sterling liabilities and a large surplus could be derived from the revenue, this would be earned at a very great cost. For instance, the fall in prices would adversely affect the agricultural classes. "It is no doubt pleasant to think of a large surplus of revenue," argued Westland, "which will arise from the enormous improvement in exchange; but that is an extremely narrow and extremely partial view of the result, for any surplus we so obtain is obtained at the cost of a heavy burden to the country and of a disaster to its commerce."[72] Elgin elucidated this point by giving another instance of the evil effects of bimetallism. The shareholders of the East India Railway got a return of $5\frac{1}{2}$ per cent on his capital, but if the exchange rate rose by 6d., the divident of the shareholder would increase by 8 to 10 per cent. This he stated would be an "unearned increment."[73]

Thirdly, in case of failure of the scheme, the whole burden would fall on India alone, because both France and the United States had sufficient gold reserves while India did not possess any. It was affirmed that a mere union of France and the United States, with no participation by England, and India lending only assistance, was a far from international agreement.

Fourthly, it was claimed that circumstances had materially changed since 1893. The exchange rate was stabilizing and Government was nearer the achievement of their aim of 1s. 4d. to the rupee. "If we are let alone," said Elgin, "I do not despair of seeing gold tendered at our treasuries before I leave India."[74] He also forcefully asserted that the time for experiments was over. The mercantile classes in India were no longer prepared to accept further drastic changes. Elgin confessed that there was already artificiality in the currency, but then there was still more of it in Bimetallism and, that in comparison, any risks the Indian Government were now running seemed to him "to sink into insignificance."[75]

Hamilton never expected such antagonism to the bimetallism scheme. He tried hard to influence Elgin by the merits of bimetallism and stressing its popularity in England; by casting doubt on the Indian Government's scheme; and by reiterating that, in India, both prices and the exchange rate had risen—a combination in recent years which was new.[76] He tried to lure Elgin into accepting the scheme by suggesting that if the exchange rate rose to 22d., it would pay for the frontier expeditions and for the military establishments. The rise in the rupee to 22d. "would give us surplus that would not only meet additional expenditure, but enable large remissions of taxation and readjustment of land revenue. I, therefore, do not want to cast away what might prove a veritable sheet anchor in financial reform."[77] It must be said to the credit of Elgin that these dubious arguments were not accepted by him.

In this round of the contest, the Indian Government under Elgin won and Hamilton confessed that the objections raised by the Government against bimetallism were "unanswerable." The cry of bimetallism as a currency system subsided and, accordingly, Lord Salisbury informed the Governments of France and the United States of the inability of the Indian Government to accede to their proposals.[78]

From this, it may be inferred that any currency system having an unnatural basis is harmful to the general public. The contracting currency or imprisoned rupee or an artificial exchange ratio, were all inadequate for the smooth working of the currency system. Whether the artificial ratio was 16d. or 23d., as long as the rupee was widely divorced from bullion, it was injurious to the interests of the people. In this long-drawn controversy, it was at no time asserted, not even once, that the currency policy had appreciably benefited the economic interest of the country.

Unfortunately, just at this time, the Indian Government was seriously involved in a large-scale frontier expedition. In 1897, the Waziris rose in revolt, and the Tochi Valley was occupied by a British force. Then followed the attack of Swat tribes on Malakand, the raids of the Mohmands near Peshawar and the seizure of the Khyber Pass by the Afridis. In a few days, the North Western Frontier was aflame from Tochi to Bunner. The British expedition against the tribes cost the Government nearly 5 crores of rupees.[79] In spite of heavy borrowing on Indian account, the years 1896-7, and 1897-8 showed a total deficit of Rupees 7 crores.[80] The deficit would have been higher but for the rising rate of exchange.

The currency question remained acutely critical. As already mentioned, as an emergency measure, it was proposed to curtail railway expenditure. This measure however could neither solve the financial problem nor end the ambiguity of the currency policy. The Indian Government was convinced that adopting the gold standard was the only way of relieving the pressure. Elgin impressed upon Hamilton that there could be only two ways of achieving the gold standard: (a) to wait till sufficient gold accumulated in the treasury at 16d.; (b) to borrow and buy gold in London and ship it to India. Of the two, Elgin preferred the latter and contended that, as the establishment of the gold standard in India was also a matter of Imperial concern, Great Britain must share the financial burden.[81] Elgin felt encouraged that both Hamilton and Beach, the Chancellor of the Exchequer, were not prepared to consider the proposals of the Indian Government.

The Indian Government's proposals concerning the gold standard were made in two despatches, of 3 and 24 March 1898.[82] The main features of the Government's scheme were: (a) a gold reserve was to be formed in India with the help of a borrowing of £20,000,000 in England; (b) the currency was to be contracted and the rupees withdrawn melted down to raise the exchange value of the rupee; (c) the silver bullion thus obtained was to be sold and gold added to the reserve; and, (d) the Government was not to part with any gold till the exchange rate reached 1s. 4d. to the rupee.

The main purpose of the scheme, irrespective of its merits or demerits, was to end the policy of "inaction"; to give Indian the same monetary standard as that of England (though, through artificial means); and to inculcate confidence in the public in the future of the exchange rate. The administration genuinely wanted to check fluctuations in exchange so as to encourage the inflow of capital into India.[83]

Hamilton could not accept the scheme at its face value. The changes demanded were so far-reaching and so vital to the economy of both India and England that it was considered necessary to submit them to an independent Commission. Hence, in April 1898, the Fowler Commission was appointed to examine the broad monetary policy in India.

It was not possible either for Hamilton or for Elgin to take the outcome for granted. Hamilton took every opportunity to remind Elgin of the beliefs and apprehensions of the British public. On the very receipt of the Indian Government's despatch, he informed Elgin that the opposition had already "guarded and trenched" themselves. The silver monometallists and bimetallists had joined hands much in advance. Hamilton said that he himself doubted the practicability of the scheme on three counts: (a) the Indian Government had taken too sanguine a view regarding the rise and fall of the exchange rate and this could not be regarded as a sure sign for the establishment of the gold standard; (*b*) the method suggested was merely to screw up the rupee, irrespective of the inconvenience it might cause to the trade; (*c*) the introduction of the gold standard on the basis of a borrowing £20,000,000 worth of gold—the greatest weakness of the scheme. Hamilton told Elgin, "Our Lombard Street friends are terribly sensitive upon anything relating to the despatch of gold from this country."[84] Both the banking and the commercial classes in London severely criticised the scheme and showed great concern for their gold interests. The scheme of the Indian Government was termed a doubtful venture —"a demand for gold as might seriously embarrass our own money market" and "materially affect our own country."[85] Lombard Street was determined to check the outflow of gold and was seriously threatening to raise the bank rate.[86] The steps proposed by the Indian Government were considered highly impractical. E.F. Marriot wrote that the scheme involved:

> initial expenditure, an increase in the amount of the sterling debt, and an increase in the weight of the whole burden of the debt due to the increased value of gold, which the demand by India for gold would lead to several years of money scarcity, dear capital, stringent markets, and currency conditions adverse to the increase of commercial enterprise and the general prosperity of the country....[87]

The Indian Government scheme, in India, was being criticised for lacking the element of convertibility. Westland realised that a gold standard scheme without convertibility would be a farce and recommended the same but at a lower rate of $15\frac{1}{2}$d. to a rupee.[88] This alarmed Hamilton and he asked Elgin not to cause any more worries and to drop the scheme of "convertibility." He wrote, "I am afraid that any idea of associating the establishment of a gold standard with the convertibility of the rupee into gold will rather increase than assuage the obstacles we have to overcome."[89] This new proposal was of course dropped.

Into this controversy plunged another group, consisting of both Indian and English men, which recommended the reopening of the Indian mints to the free coinage of silver. They believed that the step taken in 1893 had proved to be a failure and the step now contemplated would be expensive. It was impossible to put forward sound arguments in favour of a restricted currency, a false rupee and a 12 to 13 per cent bank rate, which was, in practice, equivalent to a heavy and indirect tax upon a large proportion of produce and manufactures. *The Times*, in a leading article on Indian affairs, wrote that in 1893, the problem of the Government was how, in spite of a fall in the silver ratio, to artificially enhance the rupee to 1s. 4d. In 1898, the problem of the Indian banking and mercantile bodies was how, with the rupee artificially enhanced to 1s. 4d., to avoid widespread disaster. The Government had succeeded in shifting the burden from its own shoulders to the back of the industrial and trading community, but in so doing had driven capital out of India.[90] The Bombay Chamber of Commerce contended that the contraction of money was mainly due to the closing of the mints and recommended that they be reopened.[91]

It was argued by the protagonists of the silver standard that no one had shown that India's standard coin had been deficient in any of its functions. There was no need to abandon it. The commerce of India would, rather, develop with a plentiful supply of good and cheap money and for this, it was asserted, the monetary standard had to be brought to its natural basis by reopening the mints. "We are at this moment having an unpleasant example of the partial asphyxia of commerce arising from the want of money, and the experience is one we do not wish to see repeated."[92] Dadabhai Naoroji and D.E. Wacha, of the Indian National Congress, criticised the Government for keeping in mind only the interest of foreign trade, while completely ignoring internal trade that required an abundance and not a stringency of currency.[93] The leaders of the Indian National Congress pressed for the reopening of the mints and for letting the rupee go down to its silver bullion price.[94]

Even those responsible for the Government policy, D. Barbour and J. Westland, had agreed at one time or another about the advantages of an expanding currency over a contracting one. As early as 1885, D. Barbour, in his book, *The Theory of Bimetallism*, had written that the "evils which attend a contraction of the currency are much greater than those which follow its expansion."[95] Westland said, "I do not think that anyone alleges that the depreciation of silver which has been going on for 20 or 25 years was in any way a misfortune to Indian commerce. Perhaps it was exactly the opposite."[96]

Some Englishmen, like R. Giffen, once the Assistant Editor of *The Economist*, strongly recommended that India adopt the silver standard, particularly because it suited the economic conditions of the people, their tastes, their habits and their social outlook. To force something unnatural on them would be "injudicious and injurious." The artificial currency, he said, had already penalized the people; hence, he pleaded for the opening of the mints once again.[97]

Neither the Indian Government nor the Secretary of State was prepared to revert to the silver standard. Their main reason was that there was already so much of difference between bullion and the rupee that, by going back to it, the Government would have to impose extra direct taxation. Elgin was particularly keen at this stage to realise a gold standard for India at the earliest. Fearing that the silver standard might get preference at the hands of the Fowler Commission, he took keen personal interest in selecting Indian witnesses, both official and non-official, who could impress upon the commission the need of a gold standard for India.

The Indian Government selected three official witnesses, J. Finlay, the Financial Secretary; O'Conor, Director General of Trade and Statistics; and A.P. MacDonnell, the Lieutenant Governor of North-Western Provinces and Oudh. The selection of the Indian witnesses gave some difficulty to the Government, since the choice was limited to a few who could be depended on to give the right evidence. Hamilton was specially keen that no witness should be chosen from the Indian National Congress—at least not Naoroji.[98] Elgin was keen to have Jay Govind Law, an influential Bangalee trader and a member of the Legislative Council, who had been a supporter of the Government policy; from Bombay, Shapurji Bharucha, another trader who was actively associated with the Indian Currency Association, and Ram Charan Das from Allahabad, who was a trusted friend of A.P. MacDonnell.[99]

The Fowler Committee examined the whole question of currency and came to the conclusion that the only effective currency for India would be one based on the gold standard. They recommended that the gold standard should be based on the principle of "free inflow and outflow" of gold; British sovereigns should be made legal tender and a current coin in India; the Indian mints should be thrown open to the unrestricted coinage of gold but should be closed to the free coinage of silver. The rupee was to continue as an unlimited legal tender and the ratio was to be fixed at 1s. 4d. to a rupee. The Fowler Committee held that a fixed exchange could only be secured and guaranteed by an effective gold standard.[100]

All these recommendations were accepted by the Government. In 1899 an Act was passed by which sovereigns and half sovereigns were made legal tender throughout India at a 1s. 4d. ratio. But, unfortunately, gold mints were never opened in India and ultimately it was not the gold standard but an exchange standard which came to be established in India.[101]

In the assessment of the whole currency question, it may be said that the currency policy and the high exchange ratio proved no doubt beneficial to the Government. But for the rising exchange rate, the deficit would have been greater because of famine and war; and by 1898, the Government could proudly show a surplus, though all through Elgin's period of administration, the Government was concerned about raising resources and met with extreme stringency in the money market. The salaried classes also gained with the rising exchange rate. The grant of the exchange compensation allowance at a still privileged rate of 1s. 6d. to a rupee not only increased the exchange liabilities but came at a most inopportune time, when the financial needs of the country required all possible economy on the part of the Government.

The benefits of the rate of exchange were attained at the cost of a considerable hardship to Indian cultivators and traders. Many critics asserted that the Government had improved its financial condition by merely juggling with the currency. To Dadabhai Naoroji the "closing of the mints and thereby raising the true rupee, worth at present about 11d. in gold, to a false rupee to be worth 16d. in gold, is a covert exaction of about 45 per cent more taxation all round from the Indian tax payers."[102] This allegation was not refuted by MacDonnell who wrote to Elgin after giving his evidence before the Fowler Commission that the 16d. rupee meant additional taxation, "because although the number of the rupees collected as revenue remained the same, each rupee represented more commodities. In the long run the cultivator would have to dispose of more produce to get a sixteen penny rupee. But the taxation was unconsciously paid, while from another point of view, it was only a check on a loss to which Government should not have been subjected." He further added that the taxation of the kind "which a sixteen penny rupee means will be unfelt and unknown except from the agitators."[103]

This attitude of the Government would confirm the view of many national leaders that the handling of the currency question was a political manoeuvere aimed at confusing the ignorant masses while imposing indirect and hidden taxation.[104]

To add fuel to the fire, the depreciation of silver bullion and its greater divorce from the coin caused further hardship to the poor ryot; particularly because the chief savings of the poor were in silver ornaments. During times of scarcity and famine a considerable number of silver ornaments found their way to the mints. Even the Herschell Committee had admitted that during the 1877 famine, nearly Rs 45,000,000 worth of ornaments were turned into rupees.[105] As a part of the social habit, more than half of the yearly additions to the currency before the closing of the mints went into the melting pot for conversion into ornaments or as hoards.[106] MacDonnell and O'Conor both had agreed before the Fowler Commission that a large part of the silver was used as ornament. MacDonnell had himself stated that a quarter of the peasants' savings were in ornaments.[107] It was Gokhale who remarked that the price of silver bullion had gone down even when the prices of the other commodities had not.[108] This must have enhanced the indebtedness of the poor.

Thus, where the Government gained with the rising rate of exchange, the masses lost and, during times of crisis the reserves of the people in silver could not be converted into money except at a very great loss. Merchants were unable to discount their bills except at extreme rates such as 12 to 15 per cent per annum. The resources of the Indian bankers were not available in money and they were unable to utilize their credit in the usual manner by obtaining advances freely from banks.[109]

As regards prices, there was no general fall, except in 1894, 1895 and 1899.[110] During 1893-9, many strange things happened. Whereas the rise in the value of the rupee, as measured by its purchasing power over commodities immediately after the closing of the mints, led to a fall in prices from index number 129 in 1893 to 120 in 1895, there was a fall in the average exchange value of the rupee from nearly 14d. in 1893 to 13d. in 1895. Similarly, in the period of depreciation in the purchasing power of the rupee from 1896 and 1897, the prices rose from 131 in 1896 to 153 in 1897 and, on the other hand, the rupee sterling exchange rate rose from 13d. in 1895 to 14½d. in 1896 and 15d. in 1897.[111] These paradoxes were of course the result of the operation of many other factors. As a matter of fact, the artificial appreciation of the rupee should have brought a general fall in the prices. This assumption was obviously based on the fact that shortage of rupees would enhance its purchasing power and prices would fall. This view was equally shared by the Government. In the first few years after the closing of the mints to the free coinage of silver, this trend was counter-balanced by a succession of famines and scarcities and also by hoarded rupees having come into circulation, and also probably by the rise of gold prices throughout the world during that period which helped to increase prices in India.

The impact of rising exchange rates and high prices on the general public must have been pernicious. It was Naoroji who pragmatically argued that "the real and full effect of the closing of the mints must be examined by itself, irrespective of other factors." He affirmed that the peasants had to pay a higher amount of revenue to the Government as a result of the increase in the gold and silver value of the rupee and this was "altogether independent of whatever the actual price of commodities may be." If the prices did not go down in reality because of the operation of certain other factors, he argued, it only meant that in the absence of currency changes and with the continued operation of these factors, prices would have gone up and that the peasants would have gained to that extent.[112]

The currency legislation also affected the cotton goods trade unfavourably. After the gold value of the rupee increased, the Indian cotton industry no longer possessed its former advantage and lost to China and Japan its competitive initiative, because China remained on the silver standard and Japan fixed a low ratio of exchange between silver and gold, thereby acquiring a price advantage over Indian manufacturers.[113] The decline of the Far Eastern demand for Indian cotton was one of the reasons for a five-year slump after 1890 in the Bombay mills.[114]

In the final analysis, it may be pointed out that in the 1890s, the Government of India was definitely in serious financial difficulties and some solution of the problem was essential. There could be, of course, two opinions about the methods employed. First, for example, as the Indian National Congress argued, instead a "tampering" with the currency, it would have been better to reduce the "Home Charges" and military expenditure.[115] Some others would have preferred a lower ratio as in the case of Japan which had adopted the gold standard in 1898 but had done so at a ratio with silver which was equivalent to 11d. per rupee. In the context of the low ratio, Westland made a very significant remark in an important note which he wrote on 17 October 1896. He said, "It is certainly true that falling exchange had compelled us to resort more than once to increased taxation, but it is certainly also true that falling exchange has had a great deal to do with the continual increasing produce of each of our sources of revenue."[116] In other words, a lower rate would have increased production and thereby compensated the loss in the form of additional revenues.

It is also true that many of the results of the Government's currency policy were obscured and aggravated on account of war, famine and plague. But it is equally and substantially true, as MacDonnell admitted while writing to Elgin, that effects of currency policy and the artificial value of the rupee on rural economy were not properly examined.[117]

Lastly, it was unfortunate that Elgin's period of administration was a period of trial and transition. It also fell to the administration to raise even additional money in the form of import duties and provoke the criticism of the public on account of acute scarcity of money in the market. But Elgin cannot be denied the credit for twice trying to relieve the country of the pressure of stringent money and thereby ease the financial tension and get over the period of transition as rapidly as possible. Unfortunately, British economic interests clashed with those of India.

The following table compiled by the *Department of Statistics*, Government of India, shows the course of prices in India expressed in index numbers (prices in 1873 being equal to 100):

## The Currency Question

TABLE 1

| Year | Exported articles (28) unweighted | Imported articles (11) unweighted | General index number for all 39 articles unweighted | Weight index number (100 articles) equated to 100 for 1873 |
|---|---|---|---|---|
| 1873 | 100 | 100 | 100 | 100 |
| 1883 | 93 | 79 | 89 | 99 |
| 1884 | 96 | 78 | 91 | 108 |
| 1885 | 91 | 75 | 87 | 106 |
| 1886 | 93 | 80 | 89 | 103 |
| 1887 | 94 | 83 | 91 | 104 |
| 1888 | 98 | 92 | 96 | 111 |
| 1889 | 104 | 91 | 101 | 117 |
| 1890 | 104 | 91 | 100 | 117 |
| 1891 | 103 | 84 | 98 | 120 |
| 1892 | 109 | 84 | 102 | 132 |
| 1893 | 112 | 89 | 105 | 129 |
| 1894 | 110 | 84 | 102 | 122 |
| 1895 | 111 | 87 | 104 | 120 |
| 1896 | 117 | 94 | 110 | 131 |
| 1897 | 124 | 86 | 113 | 153 |
| 1898 | 102 | 80 | 96 | 125 |
| 1899 | 100 | 87 | 96 | 121 |
| 1900 | 124 | 96 | 116 | 143 |

### NOTES

[1] H.D. Macleod, *Indian Currency*, London, 1898, p. 13.

[2] *Report of the Indian Currency Committee*, 1893, Parl. Papers, vol. 65, (C. 7060. II), Appendix ii, pp. 252-4. The average price of silver which in 1872-3 was 60. 5/16d. per ounce, went down in 1892-3 to 39 1/16d. H.L. Chablani, *Studies in Indian Currency and Exchange*, London, 1931, pp. 13-14.

[3] *Imperial Gazetteer of India*, Oxford, 1907, vol. iv, p. 195. See also *Report of the Indian Currency Committee*, 1893, op cit., Para 3.

[4] C.N. Vakil and S.K. Muranjan, *Currency and Prices in India*, Bombay, 1927, p. 40.

[5] *Financial Statement*, 1893-4, Paras 28 and 30-1.

[6] Bengal Chamber of Commerce to Indian Govt., 10 February 1892, Enc. to L. No. 60 of 23 March 1893, Financial Enclosures received from India, vol. 174. (Hereafter cited as F.E.I.).

[7] D. Barbour, *Theory of Bimetallism*, London, 1885, p. 70.

[8] *Lansdowne's Speeches in India*, vol. ii, p. 621.

⁹Indian Govt. to S.S., L. No. 68 (fin.), 23 March 1892, Paras 3, 5, 6, Financial Letters received from India, vol. 173. (Hereafter cited as F.L.I.). See Petition, Indian Currency Association to Indian Govt., 13 June 1892, Enc. to L. No. 183 of 1892, F.E.I., vol. 175.

¹⁰S.S. to Indian Govt., Despatch No. 98 (fin.), 2 June 1892, Financial Despatches to India, vol. 39. (Hereafter cited as F.D.I.).

¹¹Kimberley to Lansdowne, 16 September and 13 October 1892, Lansdowne Papers, Mss, Eur. D. 558/ix, vol. iv. (Hereafter cited as L.P.).

¹²Cross to Lansdowne, 1 July 1892, L.P., ix/vol. iv. Also Kimberley to Lansdowne, 17 March 1893, vol. v. See G.F. Shirras, *Indian Finance and Banking*, London, 1919, pp. 104-18.

¹³Indian Govt. to S.S., L. No. 160 (Fin), Confidential, 21 June 1892, Para 7, F.L.I., vol. 173.

¹⁴Enc. to L. No. 160 (Fin.) of 21 June 1892, F.E.I., vol 175.

¹⁵*Report of the Indian Currency Committee*, 1893, *op cit.*, Para 156.

¹⁶India Fin. and Com. (Fin. and Ac.) Proc., Vol. 4392, Nos. 405-7, July 1897.

¹⁷In the two major policy despatches of the Indian Government, Nos. 68 and 160 (Fin.), dated 23 March and 21 June 1892, Paras 6 and 3 respectively, *op cit.*, the words used were "decline in the gold value of the rupee."

¹⁸*L. Courtney's Minute, Report of Indian Currency Committee 1893, op. cit.*, p. 39.

See also Farrer and Welby's Minute, *op. cit.*, p. 42. Taking Sauerbeck's index, we get instructive actual figures. Gold prices fell from an average of 100 in 1867-77 to 68 in 1892, a fall of 32 per cent. The price of silver fell from 58d. in 1867-77 to 39¾d. in 1892, a fall of 31½ per cent. The price of silver, therefore, fell almost exactly with the average price of commodities. In other words, silver remained perfectly stable in value up to 1892 and yet in that year the Indian Government began to vehemently agitate for the overthrow of "this most perfect standard of value." E.F. Marriot, *The Indian Currency Question*, London, 1899 Appendix B, p. 28.

¹⁹Kiberley to Lansdowne, 16 September 1892, L.P., ix/vol. iv.

²⁰Lansdowne to Cross, 26 July 1892, L.P. ix/vol. iv.

²¹Lansdowne to Kimberley, 23 August 1892, and 5 October 1892, *ibid*.

²²Kimberley to Lansdowne, 23 June 1893, L.P., ix/vol. v. See B.W. Currie's Minute, *Report of Indian Currency Committee*, 1893, *op cit.*, p. 42.

²³Lansdowne to Kimberley, 12 October 1892, and 6 February 1893, L.P, ix/vols. iv and v respectively.

²⁴Lansdowne to Kimberley, 20 June 1893, L.P. ix/vol. V. L. Courtney, Member of Parliament and once a member of the Herschell Committee, stated before the Fowler Commission on Currency that the "raising of the rupee above its intrinsic value is a tax not merely on production ... it is an additional tax on the agriculturists and the rent payers." *Report of the Indian Currency Commission*, 1899, Parl. Papers, vol. 33, Minutes of Evidence II, (C. 9222), p. 261, Q. 13, 117.

²⁵Indian Govt. to S.S., L. No. 328 (Fin.) 4 November 1896, Para 18, Finance Departmental Papers of the Council of India, F. 5952/1896, vol. 1384 (Hereafter cited as Fin. Papers).

²⁶S.S. to Indian Govt., Despatch No. 92 (Fin.) 25 August 1892, Para 3, F.D.I., vol. 34 (Original).

²⁷Lansdowne to Kimberley, 5 October 1892, L.P. ix/vol. IV.

²⁸13 March 1893, Para 1, Enc. to Indian Govt. L. No. 99 (Fin.) Confidential, of 1893, F.E.I., vol. 177. See also C. Pritchard's Confidential Minute, 13 March 1893, ibid.

²⁹*Report of Indian National Congress*, 1893, Resolution No. xiv, p. 127.

³⁰*Poverty and Un-British Rule in India*, London, 1901, p. 532.

³¹*Report of the Indian National Congress*, 1893, pp. 127-30.

³²Elgin to Queen Victoria, 21 March 1894. Elgin Papers, MSS. Eur. F. 84, vol. 1. (Hereafter cited as E.P.).

³³Elgin to Fowler, 7 March 1894, ibid., vol. 12.

³⁴*Trade Statement of British India for 1893-4*, Parl. Papers, 1895, vol. 73, (C. 7604), pp. 6-7. See also Statistics from *The Monthly Records of Manchester Chamber of Commerce*, 1894, vol. v, p. 60.

³⁵J.M. Keynes, *Indian Currency and Finance*, London, 1924, pp. 102-3.

³⁶Telegram S.S. to Viceroy, 23 August 1893, Indian Fin. and Com. (Fin. and Ac.) Proc., vol. 4392, No. 851, March 1893.

³⁷G.F. Shirras, *Indian Finance and Banking*, pp. 144-5.

³⁸Kimberley to Lansdowne, 21 July 1893, L.P., ix/vol. v.

³⁹Indian Govt. to S.S., L. No. 307 (Fin.), 20 September 1893, Para 7, F.L.I., vol. 176.

⁴⁰Kimberley to Lansdowne, 18 August 1893, L.P., ix/vol. v.

⁴¹Kimberley to Lansdowne, 25 August and 26 October 1893, ibid.

⁴²Telegram S.S., to Viceroy, India Fin. and Com. (Fin. and Ac.) Proc., vol. 4604, No. 175, March 1894. D. Barbour had this to say regarding the suspension of the bill: "I have no hesitation in saying that all measures that could be adopted in connection with the sale of the bills, the holding of them back in order to force a higher rate of exchange than market conditions justify is the most pernicious." *The Currency Question from an Indian Point of View*, p. 18.

⁴³Vice-President Indian Currency Association to Indian Govt., 5 January 1894, Enc., to L. No. 40 (Fin.) of 1894, F.E.I., vol. 180.

⁴⁴Kimberley to Elgin, 16 February 1894, and 9 March 1894, E.P., vol. 12.

⁴⁵R. Hardie's Minute, 14 April 1894, Fin. Papers, F 1152/94, vol. 1265.

⁴⁶*The Imperial Gazetteer of India*, vol. iv, p. 168.

⁴⁷R. Hardie's Minute, *op. cit.*

Lansdowne had once prophesied that, if the change in the currency system was soon followed by additional taxation or general scarcity, the people would be persuaded that the whole misfortune was caused on account of "tampering with the rupee." Lansdowne to Kimberley, 5 October 1892, L.P., ix/vol. iv.

⁴⁸*Trade Statements of British India for 1896-7*, Parl. Papers, 1898,

vol. 74, (C. 8692), p. 6. Early in 1897 the bank rate reached as high as 12 per cent.
[49] *Annual Report of Bengal Chamber of Commerce,* 1897-8, vol. 1, p. 5.
[50] Indian Govt. to S.S. L. No. 228 (Fin.), 4 November 1896, Paras 11, 17-18, *op, cit.*
[51] Westland's Note on the Council Drawings, 17 October 1896, Para 18, E.P., vol. 135 (r).
[52] J. Finlay's Confidential Note on "Currency Question," 22 October 1896, Para 25, vol. 135 (r).
[53] Elgin to Hamilton, 4 November 1896, *ap. cit*
[54] Hamilton to Elgin, 26 November 1896, *ibid.*, vol. 14.
[55] The rate of exchange during this period had risen to 15 27/32d. But fluctuations persisted.
[56] Hamilton to Elgin, 19 November 1896, E.P., vol. 14.
[57] Hamilton to Elgin, 26 November 1896, *ibid.*
[58] Finlay's Confidential Note, 22 October 1896, Para 27, *op. cit.*
[59] Westland to Elgin, 26 January 1897, E.P., vol. 70.
[60] Elgin to Hamilton, 6 January 1897; Hamilton to Elgin, 12 February 1897, *ibid.*, vol. 15.
[61] Indian Govt. to S.S. L. No 49 (Fin.), 17 February 1897, Para 9, F.L.I., vol. 188.
[62] Para 9, *ibid.*
[63] Para 10, 11, *ibid.*
[64] S.S. to Indian Govt., Despatch No. 96 (Fin.), 13 May 1897, Paras 14-16, F.D.I. vol. 39 (original).
[65] Westland's Memorandum, 4 July 1897, E.P., vol. 71.
[66] Elgin to Hamilton (Confidential), 22 June 1897, Hamilton Collection, MSS Eur. D. 509/vol. v.
[67] Hamilton to Elgin, 24 June 1897 (appendix), 8 July (appendix), and 16 July 1897 (appendix), E.P., vol. 15.
[68] Telegram S.S. to Viceroy, 19 July 1897, *ibid.*, vol. 20.
[69] S.S. to Indian Govt., Despatch No. 129 (Fin.), Confidential, 5 August 1897, Paras 5-6, F.D.I., vol. 39 (Original).
[70] Telegram, Viceroy to S.S., 21 July 1897, E.P., vol. 20.
[71] Finlay's Confidential Note on Currency, 22 July 1897 (appendix), *ibid.*, vol. 71.
See also Indian Govt. to S.S., L. No. 261 (Fin.), Confidential, 16 September 1897, Para 5, F.L I , vol. 188.
[72] Westland's Confidential Note on Currency 22 July 1897 (appendix) E.P., vol. 71.
[73] Elgin to Hamilton, 18 August 1897, *ibid.*, vol. 15.
[74] Elgin to Hamilton, 11 August 1897, *ibid.*
[75] Elgin to Hamilton, 14 October 1897, *ibid.*
[76] Hamilton to Elgin, 1 September 1897, *ibid.*
[77] Hamilton to Elgin, 9 September 1897, *ibid.*

Earlier, Hamilton had shown the same feelings when he wrote, "We corner rupees to the detriment of trade and commerce, but to the benefit of our expenditure." Hamilton to Elgin, 19 August 1897, *ibid.*

[78] Salisbury to French and the United States Govt., 19 October 1897, Enc. to S.S. to Indian Govt., Despatch No. 218 (Fin.) of 1897, F.D.I., vol. 44 (copy).
[79] *Imperial Gazeteer of India*, vol. iv, p. 168.
[80] *Ibid.*
[81] Elgin to Hamilton, 11 November and 24 November 1897 (appendix), *ibid.*, vol. 15.
[82] L. Nos. 70 and 92 (Fin.), F.L.I., vol. 190.
[83] Elgin to Hamilton, 12 May 1898, *ibid.*
[84] Hamilton to Elgin, 25 March 1898, *ibid*, vol. 16.
[85] W. Fowler, *Indian Currency—An Eassy*, London, 1899, pp 27 and 35.
[86] Hamilton to Elgin, 13 May 1898, E.P., vol. 16.
[87] E.F. Marriot, *Indian Currency Question*, London, 1899, p. 18. See also Lord Rothschild's Evidence, *Report of the Indian Currency Commission*, 1898, Minutes of Evidence, vol. 1, Parl. Papers, 1898, vol. 61, (C. 9031), p. 268.
[88] Westland to Elgin, 19 April 1898, E.P., vol. 72.
[89] Hamilton to Elgin, 20 May and 1 June 1898, *ibid.*, vol. 16.
[90] 5 April 1898.
[91] *Report of the Bombay Chamber of Commerce*, 1898, pp. 206-12.
[92] M.D.E. Webb, Letter to the Editor, *Capital*, 6 January 1898, E.P., vol. 80 (Newspaper cuttings).
[93] Naoroji, *Poverty and Un-British Rule in India*, p. 562.
[94] R.C. Dutt, *Speeches and Papers on Indian Questions, 1897-1900*, Calcutta, 1904, pp. 103-4.
[95] P. 13. Also p. 154.
[96] Westland's Confidential Note on Currency, 27 July 1897 (appendix), E.P., vol. 17.
[97] R. Giffen, Letter to the Editor, *The Times*, 10 May 1898. See also, his evidence before the Fowler Commission, *op. cit.*, Qs. 10, 109-10, 113; 10-238—10, 248; 10, 050—10, 059.
[98] Hamilton to Elgin, 30 August 1898, E.P., vol. 16. See also Elgin to Hamilton, 1 September and 8 September 1898, *ibid*. At a later stage, when Elgin was confronted with difficulty in finding the native witnesses, he confessed to Hamilton. "I wish we could help you to keep Naoroji in the background so far as the currency question is concerned." Elgin to Hamilton, 13 October 1898, *ibid*.
[99] Elgin to Woodburn (Lt. Governor, Bengal), 19 August 1898, *ibid.*, vol. 72.
[100] *Report of the Indian Currency Commission*, 1898, Paras 54-55, Paras 59 and 66.
[101] The Gold Exchange Standard has been described by Keynes as "the use of local currency mainly not of gold some degree of unwillingness to supply gold locally in exchange for local currency, but a high degree of willingness to sell foreign exchange for payments in local currency at a certain maximum rate and to use foreign credits in order to do this—the two countries agree." J.M. Keynes, *Indian Currency and Finance*, p. 29.

[102] Dadabhai Naoroji, *Statement submitted to Indian Currency Committee of 1898*, London, 1898, Para 6.
[103] MacDonnell to Elgin, 8 July 1898, E.P., vol. 33. R. Hardie, Member of the Indian Council, had stated the same thing much earlier, "altering the rupee from a free coin to a monopoly coin, very seriously affected the financial obligations arising under all land settlements." Minute, 14 April 1894, Financial Papers, F1189/94, vol. 1265.
[104] See J.A. Wadia, *The Artificial Currency*, Bombay, 1902, pp. 53, 58, 95-9, 107-8.
[105] *Report of the Indian Currency Committee*, 1893, Para 106.
[106] G.F. Shirras, *Indian Banking and Finance*, p. 156.
[107] MacDonnell to Elgin, 8 July 1898, E.P., vol. 73.
[108] G.K. Gokhale, *Speeches*, p. 14.
[109] R. Hardie's Note on Food Stock, 9 February 1897, Enc. Hamilton to Elign, 12 February 1897, E.P., vol. 15. R. Giffen, Assistant Editor of *The Economist*, calculated on the figures of L. Probyn that ornaments before the mints were closed, were worth £350,000,000 and were now worth £256,000,000, quoted in E.F. Marriot, *Indian Currency Question*, p. 46. See also monthly Records of Manchester Chamber of Commerce, 1893, vol. iv, p. 139.
[110] C.N. Vakil and Muranjan, *Currency and Prices in India*, pp. 321-30.
[111] See the Chart on p. 25.
[112] D. Naoroji, Statement Submitted to Indian Currency Commission, 1898, *op. cit.*, Paras 7-15.
[113] *Bengalee*, 28 June 1898.
[114] D.H. Buchanan, *The Development of Capitalist Enterprise in India*, *op. cit.*, pp. 155.
[115] *India*, 11 November and 4 December 1898.
*Danyan Prakash*. 9 May 1898, Kaiser-i-Hind, 15 May 1898.
Bomb. N.N.R., 1898.
D.E. Wacha, *Report of the Indian National Congress*, 1898, pp. 98 and 101-4.
Dadabhai Naoroji, *Poverty and Un-British Rule in India*, pp. 539-46.
R.C. Dutt, *Economic History of India*, p. 582.
[116] Para 21, *op cit.*, E.P., vol. 135 (r).
[117] MacDonnell to Elgin, 27 April 1898, E.P., vol. 72.

CHAPTER II

# COTTON DUTIES

In the field of political economy, the mid-Victorian and later-Victorian periods have been called an age of free trade. But free trade in the strict sense of the term was not applied in India. Like other commodities, cotton piece goods and yarn were subjected to import duties. During 1844-74, the duty on cotton piece goods varied between 10 and 5 per cent, and on yarn between 5 and $3\frac{1}{2}$ per cent, except once, in 1860-1, when the import duty on yarn was also 10 per cent.[1]

By 1870, the circumstances changed. The Indian cotton industry began to grow. In 1854, there was only one cotton mill in India; by 1873 there were 20; and by 1876, 47. This rate of growth alarmed the Manchester industrialists. As there was great scope for the cotton industry to develop in India, thanks to plentiful supplies of raw cotton, cheap labour, and a large home market, Manchester started exerting every effort to eliminate any additional benefit, however slight, the industry received from tariff laws.[2] A fierce controversy ensued during the period of Lord Northbrook's viceroyalty on the advisability or otherwise of abolishing the import duties on cotton piece goods and yarn. Though, till the time of Northbrook's resignation, the duties remained in force, Salisbury had forcefully urged that Indian tariffs should conform to imperial interests. In 1875, to ensure that imperial interests were protected, he directed the Government not to pass any important legislation in future without previously consulting the Secretary of State.[3]

Under Salisbury and Lytton, the imperial tariff policy was effectively implemented. In 1878, import duties were remitted on certain coarser varieties of cloth and in 1879, on all cotton goods containing yarns of counts of 30 or less. Lytton enacted this legislation, overruling the majority view in his executive council.[4] It was solely the political and economic interests of England that were served by these steps.

The Indian textile industry was still in its infancy and the competition it offered to Manchester was extremely limited. The former produced only coarse cloth; the latter the finer varieties. Besides, the duties levied were too low to provide effective protection. What made matters worse was that Lytton reduced these duties in a period of deficit, famine and war.

The import duties were ultimately abolished in 1882 under the Liberal viceroyalty of Lord Ripon but the tariff holiday did not last long. The appalling growth of military expenditure[5] brought about by the frontier troubles and the expedition to Burma, the large outlay on public works; the progressive reduction in opium revenue, the exchange compensation allowance, and the fall in the gold value of silver exerted great pressure on Indian finances. In 1894, the Government was confronted with a deficit of Rs 35 million.[6] There was no means of raising further revenue except by the reimposition of import duties. The Herschell Committee in 1893 strongly urged the imposition of import duties to meet the financial shortfalls. The question at issue was whether or not to exempt cotton from the levy of the general duty. If they were exempted, nearly half the imports would be free of duty and the deficit would not be covered. Their inclusion was bound to be opposed on political and economic grounds.

There were certain other factors to be taken into consideration. The Indian textile industry had grown very rapidly. Whereas in 1882 there were 63 mills, in 1894 their number had reached 142, and this alarmed Manchester. Moreover, Elgin had come to India with specific instruction that no duty should be imposed on cotton goods. The political position of the Liberal Party which had a majority of only 34 in the House of Commons was insecure and any change in the vital cotton tariff could bring it down.

In his first private letter to the Secretary of State, Kimberley, Elgin took a realistic view of the need to reimpose import duties and wrote, "I think you may wish to know that if I concur in a course which is very distasteful to me personally, it is because I cannot see any alternative."[7] With the unanimous support of his executive council he urged the Secretary of State to allow the Indian Government to impose import duties, including those on cotton goods.

Kimberley was not amenable to the Viceroy's proposal. He

was prepared to concede the demand for general import duties but not to their imposition on cotton goods.[8] Elgin again reminded the Secretary of State of the inequity of such inclusion. He stated that if the principle of import duties was accepted, he could find no reason, even as a free trader, why cotton goods should be excluded.[9]

But the British cabinet was not prepared to take any chances with the cotton interests of Manchester. Godley, the permanent Under Secretary at the India Office, informed Elgin that the position of the cabinet was so delicate that if cotton duties were imposed, "It is possible, not to say probable, that the Government might be defeated on the subject in the House of Commons, or might revoke their consent in deference to obligation, and this would be fatal to any attempt to impose the duties for a long time to come."[10] It was feared that over 60 Members of Parliament, who represented Manchester and Lancashire, whether Liberal or Conservative, would vote against the imposition. And this would topple the Government. On 27 February Kimberley, who had earlier overruled the unanimous advice of the Indian Council against the exclusion of cotton goods,[11] finally informed Elgin by both private and official telegrams of the cabinet's decision that cotton goods were not to be included.[12]

The cabinet decision put the India government in great difficulties. The utilization of the famine insurance fund to the extent of 10 million rupees, the curtailment of provincial balances and the doubling of the duty on kerosene had brought in only enough to pay the exchange compensation allowance, which was given to Government officials to cover the loss incurred by them in making sterling remittances due to the fall in the gold value of silver. Without the import duties on cotton goods the financial position would be very precarious. Elgin pleaded again and wrote to the new Secretary of State, Fowler:

> If other import duties are to be imposed, why is not this one, and is it not expected from the consideration of home interests alone? I don't think it can be argued that it is more distinctly protective... an import duty on cotton goods would not really affect the volume of trade. On the other hand, the money is absolutely required, and I am assured... that there is no other source of revenue which would not be both inadequate

and dangerous. The real danger that is apprehended—and I think not altogether unjustly apprehended—is a coalition of British and native opposition.[13]

He emphasised that, as the Tariff Bill stood, if members of the Legislative Council were allowed a free vote, there would not be a single vote in favour of the exclusion of cotton goods. Even the members of the executive would vote for the exclusion of cotton goods from import duties only under compulsion. But Fowler did not heed his pleadings.

The Tariff proposals were taken to the Legislative Council. Though Westland had clearly stated that the proposed exemption of cotton goods was due to English pressure applied through the Secretary of State,[14] strong opposition developed and Charles Pritchard urged that the matter be reconsidered. In view of this, Elgin sought permission of the Secretary of State for the imposition of a nominal duty of $2\frac{1}{2}$ per cent on cotton goods. He also sought an assurance that, if the financial position did not improve, the matter would be reconsidered.[15] The Cabinet did not agree to the imposition of any duty on cotton goods in the first instance but agreed that, if situation demanded, the matter could be reconsidered.[16]

In the meantime, non-official members of the Legislative Council, both Anglo-Indian and Indian continued to be highly critical. When the report of the Select Committee of the Legislative Council came up for consideration on 10 March 1894, the Hon'ble Mr Playfair moved an amendment that cotton duties should be included. It was wrong, he said, to leave out one-half of the total import trade amounting to Rs 280 million annually.[17] He said that the taxation now proposed sufficed only to pay the exchange compensation allowance to the officers, which appeared "unduly onerous through the system of taxation adopted to provide the amount required."[18] He asserted that a 5 per cent duty was not against the principles of free trade, as had been admitted in the past by financial experts like J.S. Mill, Wilson, Gladstone and Lord Cromer.

The Indian non-official members, Gangadhar Rao Madhava Chitnavis and the Maharaja of Dharbanga, also strongly criticised the Government. A very powerful speech came from the official member the Hon'ble Mr Stevens. He said that the exclusion of cotton goods from the tariff list would strengthen the current belief that "in this case and perhaps in others the interests of India are sacrificed to meet the exigencies of party politics in England."[19] Westland also confessed, "if the matters were left to my discretion, I dare say, I would incline in the discretion of the Hon'ble member's amendment."[20] He admitted that Manchester's trade was not so reduced in the world that it could no longer "fight a fair fight." Both Westland and Elgin took shelter under the constitutional authority of the Secretary of State and the Cabinet. The Tariff Bill was passed in March 1894.

Public criticism was extremely hostile. Six chambers of commerce, three trade associations, and eight other public associations registered strong protests. They held that it was unjust on the part of the Government to impose a tax on kerosene, which the poor section consumed, and completely exempt cotton goods which would provide substantial revenue.[21] Lieutenant-General Brackenbury, the military member in the Executive Council, wrote to Elgin that there was a feeling of unrest among Indians over the issue. The Punjab Government wired that "exemption would be discreditable to the administration."[22]

The exemption of cotton goods from the general tariff provided an opportunity to the Indian press to make a frontal attack on the financial administration. Many newspapers denied that the exchange rate was the sole cause of the trouble. They maintained that it was extravagant expenditure on civil and military ventures, which was the prime cause and urged that at this time of financial need, it was imperative for the Government to act vigorously.[23] Many reminded the Government that it was a breach of faith to raise revenue from the people ostensibly for famine relief and use it for other purposes.[24] The *Bangavasi*, an influential Bengal paper, characterised the Indian Government as "pure nonentities" and "veritable puppets" and strongly condemned the selfishness of British rule in India.[25] Some even questioned the need of keeping "a mock viceroy" and maintaining a "sham" Legislative Council.[26] A section of the press suggested boycott of foreign goods.[27]

The criticism was not confined to India. The members of the India Council condemned the action of the Secretary of State. To sir Arbuthnot it was an action which would impair the "confidence in the justice of British rule" in India.[28] A.C. Lyall, another member of the India Council, thought that the exclusion of cotton goods from the import duties schedule could not be defended on economic grounds "having regard to the existing situation of the Indian finance."[29]

The first phase of controversy drew pointed assertion to the unsound state of India's finances. A deficit of 15 million rupees persisted. Either a curtailment of expenditure or on increase in revenue was imperative. Import duties which excluded cotton goods were an economic and political mockery. It also became clear that the political and economic influence of Manchester was unassailable. In the country, the issue caused considerable discontent.

In this situation Elgin was caught between his conscience and his politics; between positive action and expediency; between independence of action and obedience to superior authority. He had warned the Secretary of State quite early of the possible consequences of the action contemplated and had elequently demanded justice for India. He tried his best to correct the impression prevailing in England that India was rich. When Godley wrote to him that the Secretary of State did not consider the financial position of India to be so bad as to warrant the imposition of cotton duties, Elgin replied:

> You must bear in mind that we have only arrived at a solution this year by giving up the famine grant and by making calls upon the local Governments—which, I am satisfied, would not only be extremely unpopular, but also most inexpedient as any part of a permanent arrangement, and if you take out those parts of the present financial scheme, you will, I think, easily see that there is no practical alternative except the cotton duties.[30]

In this controversy, Elgin did, however, gain, one point: the question of the cotton duties could be reopened. When Fowler spoke in the House of Commons on 13 March 1894 and put out a feeler to the Government of India that import duties on cotton goods could be considered as a compromise if a countervailing excise duty were imposed on Indian cotton goods, Elgin was quick to catch on.

The Government of India, in its first major policy despatch

## Cotton Duties

on this subject of March 1894 firmly stated that the exemption of cotton goods from import duties could not be permanently maintained, particularly since the financial position was not likely to improve in the foreseeable future, and the curtailment of military expenditure suggested by Kimberley was not possible. Provincial contributions were not substantial and the suspension of the Famine Insurance Grant could not be made a permanent feature.

In May 1894, the Secretary of State and his council, in a despatch, conceded the demand for the imposition of import duties on cotton piece goods and yarn, but made it clear that this was a great concession that an excise duty on local cotton goods had to be accepted as complementary to it. In the case of imported goods which did not compete with Indian manufactures, the import duty would not be protective and no equivalent excise would be needed.[31] It further stressed that the Indian cotton industry had, during the last twelve years, developed rapidly and that, if no excise was levied, Lancashire would be adversely affected. The Secretary of State left it to the discretion to the Government of India to devise a scheme which would not be open to "serious economical objection at the outset."[32] On the receipt of this despatch, Elign asked Westland to draw up the course of action. Westland went to Bombay to study the functioning of the Indian cotton mill industry and devised a plan to meet the wishes of the Secretary of State. Westland's Minute dated 14 July 1894,[33] was painstaking, factual and revealing. He had gathered his facts by examining the records and statistics of 140 of the 141 cotton mills collected by the Indian Millowners' Association and the records of the Collector of Customs, Bombay.

Westland came to the firm conclusion that, of the total cotton manufactures in India, 94 per cent was absolutely outside the range of any competition with Manchester in view of its coarse quality, with Counts 24S[34] and below which Manchester could not hope to supply as cheaply as the Indian industry. The following table presents the then percentages of total production of clothes of fineness ranging from 10 to 40S by Indian textile mills.[35]

Manchester thus had an absolute monopoly of the finer qualities and the bulk of its trade was in piece goods of Counts of above 30S and in somewhat finer yarns.

| Fineness | % of the total production |
|---|---|
| Above 10S and under | 19.714 |
| ,, 10S and under 20S | 59.633 |
| ,, 20S and under 30S | 19.073 |
| ,, 30S and under 40S | 1.453 |
| Total | 100.000 |

Yarns imported into India[36]

| | 1892-93 | | | 1893-94 |
|---|---|---|---|---|
| From U.K. | lbs | 37,337,449 | lbs | 41,642,142 |
| Elsewhere | | 935,096 | | 1,164,849 |
| Total | | 38,276,545 | | 42,806,991 |

The value of the imports of cotton goods from United Kingdom was:

| Yarns | Rs | 26,000,000 |
| Piece goods | Rs | 220,000,000 |
| Total | Rs | 246,000,000 |

Six per cent of the above amount, or Rs 8,600,000 worth of produce, could be considered as in possible competition with Indian textiles. These not only did not compete with Rs 246,000,000 worth of goods which Manchester exported annually to India, but it also did not offer competition to Manchester's exports to China, Japan and the east coast of Africa, to which India could perhaps, have sent part of its competitive production worth Rs 8,600,000. In actual facts, it did not do so. Manchester's exports to the East were worth nearly 30 million Sterling, say Rs 450,000,000. Thus India got less than 2 per cent of the market for the finer goods and Manchester 98 per cent.[37] This point can be further substantiated by looking at the figures of exports from Bombay (as provided by the

Collector of Customs, Bombay) for the years 1892-93 and 1893-94 (see table).

*Exports of Cotton Goods from Bombay*

|  | 1892-93 Quantity | Value | 1893-94 Quantity | Value |
|---|---|---|---|---|
| Mule twist and yarn | lb | Rs | lb | Rs |
| No 15 and lower | 55,994,974 | 18,046.070 | 35,744,084 | 11,974,840 |
| No 16 to 24 | 113,700,411 | 42,758,300 | 88,372,568 | 33,810,860 |
| Total 64S & lower | 169,695,385 | 60,804,370 | 124,116,652 | 45,785,700 |
| Nos 25 to 32 | 200,358 | 94,140 | 409,185 | 197,420 |
| Nos 33 to 42 | 15,950 | 10,430 | 44,000 | 24,170 |
| Water twist |  |  |  |  |
| Nos 20S and lower | 79,136 | 32,800 | 112,365 | 46,070 |
| Nos 21S to 30S | 4,010 | 1,650 | 53,050 | 24,380 |
| No 31S to 40S (all sent to Persia) | 9,800 | 5,370 | 30,200 | 16,680 |
| No 41S to 50S (all to China) | — | — | 385 | 370 |
| Coloured | 781,890 | 460,110 | 701,990 | 410,620 |
| Total | 170,768,529 | 61,408,870 | 125,467,827 | 46,505,410 |

These figures are sufficient to show that Indian exports of Counts above 24S formed an insignificant proportion of the total export trade in yarns.

In respect of cotton goods of Counts 24S, particularly coloured, printed, dyed and fancy goods, Manchester had a more serious rival in Europe than in India. These were largely made of Indian raw cotton, mixed with American cotton to produce quality goods. In 1892-3, exports of new cotton from India were 4,789,201 cwt, of which 528,403 went to the United Kingdom, 443,988 to Japan and nearly all the rest, say $3\frac{3}{4}$ million cwt to Continental Europe.[38] This showed that while the exports of Indian raw cotton were rising, the share of the United Kingdom in the import of these inferior grades of cotton was declining as it paid Manchester better to go in more for the manufacture of finer quality of goods. On the other hand, because the inferior Indian cotton was more suited to the manufacture of coarse cloth, the Indian cotton industry concentrated on the manufacture of coarser varieties and did not manufacture finer cloth. To import American or Egyptian cotton was expensive, and in this India could not compete with Lancashire.

In a nutshell, it was only 6 per cent of the total Indian production which could compete with Lancashire for markets. Westland clearly regretted that an excise duty should be levied on such slender grounds. He wrote:

> I accept the fact that we are directed to impose an excise duty so as to prevent this amount of disadvantage in respect of these competitive goods occuring to the Indian Millowners. I do not alter my opinion that an excise duty on cotton manufactures taken *per se* is an expedient worthy of the middle ages.[39]

He added:

> ... but I assume that if we require to raise money by imposing import duties on cotton yarns and fabrics, we have to accept the condition that we must deprive them of a protective character by levying an equivalent excise duty on those classes of Indian manufactured goods which come clearly and directly into competition with dutiable imported goods from England.[40]

Westland observed that a dividing line drawn at 24S would leave Manchester absolutely unaffected. His suggestions were:

(a) An import duty of 5 per cent *ad valorem* on all cotton piece goods.

(b) An import duty of $3\frac{1}{2}$ per cent on all cotton yarns of of counts above 24S.

(c) An excise duty of $3\frac{1}{2}$ per cent *ad valorem* on cotton yarns counts above 24S produced in mills in India.

Westland's minute was welcomed and was accepted in full by the Government of India, which forwarded it to the Secretary of State.[41] Elgin advised Fowler privately that the question of a countervailing excise duty should not be pushed too far.[42] But the Secretary of State was not prepared to give up the idea of an excise duty though he admitted that effective competition between India and Lancashire was limited.[43] On the whole, the first reaction of the India Office appeared encouraging.[44] But that was all. The influence of power began to work, and the Manchester and Party interests were predominant. The Manchester Chamber of Commerce, which knew well that the exemption of cotton goods from duty was a temporary matter, kept on pressing the issue and sent one resolution after the other to the Prime Minister and the Secretary of State.[45]

Fowler informed Elgin that, as the matter was of "prime importance," the final decision would be taken by the Cabinet, but he left Elgin in no doubt that the scheme of the Government of India was to be modified. Godley prepared the agenda for the Cabinet meeting which was held on 9 November 1894. Fowler informed Elgin of the Cabinet decision: "I want you to understand, as the matter now stands, I think the duty on both yarns and piece goods should be 5 per cent —that the excise duty should be 5 per cent—and that the Excise Duty should cover all yarns above 20S."[46] Elgin accepted this as a *fait accompli*.[47] In so readily accepting the decision, Elgin seems to have been deeply influenced by two men: Fowler, who was strong, unyielding and decisive; and Godley, who was as "rational" as he was persuasive. In the early stages, these men dominated the Viceroy.

Although Elgin had accepted the position, some Members of his Executive Council, particularly Pritchard and Miller,[48] did not agree with the Secretary of State's decision to impose an excise on Indian cotton goods and claimed the right of abstention from voting on the Bill in the Legislative Assembly. This request at once raised a constitutional issue concerning the position of the Viceroy's Executive Council *vis-a-vis* the Home Government. The Secretary of State, Fowler, made the constitutional point in very clear and strong words, which have been termed the "Mandate" of the Secretary of State:

> The existing law subjects the Government of India to the control of the Imperial Government; and the Secretary of State, who exercises that control, is responsible to the Parliament... India is, under the Act of Parliament, governed by, and in the name of, the Queen, and she governs by the advice of a responsible Minister. All the powers of the Directors of the East India Company, and of the Board of Control in relation to the Government of India and its officers and its servants

> are by statute vested in the Secretary of State. There is not, and there cannot be, any foundation for the theory that "the loyal cooperation" of an officer of the Indian Government is due only to the Viceroy and to the Council, and not to the Secretary of State as representing the Queen . . . . So long as any matter of administration, or policy, is undecided, every member of the Government of India is at liberty to express his own opinion, but when a certain line of policy had been adopted under the directions of the Cabinet, it is the clear duty of every Member of the Government of India to consider, not what the policy ought to be, but how effect may best be given to the policy which has been decided upon; and, if any Member of that Government is unable to do this there is only one alternative open to him.[49]

And he further emphasised in another letter:

> I should be very sorry to think that you have in your Council any man who would dispute the supreme authority of the Cabinet on a constitutional question of this description, and by withholding his resignation necessitate his dismissal. However, my position is very clear and with the cordial support of my colleagues I shall immediately advise the Queen to dismiss any Member of the Council who so far forgets what is due to his own position and the position of the Viceroy as to the attempt to continue a member of the Government whose policy he is unable to support.[50]

There was a two-fold significance in Fowler's statement of the constitutional issue. First, even before this, there had been no doubt about the power of the Secretary of State and the Cabinet, the importance of the statement lay in the fact that it was for the first time explicitly defined during Elgin's tenure.[51] Secondly, the Secretary of State by his statement definitely weakened the powers of the Viceroy's Executive Council and the Viceroy's Legislative Council. To his own embarrassment Elgin stated:

> It is not for me to deny that; but, on my own behalf, I would say that it does not altogether smooth the difficulties in a

## Cotton Duties

Viceroy's path (which I doubt if anyone who has not been a Viceroy can fully appreciate) if he has too often to say to his colleagues "you must submit or resign." It so happens that this is the second case in my short tenure of office when such a question has arisen, not as affecting a single individual, but several Members at the same time.[52]

The strong stand taken by the Secretary of State humbled Elgin who accepted a subordinate role. It was from this period that he earned the reputation of being "subservient to Whitehall."

It was against this background that the legislation based on the Secretary of State's decision was introduced on 17 December 1894 in the Viceroy's Legislative Council. In the presentation of the Tariff Amendment Bill and the Cotton Duties Bill, J. Westland was frankly apologetic.[53] Opposition to the Bill came from official and non-official members alike. The Hon'ble Fazul Bhai Vishram unsuccessfully pressed for the raising of the limit for excise from 20S to 24S count in the Select Committee. When the Bill came up for discussion in the Legislative Council on 27 December 1894, Stevens, a nominated official member, spoke against the Government measure. Playfair also made a strong attack on the introduction of the principle of excise which was imposed on Indian goods. It seemed to Playfair that the Indian export trade in cotton yarn would diminish because the excise would inflate prices. The increase in the level of taxation would also affect the sale of coarser yarn within the country. He held that "the manufacturing industry may languish to the detriment of the grower as well as of the spinner of Indian cotton." Fazul Bhai Vishram, Mohiney Mohan Roy, Griffith Evans and Phirozeshah Mehta did not lag behind in making a strong attack on the Government measure.[54] The Bill was defended by the Lieutenant Governor of Bengal and Lieutenant General Brackenbury. The solid and united opposition of all non-officials, alarmed Elgin. He took the unusual step of exercising his vote when an amendment was moved.[55] He also made a speech which was not without significance either in respect of the position of a Viceroy or in the constitutional history of British India. He explained the mandate of the Secretary of State *vis-a-vis* the right of the members to vote:

In every legislative body, a man must sit ... by what in modern parlance is called a mandate, and that mandate must be given by some authority. ....Here we have no election, and I am glad to say no party, but every man who sits by the authority and sanction of Parliament, and to say that he can refuse to obey the decisions of Parliament would be absurd. But that is not all. Parliament has provided for the Government of the Indian empire. The British Raj can be provided for in no other way.[56]

He went on to say that this power of Parliament was exercised through the Secretary of State and his Council and it was but proper to obey its orders. Exhorting the Council to vote for the amendment he said, "If this Council does not adopt this amendment, it will take upon its shoulders the responsibility of losing this bill and of losing perhaps altogether the financial resources which we so much need."[57] Such a statement, coming as it did from the head of the administration, could not but influence the members.

A highly controversial measure was thus imposed, involving of excise on a developing industry, the burden of which would fall on the poorest of the poor. Such action by the Imperial Government had had no precedent. Even Samuel Laing and Lord Lytton,[58] the two great free trade enthusiasts had rejected it. In March 1894, Westland had assured the Legislative Council that Government neither could nor would sanction the imposition of an excise on the local manufacture as such a tax could be neither productive nor economic. It had been proved beyond doubt that there was no competition between Indian cotton goods and Lancashire goods. Westland had stated that import of English goods of the affected categories was only 2 per mile and yet it was proposed to put 20 per cent of Indian production to unnecessary hardship.[59]

It may be observed here that the scope for earning a margin of profit on spinning yarn of counts above 24S from Indian cotton was exceedingly circumscribed and the result of the imposition of an excise duty could only be a fall in the production and consequently, the revenue from the excise, to a level which would render the whole exercise futile. Also, the benefit could not be confined to English manufacturers alone. Although the proportion was still small, an appreciable quantity of both cloth and yarn was being imported from both America and the European Continent, where heavy protective duties were levied on all Indian produce. In a country like India, where a large majority of the population depends on agriculture for their subsistence, manufacturing industries required the careful fostering by the Government by every legitimate means at its disposal—not the discouragement that the excise brought in its train. The excise duty was thus a totally retrograde measure, politically and economically unjust both in its conception and incidence. Financially, as a source of revenue, it did not prove useful. Its imposition at the behest of the totally external authority of the British Secretary of State for India, took away from the Legislative Council even the very circumscribed independence and representative character it once possessed.[60]

If the agitation in India against the imposition of the excise was vigorous, the uproar in England was no less so, the grouse being that the excise was not sufficient to exclude all possibility of protection to the Indian industry.[61] The agitation was as strong in Manchester as it was in Parliament. Fowler had a hard job handling the turbulent "House." He feared that members of his own party might vote against the Government. R.G.C. Mowbray, a Conservative Member, informed Elgin that a big meeting was held at Manchester on 14 February under the presidentship of Sir Henry James, that Lancashire was in a very agitated mood and that, at the meeting, "for two hours I felt like Mary Queen of Scots being thundered by John Knox."[62] Lancashire wanted either customs duty exemption for counts below 20S or that the excise levy should begin at a lower count.[63]

Sir Henry James did not lose any time and moved an amendment in the House of Commons on 21 February, which was supported by Lord George Hamilton.[64] He stated that the legislation of December 1894 was against the principle of free trade and was harmful to the trade of Lancashire and to the commercial interest of England. Fowler denied this and stoutly defended the Indian Government's measure. He also pointed out that Great Britain raised £20 million of her revenue from custom duties, including £3 million on tea imported from India.[55] G.J. Goschen supported the Liberal Government[66] and Government triumphed by 304 votes to 109. In a leading editorial, *The Times*

(London) fully supported the Government, praised Fowler and defended the action of the Government of India as "just, equitable and impartial."[67]

Before the controversy had fully subsided, the Scottish manufacturing interests also protested. They contended that they sent "large quantities"[68] of dyed yarn of low counts to Burma on which they had to pay duty, whereas Bombay yarn did not pay any. This, they asserted, was a clear case of protection. Sir Henry Fowler, who had defended the Indian Government measure on 21 February in the House of Commons, wrote to Elgin the very next day to say: "My own inclination is towards exempting the coarse counts from customs."[69] As a consequence, the Indian Government agreed to, in effect, exempt imports into Burma of coloured yarn of 20S fineness and under and reduced the duty from 5 per cent to $\frac{1}{2}$ of one per cent through executive action.[70] The $\frac{1}{2}$ of one per cent was retained to compensate for the import duty paid by Indian manufacturers dyeing materials. However, it was stated by the Indian Government that there was absolutely no evidence, or even allegation, that any other duties could have a protective effect.

The exemption from duties of certain goods imported into Burma involved two anomalies: one, that the exempted yarn imported into Burma could be transported to India freely; and, two, it was contrary to the principle and practice of customs legislation to levy duties at different rates at various ports. The Government of India tacitly admitted this in their despatch:

> Though it would introduce a new principle in levy of duties on transit from one part of India to another, that anomaly is not greater than the levy of the excise duty itself and must be accepted as the excise duties are not on its own merits, but as the condition of the fairness of the imposition of cotton import duties.[71]

But Fowler did not want the retention of even $\frac{1}{2}$ of one per cent and informed Elgin that he was being pressed with repeated representations from the Scottish and Lancashire manufacturers. But, at that stage, Elgin was not prepared to yield, for he was again being faced with opposition in the Viceroy's Executive Council. Fowler, however, would not unbend and he accepted the retention of the ½ per cent duty only reluctantly as a temporary measure. He informed Elgin that he was under pressure to meet the deputation from Lancashire on 27 May 1895.

The deputationists held that they had been unjustly treated,[72] but did not seem to have made much impression on Fowler. Reporting the interview to Elgin, he said that Lancashire argued on the same lines as Scottish manufacturers and that their case was not based on facts. He had assured them that if facts supporting their case were forthcoming, he would take steps to end the justice. As a result, Manchester drew up a formal statement of their case and sent it to the Secretary of State on 9 July 1895.[73]

In the meantime, the Liberal Government was overthrown. The Conservatives came back to power, which was a matter of very substantial significance for cotton duties controversy. Godley informed Elgin that the Conservative had won with an overwhelming victory and stated, "One feels safer and less likely to see experiments tried which were considered dangerous, by those who knew India best." But he added a warning that the question of cotton duties might continue to cause trouble.[74] But the most revealing letter to Elgin in this context came from Lieutenant General Brackenburry. He wrote: "I am rather anxious as to the effect this change may have on the Cotton Duties question. Lord George Hamilton, you may remember, voted with and spoke in favour of Sir Henry James' motion. His brother is one of the M.P.s for Manchester. Sir Henry James is in the Cabinet; Lord Salisbury had the Cotton Duties repealed. Lord Cross is strong on Lancashire interests."[75]

Lord George Hamilton, the new Secretary of State for India, in his first private letter to Elgin, clearly opened his mind on the long drawn controversy.[76] With this letter he sent on the Lancashire memorial. The contention of the memorialists was that the Indian manufacturer had a very substantial advantage over Lancashire as he paid excise duty on the grey yarn value only, while the Lancashire manufacturer had to pay an import duty on the value of the finished goods, bleached, woven, dyed or printed. They represented that Indian woven goods made from yarns just below the excise line could compete with and take place of imported woven goods liable to a 5 per cent duty. They stressed that it was impossible to be fair to both Indian and British manufacturers with an artificial dividing line at 20S or at any other count and they cited the experience in India of 1878-82 to show that any attempt to draw such a line would break down and would result in fiscal inequality.[77] Commenting on the memorandum, Hamilton fully agreed with the deputationists that the excise on yarn was insufficient to redress the balance in favour of Lancashire and stressed on his predecessor's pledge to Parliament "that no savouring of protection should be associated with these customs duties, and that the excise duties should completely counter-balance the customs duties.... The unconditional promise Sir Henry Fowler gave as to the removing of all protective tendency cannot be escaped, and it is obligatory upon both of us."[78]

Elgin assured Hamilton that he would do his best to accommodate his views. He wrote, "you could find no one more ready to acquiesce in the extreme gravity of any decision."[79] He sent all the papers to Westland for information and comment. Westland's first impression was that the "Manchester case was greatly overdrawn and open to challenge even in its general features; but... I admit they have enough of a case, in the eyes of the public at all events, to render it necessary for us to do something towards meeting their claim."[80] Westland also discussed the question of the abolition of the duties but proposed only the exemption of imports of yarn of fineness 20S or less. Elgin agreed that something had to be done to meet the claims of Lancashire.[81] In the meantime, Hamilton kept on pressing that Lancashire's trade was in a depressed condition and he was under obligation to meet another Lancashire delegation. He emphasised that the customs duties should be abolished.[82] Elgin sent Hamilton the note prepared by Westland on the representation of Manchester.[83]

Hamilton was not entirely pleased with Westland's note and to a letter to Elgin he attached his comments on Westland's Memorandum. He admitted that a certain but very limited amount of goods under 20S were imported into India from England, but asserted that the small value of the goods did not "justify the infringement of the parliamentary engagement made nor would such a plea be listened in the House."[84] Hamilton held that Lancashire's arguments, as to the difference between the initial value of the yarn and the final value of the completed cloth constituting protection for Indian goods, was unanswerable. In principle, he argued, Lancashire was correct, though he agreed with Westland that the actual difference and consequent amount of protection given had been overstated by them. Hamilton appreciated Westland's proposal that both the import duties and the excise be abolished and be replaced by an all round tax levied by weight rather than by value of piece goods. "Assuming that the substitution of weight for value affects actually equally both sides, it seems a basis for settlement."[85]

Westland explained to Elgin that the reason for suggesting assessment by weight was to make excise assessment exactly equal to the import duty. Moreover, it could be easily fitted into the working of the excise system. Two-thirds of the imports were of grey shirtings in which value by weight was almost uniform and the value of Indian made fabric over counts twenty was almost the same. There could be loss of revenue only if it was necessary to apply the same system to white goods, but Indian competition in these was very limited. Under this scheme, the coarse goods consumed by the poor, being mostly under count 20S, would escape taxation altogether. In this respect, Westland won a great but short-lived victory.[86]

Hamilton soon realised that he had misunderstood Westland's note and had interpreted the suggestion contained in it as applying to all piece goods above 20S, including bleached goods. It was George Lord, an influential Manchester merchant, whom he later consulted notwithstanding the fact that he had prohibited the Indian Government from consulting Indian Chambers on matters of policy,[87] who drew his attention to his error. Lord was of the view that the *ad valorem* principle was the only practicable one for bleached and printed goods.[88] Hamilton insisted on this and the Government of India yielded.

The Government of India now proposed taxing only cloth, exempting yarn—by way of import duty and excise on local production. Hamilton agreed and suggested that, in view of the rising exchange rate, the duty might be reduced to $3\frac{1}{2}$ per cent and advised the Indian Government to do so by an executive order.[89] Surprisingly, Hamilton found in Lord Northbrook a great sympathiser with the proposal for taxing the cloth and exempting yarn and maintaining a uniform duty on cloth for customs and excise. Northbrook even wrote to Godley expressing his full concurrence with and support to Government's proposal. He wrote:

"The Indians really want protection, and are quite incapable of understanding (or of admitting their validity if they do understand) any arguments based upon the most ordinary rudiments of political economy."[90] The support of Northbrook strengthened the hands of the Government. Elgin agreed to the proposal, but did not agree to implement it by executive order and asked Westland to prepare for legislation.

The controversy about cotton goods and yarn raises some basic questions. What constitutes protection? How far was the Manchester's claim justified? Was there any scope for compromise? The answer to all these questions requires an analysis of reliable facts and figures and an analysis, in their light, of the arguments of the Home Government and the Manchester group.

It was claimed by Lancashire that 250 million lb of yarns of 20S and under were annually manufactured in England and that they therefore had a substantial interest in the trade.[91] But it was nowhere asserted that more than a very limited portion of that manufacture was destined for, or found its way to Indian markets. There was no statistical information available to that effect. It was, in fact, well known that, save in the one instance of drills, it was not represented to any appreciable extent in the cloth imported into India.[92] If any misapprehension existed on this point, it was the manifest duty of the representatives of the English cotton manufacturing interests to remove it, and they could have had no difficulty in doing so, as English spinners and manufacturers were perfectly well informed as to the ultimate destination of their production. That they did so only in the case of drills, was alone sufficient to dispose of the allegation that competition either existed or could exist in yarns of 20S and under or goods made from there of. As to goods woven from the higher counts, there was not only "no instance given of existing competition but no suggestion of possible competition in the future except by means of substitution."[93]

It was asserted by Lancashire that the exemption from the excise duty of yarns of 20S fineness and less would encourage the manufacture of duty free cloths. As such, exemption would result in Indian manufacturers avoiding the excise duty altogether by substituting the manufacture of cloth from excisable yarns by manufactures from non-excisable yarns.[94]

*Cotton Duties*

If there was any substance in this view and buyers could be so easily persuaded to transfer their preferences, coarser goods of Indian manufacture could have displaced the heavily sized shirtings of Lancashire years ago. Moreover, as the Indian millowners asserted, certain cloth could not be substituted. Some modification did take place in 1878, when the bait of 5 per cent difference induced Lancashire manufacturers to strike out on a new line for themselves. What was practicable then, however, in making a purer 30S/30S was now no longer so when dropping from 30S to 20S. The change in appearance and quality would be too great. Besides, in going above 20S, the increased cost of spinning Indian cotton, owing to its short and weak staple, could be very heavy. On the other hand, Lancashire, on going much below 28S to 30S would, while employing highly, skilled labour, be operating uneconomically. In any case, there was no evidence that substitution had already taken place.

It was stated by Lancashire on the strength of Westland's statement in the *Blue Book* that with American cotton at 3d. per 1b they could produce coarse counts of 20S or under as cheaply as was done in India.[95] This contention was obviously wrong because it had not taken into consideration the cost of either American or Indian cotton. This can be seen from the average prices of standard qualities of American (mid-uplands) and Indian (good Dhollera) cotton per 1b during 1891-5.[96]

COTTON PRICES, 1891-95

|  | 1891 | 1892 | 1893 | 1894 | 1895 |
|---|---|---|---|---|---|
| Mid uplands | $4\frac{5}{8}$d. | $4\frac{17}{64}$d. | $4\frac{1}{2}$d. | $3\frac{11}{16}$d. | $4\frac{3}{64}$d. |
| Good Dhollera | $3\frac{25}{32}$d. | $3\frac{19}{32}$d. | $3\frac{15}{16}$d. | $3\frac{3}{64}$d. | $3\frac{11}{32}$d. |
| Difference | $\frac{54}{64}$d. | $\frac{43}{64}$d. | $\frac{36}{64}$d. | $\frac{41}{64}$d. | $\frac{45}{64}$d. |
| Percentage of difference | 18.24 | 15.75 | 12.50 | 17.37 | 17.37 |

Average difference 16.24 per cent

The most important feature of Lancashire's protest was the statement that their exports of piece goods to India for February 1895 were 28.62 per cent less in quantity and 39.12 per cent less in value; for March, 44.12 per cent less in quantity and 50.96 per cent less in value; for April 31.26 per cent less in quantity and 42.32 per cent less in value, than the corresponding month of 1894; and that this was due to the customs duties and insufficient excise levy.[97]

The year 1894 could not really be taken as the basis for comparison in view of two exceptional events. First, the closure of the mints in June 1893, which temporarily advanced the exchange rate from 14½d. to 16d. per rupee. Exporters in England took advantage of the temporary rise in the rate as they had done in 1890-1 to push their goods in the Indian market as fast as possible. The imports continued to be substantial long after the exchange rate had begun to fall and, indeed, the trade was carried on up to the end of the year with unusual vigour, importers being apprehensive that the rupee might continue to fall until it reached the level of its intrinsic value in silver. The result was that the value of imported merchandise by the end of the year exceeded that of preceding year by no less than 18 per cent.[98] Among the imports, the largest increase, amounting to more than half of the whole—Rs 60¾ million out of an aggregate increase of Rs 111⅓ million—occured in cotton goods, including yarns. The increase in the case of cotton goods thus accounted for 68 per cent of the total increase.[99]

It is probable that this great spurt in speculative trade would have been followed by a pause in 1894-95, but a new incentive to speculation was provided by the prolonged discussion of the propriety or otherwise of including cotton goods in the import tariff,[100] a discussion conducted in the background of the knowledge that the Government of India were in favour of such an inclusion. This anticipation that an import duty would soon be levied on them also led to further speculative imports of the grey and white goods much in excess of immediate needs and even of the inflated imports of 1893-4.[101] This was the second factor that made 1894 an exceptional year for imports of cotton goods.

During the first four months of 1895, the trade fell as was to be expected after two years of administratively induced inflation.[102]

It would thus be wrong to attribute any portion of this decline to the effect of the customs duty. Import duties which had been levied on cotton goods before 1882 had not restricted consumption and it was not likely that they had done so in 1895.[103] The recession could, with greater reason, be attributed to the disinclination of traders to pay duty on goods which they could not sell until the market was cleared of the accumulated stocks, imported before the imposition of the duty. The combination of these two factors—over-supplied markets and fiscal uncertainty —resulted in a substantial contraction of trade.

But there is yet another way of looking at this question. Even if there was a decline in the general volume of trade between the United Kingdom and India to the full extent claimed, "It could not in justice be written down to the maleficent influence of an insufficient excise until it could be shown that the deficiency had been supplemented by the products of the Indian mills."[104]

It was also alleged by Lancashire that the arrangement for countervailing excise duties failed to exploit a very important source of revenue. But it was amply known that the countervailing excise was never intended as a source of revenue. It was imposed only to counteract the alleged protection effect of the customs duties on cotton goods.

Lancashire claimed vaguely that they had a "large trade" with India in grey, bleached, dyed and printed goods of 20S fineness and under. In the examples presented, they claimed that the Indian manufacturer was protected to the following extent:

| | |
|---|---|
| On grey goods | 2.31 per cent |
| On bleached goods | 2.62 per cent |
| On dyed goods | 2.92 per cent |
| On printed goods | 3.92 per cent |

This was not supported by any substantial evidence drawn from authentic documents and the contention was summarily dismissed by Westland.[105] Even if 60 million yards of Lancashire cloth had been imported into India, as was claimed, it represented an insignificant portion of total British textile exports to India which amounted to nearly 1,000 million yards annually. It was, therefore, unfair, on such specious grounds, to penalize 94 per cent of Indian cotton manufacturers which were of counts below 24S.[106] Besides this, the Government of India had already reduced the import duty on dyed yarns of 20S count and under to $\frac{1}{2}$ of one per cent, which was too trivial to deserve special consideration.

It was further held by Lancashire that the statement in the

*Blue Book* that the cost of the mill stores and dyeing materials imported constituted 25 per cent of the price of Indian manufactures of coarse yarn and cloth, was erroneous, and hence the argument based on it was fallacious.[107] That the statement in the *Blue Book* was not correct was a fact, but the duty on stores used in Indian mills in making cloth was levied at more than three times the rate stated by representatives of British textile interests.

If competition existed, as was alleged by Lancashire, then their demands could perhaps be justified in the context of the colonial status of India. Since Lancashire, in theory, if not in practice, had a valid case in respect of coarser varieties, the Indian Millowners' Association and the Bombay Chamber of Commerce were willing to agree to the exemption from import duty all cloth and yarns of 20S fineness and under (although they had to bear an import duty on mill stores), and thus put them on the same footing as similar local produce. They also suggested that the excise should be imposed on the market value of all India cloth made from yarns over 20S instead of on yarn only.[108] This, if accepted, could not have resulted in the loss of much revenue. It would also have been an equitable tax. Above all, the poorer classes, who consumed the coarse cloth, would not be burdened with extra taxation.

But that was not to be.[109] The views of the Bombay Millowners' Association were not even considered. As Westland noted, "We would be too obviously setting it aside."[110] This was another clear indication that the Government was under the mandate of the Secretary of State.

Against this background, Westland introduced the Cotton Duties and Tariff Bill in the Legislative Assembly on 23 January 1896. The presentation was a routine one. He stated that much of the Manchester case was overdrawn, but they had a case on two issues. First, that a substitution could take place and Lancashire goods could be prevented from competing with coarser kinds of cloths. Secondly, that the tax levied on yarn was higher than that levied on completed articles. He said:

> If Lancashire trade were in flourishing condition, I cannot help thinking that these differences would have been considered to be more theoretical than practical. But we cannot conceal from ourselves the fact that Lancashire trade has recently

been in a depressed condition, although we certainly contend that circumstances out of which this depression arises have nothing to do with Indian cotton duties.[111]

If that was the excuse of the Government of India, how did they justify so very sweeping a measure as the subjection of all of Indian mill cloth to excise. The Bombay Chamber had unequivocally stated that if Lancashire wished to export coarse cloth, it could do so and they had no objection to their goods coming in freely.

Westland had made the best of a bad job. He reduced the duties all around to $3\frac{1}{2}$ per cent. On the burden of the excise tax, he said that he did not call it a burden because the Indian millowner would pass it on to the consumer. There was no boubt that in all cases the consumer had to pay, but why was this consolation not offered to the Lancashire millowners? Probably because such an offer would never have been accepted by them.

On 3 February 1896, the Cotton Duties Act was amended and so was the Tariff Act. The Tariff Act abolished the altogether duties on yarns of all kinds and reduced those on other cotton manufactures from 5 per cent to $3\frac{1}{2}$ per cent *ad valorem*. The Cotton Duties Act similarly exempted yarns of Indian manufacture and imposed a duty of $3\frac{1}{2}$ per cent on woven goods of all counts manufactured by Indian mills. A minor change was introduced to rectify the objections of Indian millowners. Westland imposed *ad valorem* duties on all imports and "tariff values" for the chief classes of mill goods. These "values," he explained, would approximate closely to the actual values and would not be dependent on day to day changes in prices or in estimates of prices by different millowners.

This amendment involved a remission of taxation of Rupees $51\frac{1}{2}$ lakhs (37 per cent) on Manchester goods and an increase of Rupees 11 lakhs (300 per cent) on taxation on Indian made goods.[112] What this meant was poignantly stated by J. Piele:

The Act puts an excise on all the coarse cloth manufacture of the Indian mills. On what similar manufacture does it put a duty on the other, the Lancashire side? On none whatever. For there is none. There is no import trade of coarse goods from Lancashire, so that "tax all cloth" means "tax Indian cloth," and free all yarn? But Indian yarn has always been free. It is Lancashire yarn which is freed, so that formula really means "tax Indian cloth and free Lancashire yarn."[113]

What prompted Lancashire to press for such "equal status" (in real effect, preferential status) *vis-a-vis* Indian textiles? Lancashire had never cost a friendly eye on the growth of the Indian textile industry ever since its birth; it was always opposed to India gaining industrial strength. That was implicit even in the Lancashire memorandum:

> Lancashire would hail with satisfaction legislation of a kind that would tend to make India prosperous and wealthy by encouraging agriculture and larger exportation of the produce of its own soil, which would prove the best source of wealth of such a country, also by a free admission of its products into this country, thereby developing a free exchange of trade such as would bring comfort and contentment to the inhabitants there as well as here.[114]

It was universally accepted that, with a famine economy, it would be impossible to achieve prosperity without industrialisation. But this made no difference to the victorian capitalist, who, in the words of G.D.H. Cole looked at the world with the eyes of traders in finished consumable commodities and whose "creed of laissez faire followed logically from their economic ambitions."[115]

Further, other European countries were developing industrially very fast and England was losing the industrial monopoly which she once enjoyed. That the pace of the Industrial Revolution in England would continue unabated was a vain hope. The "great depression" in England of 1873-96 was a clear indication of the dangers ahead. British productivity in this period had shown clear signs of relative stagnation and there was a considerable weakening of Britain's economic position.[116] Hoffman estimated that the annual rate of expansion which had been 3 to 4 per cent had fallen during this period to 2 per cent.[117] The cotton industry also experienced a declining rate of growth of production.[118]

All this naturally had its effect on the pattern of British trade, particularly on exports. While British exports were falling everywhere on account of the stiffer competition, it was inevitable that that attempts at expansion would be directed to neutral or non-protected markets,[119] like India. The natural tendency in the face of foreign competition is towards protection and British trade policy towards colonies and dependencies therefore stiffered—"a return during this period to the idea of empire, in the hope of finding salvation in colonial markets "[120]

To sum up, it may be said that cotton duties controversy brought to the surface many crucial issues and forced all concerned to take clean and unambiguous positions on them. It was clearly demonstrated that the political and economic interests of England would always be paramount and "raised serious doubts about the British Government's claims to disinterestedness and impartiality in governance of its great dependency."[121] It led to the acceptance of the principle of internal excise which would not at that time, have been approved by any serious student of economics. Valentine Chirol wrote: "No measure has done greater injury to the cause of free trade in India or more permanent discredit to British rule than this excise duty on Indian manufactured cotton, for none has done more to undermine Indian faith in the principles of justice upon which British rule claims and on the whole most legitimately claims to be based."[122] By its action and its clear discrimination, the Government antagonised the Indian industrial class.[123] It was also demonstrated more than once during the controversy that the Indian administration was entirely subordinate to London. Unfortunately for Elgin this first bill to be enacted during his first year term as Viceroy went against the Indian interests, thus starting his administration on the wrong foot. It may be noted, however, that the policy followed in connection with the cotton duties was a mere continuation of the policy which was laid down in 1875; even a change in the British Government, during Elgin's viceroyalty did not bring any change.

While concluding this discussion of the controversy, it is necessary to attribute the policy adopted to pressure from Manchester alone. Manchester no doubt exercised a special and powerful influence, using what McDonagh described the "Manchester technique of exercising pressure...upon susceptible statesmen."[124] Yet, the Manchester's opinion was shared by the majority of influential circles, whether in England, Scotland or Wales; whether in Oldham or London, whether Liberal or Conservative; industrial or a labour. Even among the working classes, Toryism dominated. As H.J. Hanham says in his book *Elections and Party Management*: "Several of the leading cotton union officials were Tories, including the most able of them, Thomas Birtwistle."[125]

The controversy sowed the seeds of discontent, if not of unrest, in India. Of this aspect J. Piele said:

> It supplies a weapon to our enemies on the platform and in the press. It is a dangerous thing to set a sense of wrong, which we can neither deny nor entirely explain away, circulating above ground or underground among the millions of India. The safety and strength of our empire rests on our being unscrupulously and fearlessly just.[126]

### NOTES

[1] A Note prepared by Sir Henry Waterfield, Finance Secretary, India Office, on the history of cotton duties up to 1879; November 1894, Revenue and Statistics and Commerce Department Papers of the Council of India, 1443/94, vol. 336 (Hereafter cited as R and S Papers).

[2] E.C. Moulton, *Lord Northbrook's Indian Administration, 1872-1876*, Bombay, 1968, p. 178.

[3] *Ibid.*, 174.

[4] For details see L.M. Gujral, *Internal Administration of Lord Lytton, 1876-80*, unpublished, Ph.D. thesis, London University, 1958, Chap. I.

[5] An analysis of expenditure on the army in India 1884-5 to 1892-3 was forwarded to the Secretary of State in Indian Government L.No. 63 (Mil.), 5 April 1893, Military and Marine Letters from India, vol. 69.

[6] Westland's Statement, *Proc. of the Council of the Governor-General in India*, 1894, vol. 33, p. 118. Writing a letter to the Editor of *The Times*, 19 February 1895, David Barbour (former Finance Member of the Government of India) pointed out that all budgets from 1892-3 to 1895-6 had shown deficits, in spite of the fact that increases in taxation in the form of income tax, salt tax, petroleum tax and import duties had brought in additional revenues amounting to Rs 55 million. In addition to this Rs 15 million were absorbed to central revenues from the famine relief and provincial funds.

[7] Elgin to Kimberley, 31 January 1894, E.P., vol. 12.

[8] Telegram S.S. to Viceroy, (Pr.), 30 January 1894, *ibid.*, vol. 17.

## Cotton Duties 61

⁹Telegram Viceroy to S.S., 16 February 1894, *ibid.*
¹⁰Godley to Elign, 22/23 February 1894, *ibid.*, vol. 29.
¹¹All the 11 Members dissented. Minutes of the Council of India, vol. 72, pp. 98-9.
¹²Telegrams S.S. to Viceroy, 27 February 1894, *ibid.* vol. 17.
¹³Elgin to Fowler, 7 March 1894, E.P. vol. 12.
¹⁴*Proc. of the Council of the Governor General in India*, 1894, vol. 33, p. 119.
¹⁵Telegram Viceroy to S.S., 6 March 1894, E.P., vol 17.
¹⁶Telegram S.S. to Viceroy, 8 March 1894, *ibid.*
¹⁷*Proc. of the Council of the Governor-General in India*, 1894, vol. 33, pp. 143-4.
¹⁸*Ibid.*, p. 145.
¹⁹*Ibid.*, p. 163.
²⁰*Ibid.*, p. 180.
²¹Indian Government sent 29 Enclosures with L. No. 27 (Fin.) of 21 March 1894, all condemning the exclusion of cotton goods from the general tariff Act. F.E.I. vol. 180.
²²Telegram Punjab Govt. to Viceroy, 3 March 1894, E.P., vol. 64.
²³*Kaiser-i-Hind*, 11 March 1894, *Bombay Samachar*, 13 and 14 March 1894, *Bomb. N.N.R.* 1894.
²⁴*Maharatha*, 4 March 1894; *Gujarati*, 4 March; *Kaiser-i-Hind*; 4 March, *Bomb. N.N.R.* 1894.
Samachar, 7 March 1894; *Hitavadi*, 15 March 1894; *Bengal N.N.R.* 10 March 1894; *Madras N.N.R.* 1894.
²⁵15 March 1894, *Beng. N.N.R.*, 1894.
²⁶*Sulabah Dainik*, 7 April 1894, *ibid.*
²⁷*Hindu Panch*, 22 March 1894; Poona *Vaibhava*, 15 April; *Danyan Prakash*, 16 April 1894; *Bomb. N.N.R.* 1894.
²⁸Arbuthnot's Note of Dissent, 1 March 1894, India Council Minut Book (copies), vol. 5, p. 1-2.
²⁹*Ibid.*, p. 3. See also Memorandum by Lord Farrer on the Indian cotton duties, R and S papers, No. 518/94 vol. 324. Only a few voices were raised against the measure in the House of Commons. Sir George Chisney deplored the action of the Secretary of State.
³⁰Elgin to Godley, 21 March 1894, E.P., vol. 64.
³¹S.S. to Indian Government Despatch No. 65 (Rev.), 31 May 1894, Para No. 10 Revenue Despatches to India, vol. 15.
³²*Ibid.*, Para 16.
³³J. Westland's Minute, 14 July 1894 (Confidential), India Fin. and Com. Proc. (Statistics and Com.) vol. 4606, No. 378, August 1894. The original minute contained 52 paragraphs. 27 were omitted from the Parliamentary Papers issued as a *Blue Book*, vol. 72 (C. 7602) 1895. The unexpurgated minute was not made public.
³⁴The Count of a yarn is the number of yards of that yarn which required to make up weight of 1/840 of a pound. 20S are therefore exactly twice as fine as 10S and 30S are three times as fine. Of these

Counts it would require 10 yards, 20 yards and 30 yards, respectively to make up the weight of 1/840 of a pound.

[35] *Op. cit.*, Para 11.

At that time, only a small proportion of the yarns produced by Indian mills was used for mill weaving. Of the 141 mills than in existence, only 64, or less than half, possessed any looms at all; the rest were occupied solely in producing yarns for export and for handloom consumption. Among the 64 mills with looms, the weaving department absorbed only a portion of output of yarns: 373 million lbs were exported, 129 million lbs were sold to handlook weavers and 74 million lbs were used for weaving. J. Westland, Minute, Para 15.

[36] Of the imports, Bombay, Madras, and Calcutta each received a little over 10 million lbs. Of the imports into Bombay, a complete analysis extending over 24 years was made by the Bombay Chamber of Commerce and the result of that analysis showed that

(a) of grey mule twist, only 0.4 out of 27.21 or 15 per cent of the imports was of 24S and under;

(b) of grey water twist, only 15 out of 26.19 or p. 57 per cent of the imports was of 24S and under;

(c) and the percentage in both cases had been for years, gradually decreasing. *Ibid.*, Para 17.

[37] *Ibid.*, Paras 27-8.

[38] *Ibid.*, Para 23. Even of the exports to the U.K., about half, Westland believed, were re-exported to the Continent.

[39] Westland's Minute, Para 29. It was to these remarks that Fowler had taken exception and asked Elgin to properly edit and excision the Minute. Fowler to Elgin, 13 December 1894, E.P., vol. 12.

[40] Westland's Minute, Para 29.

[41] Indian Government to S.S., L. No. 210 (Fin.), Confidential, 7 August 1894, F.L.I., vol. 179.

[42] Elgin to Fowler, 24 July 1894, E.P. vol. 12. He wrote, "It does not seem to me that it is shown to be in a condition to be a serious rival to Lancashire and the accounts of the Mills in Native states are not encouraging as to the prospects of Natives carrying on successfully the better class of manufactures; but still it gives employment to a large number of workmen, more in proportion, as Westland points out, than in England, and I think it deserves every encouragement we can legitimately give it."

[43] Fowler to Elgin, 17 August 1894, *ibid.*

[44] Godley to Elgin, 23 August 1894, *ibid.*, vol. 29.

[45] *Monthly Record of the Manchaster Chamber of Commerce*, Res., 19 March, 13 June, 5 November 1894, 1895, vol. vi, pp. 1-2.

[46] Fowler to Elgin, 9 November 1894, E.P., vol. 12. See also Note prepared by M.A.N. Woolaston (Assit. in the Rev. Statistics Dept. of India Office) on exercise, 10 September 1894, R and S Papers No. 1443/94, vol. 336.

[47] Telegram viceroy to S.S., 28 November 1894, E.P., vol. 17.

## Cotton Duties

[48] Members for Public Work and Law.
[49] Fowler to Elgin, 12 October 1894, E.P., vol. 12.
[50] Fowler to Elgin, 30 November 1894, *ibid.*
[51] Even Godley wrote to Elgin, "I wish the principle had been settled by one of your predecessors." Godley to Elgin, 28 November 1894, *ibid.*, vol. 29.
[52] Elgin to Fowler, 14 August 1894, Wolverhampton Papers, MSS. Eur. C. 145.
[53] *Proc. of the Council of the Governor General in India,* vol. 33, pp. 384-92 and p. 404.
[54] *Ibid.,* pp. 402-38.
[55] Nine votes were in favour of the amendment and 11 against (including Lord Elgin) one abstained (Stevens).
[56] *Proc. of the Council of the Governor General of India,* 1894, vol. 33, p. 447.
[57] *Ibid.,* p. 449.

Later, Elgin tried to clarify his position and denied to Fowler that he argued for his "Mandate theory." "I assert the supermacy of Parliament and allege that the Secretary of State is the only proper exponent of what Parliament means, I reserve absolutely the right of voting to men who act under a due sense of their responsibility. I only mention these points because it is generally assumed that I argued for your 'mandate' overriding everything. Even as regards the Members of the Executive that is not what I said or intended." Elgin to Fowler, 9 January 1895, E.P., vol. 13.

[58] During Lytton's of Indian administration, when Manchester demanded that an excise duty be imposed on India cotton goods, he termed it an "abominable proposal" and added "I think that the Manchester gentlemen who made it ought to be ashamed of themselves." Lytton to Louis Mallot 15 March 1878, vide L.N. Gujral's, *International Administration of Lord Lytton, op. cit.,* p. 38.

[59] *Proc. of the Council of the Governor General in India,* 1894, vol. 33, p. 425.

See also Secretary Millowners Association, Bombay, to India Government, 10 September, 1894, India Fin. & Com. (Statistics of Com.), Proc. vol. 4606, No. 796, November 1894.

[60] "It is a gratuitous insult to the Government of India that the Council should be asked to pass it and the insult is greater, and its infliction the more unpardonable, that the circumstances are such that the Government of India is required to choose between becoming the instrument of its own humiliation and furnishing a practical proof of the justice of the imputation which constitutes the insult." *The Friend of India,* Calcutta 16 January 1895, E.P. vol. 76 (Newspaper cuttings).

[61] Fowler to Elgin, 2 January 1895, *ibid.,* vol. 13.
[62] Mowbray to Elgin, 14 February 1895, *ibid.,* vol. 30.
[63] Fowler to Elgin, 15 February, 1895, *ibid.,* vol. 13.
[64] *The Times,* 22 February 1895.
[65] *Ibid.*

In the course of the debate, Sir George Chesney further elucidated the point, stating that England imposed 200 per cent import duty on Indian tea and five times that on Indian cigars.

[66] Parliamentary Debates, 4th Series, vol. 30, Col. 1349, 21 February 1895.

[67] *The Times*, 22 February 1895.

[68] No statistics covering such goods entering Burma were maintained.

[69] Fowler to Elgin, 22 February 1895, E.P., vol. 13.

[70] Telegram Viceroy to S.S., 22 March 1895, *ibid.*, vol. 18.

[71] Indian Government to S.S., L. No. 98 (Fin.), 1 May 1895, F.L.I., vol. 182.

[72] Lancashire deputation to Rt. Hon. H.H. Fowler, 27 May 1895. India Sep. Rev., Proc., 5031, No. 785, July 1896. The Lancashire arguments were conspicuously loaded with threats of use of their political and economic strength. During the discussion, Fowler was reminded of this at least five times by succession of the deputationists.

[73] Statement drawn up by John Whittaker on behalf of Joint Committee of Cotton Manufacturers, 9 July 1895. India Sep. Rev. Proc., vol. 5031, No. 791, July 1896.

[74] Godley to Elgin, 30 July 1895, E.P., vol. 30.

[75] Lt. Gen. Brackenbury to Elgin, 30 June 1895, *ibid.*, vol. 66. The new Cabinet consisted of three former Secretaries of State besides Hamilton, Lord Salisbury, Lord Cross and Lord Devonshire.

[76] Hamilton to Elgin, 16 August 1895, *ibid.*, vol. 13.

[77] Lancashire Memorial, Enc., *ibid*.

[78] Hamilton to Elgin, 16 August 1895, *op. cit.*

[79] Elgin to Hamilton, 3 September, Hamilton Collection, MSS. Eur. D. 509/1 vol. 1. (Hereafter cited as H.C.).

[80] Westland of Elgin, 6 September, 1895, *ibid.*

[81] Elgin to Hamilton, 10 September 1895, H.C., D. 509/1, vol. 1.

[82] Hamilton to Elgin, 3 October and 31 October 1895, E.P., vol. 13.

[83] Elgin to Hamilton, 16 October 1895, H.C., D. 509/1, vol. 1.

[84] Hamilton to Elgin, 7 November 1895, E.P., vol. 13.

[85] *Ibid.*

Hamilton, after duly consulting Lancashire, had agreed to Westlands proposals, providing that weight was substituted for value in assessing the tax, that is substitution of a tax per pound of cloth in place of 5 per cent *ad valorem*. Hamilton to Elgin, 29 November 1895, *ibid.*, vol. 13.

[86] Telegram Westland to Pr. Secy. to Elgin, 17 November 1895, *ibid.*, vol. 67.

[87] Hamilton to Elgin, 7 November 1895, *ibid.*, vol. 13.

[88] Telegram S.S. to Viceroy, 5 December 1895, *ibid.*, vol. 18. George Lord to Hamilton, 3 December 1895.

Enc. Hamilton to Elgin, 6 December 1895, *ibid.*, vol. 13.

[89] Hamilton to Elgin, 13 December 1895, E.P., vol. 13.

[90] Northbrook to Godley, 29 January 1896, Encl. Godley to Elgin, 1 February 1896, E.P., vol. 31.

## Cotton Duties 65

⁹¹Lancashire statement submitted to S.S., Objection No. I & II, 9 July 1895, India Sep. Rev. (Fin. & Com.) Prof., vol. 5031, 791, July 1896 (Hereafter cited as Lancashire statement).

⁹²*Percentage volume of grey drills imported into Bombay to the total value of total cotton goods imports 1890-5.*

| Calendar Year | Value of all cotton goods imported excluding yarns Rs | Approximate average value of grey drills imported | Percentage |
|---|---|---|---|
| 1890 | 8,75,64,722 | 15,21,241 | 1.73 |
| 1891 | 8,03,80,929 | 20,83,559 | 2.59 |
| 1892 | 7,08,68,829 | 13,51,091 | 1.90 |
| 1893 | 7,78,42,481 | 18,63,602 | 2.39 |
| 1894 | 10,01,13,677 | 19,43,648 | 1.94 |
| Average of 5 years | 8,33,54,127 | 17,52,628 | 2.11 |
| 1895 (11 months) | 6,14,04,294 | 14,55,654 | 2.37 |

Bombay Millowners' Association, 7 January 1896, Para 39, India Sep. Rev. (Fin. & Com.) Proc., vol. 5031, 879, July 1896 (Hereafter cited as Millowners' statement).

⁹³*Ibid.*, Para 8.

⁹⁴Lancashire statement, objection v. *op. cit.*

⁹⁵Noble to Fowler, Lancashire Deputation, *op. cit.* As a matter of fact Noble had misquoted Westland. What he actually said was, "It would obviously never pay "Manchester to use up American cotton at 4d. a pound in making a class of goods which their Indian competitors can make up as well as out of cotton that only costs 3d." *Parl. Papers,* 1895, vol. LXXII, (C. 7602) (called *Blue Book*), p. 8.

⁹⁶Millowners' Statement, Para 24, *op. cit.* This statistical data was based on Reuter's Telegram. As a matter of fact, on 15 February 1895, when American cotton was quoted in Liverpool at 3d., good Dhollera was quoted at 2 9/16 per lb Reuter's Telegram, 15 February 1895.

⁹⁷Thompson to Fowler, Lancashire Deputation, 27 May 1895, *op. cit.*

⁹⁸*Trade Statements of British India,* 1893-4, Parl. Collection, No. 194 (C. 7604), p. 6.

⁹⁹*Ibid.*, p. 6.

¹⁰⁰Elgin had informed Fowler that, in anticipation of the proposed import duty on cotton goods, large stocks were being sent to India. Telegram Viceroy to S.S., 7 December 1894, E.P., vol. 17.

¹⁰¹*Trade Statements of British India, 1894-5,* Parl. Collection, No. 194 (C. 7997), p. 19.

¹⁰²Fowler had told the deputationists that the trade in the first four months of 1895 was higher than in the first four months of any previous year except 1894. Fowler to Lancashire deputation, 27 May 1895, *op. cit..*

[103]*Trade Statement of British India*, 1894-5, Parl. Collection, No. 194 (C. 7997), p. 19.

[104]Millowners' Statement, Para. 73 *op. cit.*

In course of conversation with the Lancashire deputation, even Fowler had stated, "I do not know where the trade has gone because there is no corresponding manufacture in India." Fowler to Lancashire Deputation, 27 May 1895, *op. cit.* For Statistics, see India Sep. Rev. (Fin. & Com.) Proc., vol. 5031, Nos. 880-1, July 1896.

[105]Westland of Elgin, 6 September 1895, E.P., vol. 67.

[106]Fowler to Lancashire Deputation, 27 May 1895, *op. cit.*

[107]Lancashire Statement, objection No. 3, 9 July 1895, *op. cit.*

[108]J. Monteath, Act. Secy. to Bombay Govt. Rev. Dept. to the Secy. Indian Govt. 23 January 1896, Para 4, India Sept. Rev. (Fin. & Com.) Proc., vol. 5031, 865, July 1896.

[109]Godley to Elgin, 3 January 1896, E.P., vol. 31.

[110]Westland to Babington Smith Pr. Secy. to Viceroy, 8 January 1896, *ibid.*, vol. 68.

[111]*Proc. of the Council of Governor-General*, 1896, vol. 35, p. 35.

[112]R.C. Dutt, *Economic History of India*, p. 543, C.N. Vakil, *Financial Development of Modern India*, p. 433.

[113]J. Piele, Minute of Dissent, 10 April 1896, Dissent of Indian Council, Minute Book (copies) vol. 5, p. 33. All the unofficial members of the legislative Council vehemently criticised the government action but without any avail. For Indian National Congress reaction see P.C. Ghosh, *The Development of Indian National Congress 1892-1909*. Calcutta, 1960, chap. IX. Without any exception, all the newspapers, Native and Anglo-Indian, severely criticised the Government.

[114]S.S. to Indian Government Despatch No. 99 (Rev.), 5 September 1895, Enc. No. 3, Revenue Despatches to India, vol. 16.

[115]G.D.H. Cole, *Introduction to Economic History, 1750-1950*, London, 1953, p. 93.

[116]A.E. Musson, "The Great Depression in Britain, 1873-96; a Reappraisal," *The Journal of Economic History*, vol. XIX June 1959, p. 206.

[117]W. Hoffman, *British Industrial Production, 1700-1950*, Oxford, 1955, pp. 31-5.

The annual rate of manufacturing growth of the U.S. between 1873 to 1913 was 4.8 per cent, of Germany 3.9 per cent, 3.7 per cent for the world as a whole, and only 1.8 per cent for the United Kingdom. (Folke Hilgerdt, *Industrialization and Foreign Trade*, League of Nations, 1945, p. 132.) Not only this, the U.K.'s share of world manufacturing production was sharply declining: in 1870 it was 31.8 per cent between 1896-1900 it had fallen to 19.5 per cent, whereas that of the U.S. had grown from 23.3 to 30.1 per cent and that of Germany from 13.2 to 16.6 per cent. (*Ibid.*, p. 13. See also William Ashworth, *A History of the International Economy 1850-1950*, London, 1954, pp. 35-8.

[118]See S.J. Chapman, *The Lancashire Cotton Industry*, Manchester, 1 04, pp. 23-33, and 70-71.

[119]As a matter of fact, it was with such countries that British trade expended. The Board of Trade's statistics clearly show this shift in the distribution of British exports. See *Annual Statement of Trade Statistical Abstracts*, Par 1. Paper, 1903, vol. LXVII (ed. 1761), 1904, vol. LXXXIV (ed. 2337).

[120]A.E. Musson, *op. cit.*, p. 228.

See J. Gallaghar and R. Robinson, "The imperialism of the Free Trade," *Economic History Review*, vol. vi, 1953-54, pp. 1-15. Parker Thomas Moon, *Imperialism and World Politics*, New York, 1927, chap. iii. J.A. Hobson, *Imperialism: a study*, London, 1954, ed., Part I, chap. iv.

[121]P. Harnety, "The Indian Cotton Duties Controversy," *English Historical Review*, October 1962, vol. 77, p. 701.

[122]*Indian Unrest*, London, 1910, pp. 276-7.

[123]Percival Spear, *India: A Modern History*, Michigan, 1961, p. 337.

[124]O. MacDonagh, "The Anti-Imperialism of Free Trade," *Economic History Review*, 1961-2, vol. xiv, p. 492.

[125]H.J. Hanham, *Elections and Party Management*, Manchester, 1959, pp. 326-7.

[126]J. Piele, Minute of Dissent, 10 April 1896, Dissent of India Council, Minute Book, vol. 5, p. 39.

This part was ordered to be omitted by the Secretary of State when it was printed on the orders of the House of Commons.

CHAPTER III

# RAILWAYS

The period of Elgin's viceroyalty was one of considerable activity in the field of railway expansion in India. He viewed the expansion of railways to be the most important and "legitimate" of tasks for a Viceroy, "far more so, in my opinion, than wars or expeditions."[1] He was of the opinion that new railway lines in India would improve the trade and prosperity of the people. This expansion, Elgin believed, was not possible without the substantial participation of private enterprise. But private capital in Britain was reluctant to invest in India on account of the falling gold value of the rupee. This could only be overcome by a firm and direct guarantee of protection against losses arising out of such decline. Elgin boldly acknowledged this and, to ensure proper and speedy utilisation of private investment, and to protect investors against exploitation by unscrupulous company promoters, he also thoroughly reorganised the railway branch of the Public Works Department and inaugurated a policy of railway planning in India. In this and other dispositions about railways he was abundantly successful. Railway mileage was extended from 18,459 in 1893 to 22,491 in 1899.[2]

To place railway activities during Elgin's administration in perspective, it would be useful to trace briefly the earlier history of railways in India.

The first sod was turned for the construction of Indian railways in 1849, but it was 1853 before the first line, between Bombay and Kalyan, was opened to traffic. It was Lord Dalhousie who was largely responsible for giving the first fillip to railway construction in India.[3] He was convinced for the importance of railways both for preserving internal order and external security. He accurately gauged the important role India would play both as a supplier of cheap raw materials to British industry and as a market for its finished goods.[4]

In a well known Minute of April 1853, Dalhousie laid great

emphasis on the necessity of laying a system of "trunk lines" connecting the interior of each presidency with its major towns and the presidencies with each other. To this end, he maintained, it was the duty and interest of the state to encourage the investment of "English capital and English energy" in India.[5] The earliest railway construction was by the "guaranteed companies" incorporated in England.[6]

The terms of agreements with the guaranteed companies were onerous to the Government. The first of such agreements were with which the East Indian and the Great Indian Peninsula Railway Companies. Interest at 5 per cent per annum for 99 years was guaranteed to the Company on capital paid into the Treasury. The guarantor was to be given an advance, which was to be repaid with interest at 5 per cent from profits above the guaranteed minimum, in such a way that half of the profits were to be credited to the company and the other half were to be applied, first towards payment of interest on the debt, and then towards the extinction of the debt. When both the debt and interest were discharged, the companies were to take the whole of the surplus net receipts. At the expiration of the term of 99 years the ownership of the whole assets of the railways would pass to the Government.[7]

Up to 1869, when the policy of guaranteed companies was given up, 4,255 miles of railway were opened in India. Though the railways greatly improved the political, military and commercial situation, financially they were a liability.[8] Soon, the drawbacks of the guarantee system began to show. It was found that the guarantee had been fixed at too high a rate, which deprived the companies of all incentive to economy in construction.[9] It was realised that the greater the amount spent, the greater would be the amount of stock which would stand at premium. "Consequently, the earnings which might have been sufficient to pay interest charges on a reasonable expenditure, proved inadequate to meet the guarantee on the outlay actually incurred and the Government had to make good the deficit."[10]

The failure of the guarantee system and the increasing financial burden of the guarantee forced the authorities to seek a solution. In January 1869, Lawrence scrapped the system under which "the whole profit goes to the Companies, and the whole loss to the Government."[11] Lawrence and his advisers recommended that all future railway extension should be carried out by the direct agency of the Government. This was agreed to by the Home Government with a proviso that a definite annual sum should be devoted to this purpose, which was then fixed at £2,500,000.

The experiment of railway construction exclusively through the agency of the State lasted only a decade. Though financially cheaper, it came under severe criticism for tardy progress of construction. Between 1869 and 1880, only 2,493 miles of railway were constructed.[12] This slow growth was primarily due to the fact that the State revenue had proved insufficient for railway construction, particularly as a result of the famines of 1874 and 1879, the Afghan War and the fall in the gold value of silver.[13]

The Famine Commission of 1880 underlined the paramount importance of railways for famine relief. The commissioners urged an immediate addition of not less than 5,000 miles and subsequent construction of 20,000 more miles for protective purposes.[14] Besides, British mercantile opinion was rapidly growing more favourable towards large railway expansion in India and urged more and fuller participation of private enterprise in the process.

Between 1880 and 1884, the elements of a new policy were formulated. The agency of the companies was reintroduced for the construction of new lines as well as for the working of the State-owned railways. The policy of State construction also continued. Assistance to companies took the form of a "limited guarantee" or "safe or reasonable guarantee," terms difficult to define. The departure in railway policy dating from 1881 may be regarded as the beginning of a "new policy" which implies a complete abandonment of the policy of 1869-70.[15]

In 1881 and 1882, four companies were brought into existence to undertake new construction and manage the lines without any guarantee at all. These lines were the Bengal Central, the Rohilkhand Kumaon, the Bengal and the North-Western, and the Southern Mahratha railways. This policy too did not prove a success. The first two companies were soon bought by the State; the third was subsidised by the Government by adding the Tirhoot State Railway, a profitable line; the last was given a Sterling guarantee of $3\frac{1}{2}$ per cent in the form of "assistance"—

the assistance, however, "taking the very substantial and attractive form of a Sterling guarantee, somewhat above the English market rate, together with a prospective share of surplus profits and free grant of land."[16] The main terms of the guarantee[17] were: (1) the railways were to be the property of the State, only the capital being provided by the company; (2) the interest on the capital raised was to be $3\frac{1}{2}$ per cent; and (3) the State retained nearly $\frac{1}{4}$ of the surplus profit. These companies, therefore, unlike the old guaranteed companies, were merely agents appointed by Government to raise capital to construct the lines, and then work them for Government.

Failing to attract foreign capital without a Sterling guarantee, the Indian Government proposed, on 19 March 1893, that capital be invited, on a rupee basis, for the construction, "principally" of branch lines.[18] The Secretary of State agreed to the terms suggested and the Indian Government issued a Resolution on 15 September 1893, with a view to encourage the construction of feeder railway lines by private enterprise.

The essential features of the new Resolution were: (1) the investor was to select the general direction of the branch lines; (2) he was to raise his capital and place that capital in the hands of the Government; (3) the branch line was "to be worked by the state for not more than 50 per cent of gross earnings, including the provision of rolling stock and the free use of land"; and (4) a rebate was to be given by the parent line to the branch line on traffic inter-changed with it, so as to provide a return of four per cent on the approved capital.[19]

This Resolution failed to get any response. It was considered by the investors whom it was intended to attract that the conditions imposed were neither clear nor certain. Secondly, the investors who had looked forward to some sort of guarantee as a "convenient" system, professed doubt concerning its sufficiency. It was also asserted that the limit set at ten per cent of the gross earnings of the main line from traffic interchanged between the main line and the branch was unsuitable for universal application; for, in some cases, it could be either too little or too much.[20] Added to this was the obvious difficulty of estimating the value of the rebate or the probable receipts from local traffic.[21] A further discouraging factor was that the exchange value of the rupee was moving towards its lowest point, (1s. $0\frac{1}{2}$d.) in June

1894 and, in the circumstances, the terms offered could hardly be received favourably.

Thus, it was the unsettled condition of the currency situation that greatly hindered the expansion of India's railways. On the one hand, Sterling capital could not be freely employed without unduly increasing Sterling liabilities; on the other, private English capital would not be forthcoming until assured of the risks being covered. When Elgin took office, railway policy was at the crossroads: there was urgent need of a well considered policy and an organisation to implement it.

Elgin considered the Resolution of September 1893 as the first obstacle towards a resolute railway policy and the utilisation of private enterprise for railway expansion. He was aware that the Secretary of State had in 1884 imposed a limit of £$2\frac{1}{2}$ million on Government borrowing for public works. He believed that, if rapid expansion of railways was to take place, this amount was inadequate and the aid of private enterprise was essential. He believed personally from the point of view of the general progress of the country, the immediate returns were of little significance and he was therefore eager to "give more encouragement to private enterprise."[22] The Secretary of State, Fowler, was of the same opinion and stated that, until a way could be found to offer more attractive terms than those of September 1893, little progress could be made.[23] It was in an attempt to offer better terms to private enterprise for branch lines that a new railway policy was laid down and an important departure from the prevailing policy effected.

The realisation of the need for the change was growing both in England and in India. The first move came from the Indian Government, when Lt. Col. Bisset, Director General of Railways, asked for revision of the terms. But it was the Secretary of State who officially recommended the alteration of the resolution. This was the result of constant pressure on the Secretary of State from mercantile interests in England The London Chamber of Commerce, in its letter of 19 June 1894, and Duff Bruce, Consulting Engineer to the Assam-Bengal Railway, in his letter of 6 June 1894 to the Secretary of State, advocated an enlargement of the terms of the Resolution.[24] Duff Bruce suggested the replacement of the rebate on account of inter-line traffic (section 7 of the Resolution) by a fixed guarantee of $3\frac{1}{2}$ per cent on their capital to be paid by the main line to the branch line shareholders. After the payment of the fixed guarantee, other fixed sums and working expenses, the profits should be divided in the proportion of 2/3 to the owing (branch) company and 1/3 to the working (main line) company.[25]

The London Chamber of Commerce suggested that the "rebate of traffic" principle should be maintained, but the existing maximum of 10 per cent on interchanged traffic should be raised to 40 or 50 per cent and that this would be without any real risk of loss to the State.[26]

These notes were discussed by C. S. Colvin, Secretary, Public Works, at the India Office. In his note of 8 June 1894, he stated that Bruce's suggestion would be a "too radical departure from the policy under trial." He believed the limit of 10 per cent for the rebate in question "to be too low an one," and sought "for relief in enlarging this limit."[27] He supported the London Chamber of Commerce's proposal, which the Public Works Committee had accepted in full, and suggested to the Secretary of State that to write to the Indian Government instructing revision of the terms of the Resolution of 15 September 1893.[28] In August 1894, the Secretary of State moved for the amendment.[29]

Calcutta and Bombay were equally restive for a change. In his Presidential Address to the Bengal Chamber of Commerce, Arthur Allan underlined the importance of feeder lines and pressed the Government to offer favourable terms to the private enterprise and advocated the cause of the guarantee system.

The decisive step towards the change was taken by Lord Elgin in his Note of 31 December 1894. He emphasised the general principles underlying Government's railway policy of encouraging private interprise to undertake expansion. As a first step he agreed to alter the Resolution of September 1893 as proposed by the Secretary of State and increase the terms of rebate. Though he was convinced that, without some sort of guarantee, the situation was not going to improve, he was not immediately inclined to advocate anything beyond an increased rebate. The Indian Government suggested to the Secretary of State that the returns to branch lines from gross earnings on the traffic interchanged with main line be increased from 10 to 15 per cent.[30] But Fowler considered this to be too meagre a concession to warrant a change and recommended steps "to enlarge the rebate to the extent required to make up to 4 per cent return, provided that rebate shall in no case exceed net earnings of the main line from interchanged traffic."[31]

The Secretary of State's view was opposed very strongly by both the Public Works Member, Charles Pritchard, and the Finance Member, James Westland.[32] They objected to his suggestion on the ground of its being "equivalent to a firm guarantee,"[33] as also on two other counts. One was that such a scheme necessarily meant increasing the capital value of the line, if owned or built by a private company; and the second that it could adversely effect State revenues in case the Government decided to buy a line.[34] Pritchard tenaciously held to the spirit of the Resolution of 1893 and Westland discouraged anything which involved additional expenditure.[35]

The Viceroy concurred with his colleagues' opposition to the "firm guarantee," as implied in the proposal of the Secretary of State, but notwithstanding this, he preferred the construction of branch lines by "separate companies." He also suggested that the percentage of net earnings rebate to the branch should not exceed $3\frac{1}{2}$ per cent.[36]

Elgin had two motives in restricting the Secretary of State's proposal to small branch lines and their construction by separate companies. One was to mitigate the fears of his colleagues and another was his desire to see feeders develop quickly.[37] In the case of major lines, he did not want Government to offer such a high dividend, particularly when Government could get capital at a lower rate of interest in the market or by giving a direct guarantee of returns of 3 or $2\frac{1}{2}$ per cent.[38] Fowler accepted the suggestion concerning a lower dividend but did not agree to restrict either the lengths of branches or construction by separate companies.[39] The Indian Government accepted proposals for the construction of branch or feeder railways "provided that capital is in rupees" and further that it be "clearly understood that offers in sterling on this basis, whether in London or India, will not be admitted."[40] But Fowler was not prepared to agree to a general exclusion of Sterling capital and stated, "each offer in London must be considered by me on its merits."[41] Accordingly, the Indian Government published the amended Resolution on 29 March 1895 which did not mention any rebate or dividend for sterling offers.[42]

The result of publishing the amended resolution without any reference to Sterling capital was unfortunate. The press and the public, particularly the English mercantile community, objected to the reduction from 4 to $3\frac{1}{2}$ per cent of the dividend to the branch lines, whose capital was in rupees. They stated that the Government, instead of encouraging rupee capital, boosted Sterling interests, for whom the dividend remained at 4 per cent.[43] They would have preferred its reduction to $3\frac{1}{2}$ per cent. The Bombay Chamber of Commerce showed its annoyance when it wrote, "The Chamber thinks that the effects of the alteration, as proposed by the Government of India Resolution of 29 March, will be to render the conditions more complex and obscure than ever, as sterling and rupee capital are to be differently treated."[44] Even Elgin agreed that "sterling dividend on sterling schemes ought to be somewhat less than $3\frac{1}{2}$ per cent on rupee schemes."[45] On the whole, the amended resolution was an improvement over the Resolution of 1893. The intention of the alterations was to provide increased inducements for investment of the rupee capital, but the public misunderstood the offer and, instead of welcoming the very substantial increase in the security (which was as good as a firm guarantee), the public persistently fixed upon the difference of rate, $3\frac{1}{2}$ per cent instead of 4 per cent, ignoring altogether that they were the minimum rates. What this resolution suffered from was not lack of the element of inducement but want of clarity.

The significance of this resolution should not be underestimated. It was the first step towards the reintroduction of the guarantee system, though, at that stage, only an indirect or imperfect guarantee to be met from the net earnings of the railway line and not from the whole revenue of the State. This in itself was, nevertheless a big change and quite a departure from the previous policy.

The need for further change in the branch line policy was soon felt. Private enterprise was not yet satisfied; they continued to press for a more effective guarantee. The Government of India realised that a fresh resolution defining more clearly the terms to be offered to private enterprise was required.

On the initiative of Elgin, who was resolved to give an absolute guarantee for branch line construction, the Indian Government decided to cancel the resolutions of September 1893 and March 1895, and issued a new resolution on 17 April 1896.[46] Its main feature was that the Government allowed the promoter of a company an option between a rebate sufficient to make up a dividend of $3\frac{1}{2}$ per cent (on the terms stated in the resolution of March 1895) and an "absolute guarantee" of interest, the rate being 3 per cent.[47] In either case, it was provided that any assistance given by the government was to be on a silver basis, whether the capital was raised in silver or Sterling.[48] the new resolution also limited the length of a branch line to 100 miles. This definitely ended the ambiguity of the previous resolution and clearly demarcated the difference between branch and main line construction.[49] The success of the resolution was immediate. As many as seven branch line constructions came up under the purview of the new resolution.[50]

Until the old resolution was cancelled, there was only one "statement of terms" open to the promoters. That was in the resolution that dealt with branch lines only. Yet, in practice, proposals had been made "to apply its terms to lines which by no possibility could be called branches or even extensions" like the South Punjab Railway which was 400 miles long. There was, therefore, need to simplify and declare the general policy applicable to all construction.[51] As stated earlier, it was in lieu of the branch line resolutions that a railway policy towards private enterprise came to be firmly established. No doubt in its making, it had taken a hammering for nearly two years, during which period the efforts of Elgin were singular. As early as 31 December 1894, he had stated that larger lines, if to be constructed by private enterprise, must be given an absolute guarantee of interest.[52] At that stage, neither his Executive Council nor the Secretary of State was inclined to come forward publicly in favour of such a policy. But soon the opposition began to waver. Fowler promised to consider the question of guarantees.[53] The new Secretary of State, Hamilton, seemed to be in agreement: "A limited guarantee, with a prospective increment, is what the public would like, and this, I think, we could give."[54] By July 1895, Elgin was gratified to find that there was substantial agreement in his Council on the policy of guarantees. By September 1895, Elgin was delighted to hear that the Secretary of State and his Council were convinced of the need for the change.[55] On 9 October 1895, the Indian Government officially proposed an announcement of adherence to the guarantee system for the construction of the railways by companies.[56] The offer for the larger lines was made on the basis of a "plain guarantee," "which was presumed to be in sterling."[57]

The Public Works Department at the India Office, in its departmental minute of December 1895, counselled the Secretary of State to approve the guarantee system.[58] The joint Finance and Public Works Committee recommended on 9 January 1896 the following terms for construction of main line railways:[59]

(1) On a sterling basis, a limited guarantee of 3 per cent plus such share of surplus net profits as may be agreed upon.

(2) On a rupee basis, a somewhat higher guarantee ($3\frac{1}{2}$ per cent) plus such share of surplus net profits as may be agreed upon.

The proposal of the Indian Government was thus endorsed and accepted by Hamilton and his committee.[60]

For a correct appraisal of the "guarantee" policy, it is necessary to examine and analyse the reasons which impelled the Government to adopt it. For this purpose, it is imperative that we place this step in its historical perspective. The policy, at least in theory, after 1880 was to refuse guarantees and either to construct lines with State money and through a State agency or through unaided private enterprise. But private enterprise had failed altogether to come forward. For example, the Bengal Central Railway was started as an independent line, but the moment it failed to pay, pressure was brought to bear on government which induced the Secretary of State to take it over. Similarly, the Bengal and North-Western line had to be aided by leasing to them the Tirhoot State line in order to make the concern a paying one. In 1889, the Delhi-Kalka Railway was formed as an independent line, but as soon as it was opened, the company demanded exemption from the contract.[61] It is, perhaps, safe to assume that unaided companies did not exist.

In many cases, either a direct sterling guarantee was given, as in the case of the South Mahratha Railway and Assam-Bengal Railway, or the promoters tried to get guarantees in a round about way. An example could be cited. It was J. Westland[62] who examined this point when a promoter (Col. Filgate) offered to take over and complete the East Coast line on the basis of capital constituted as follows:

(A) Rs 450 lakhs Government money
(B) Rs 500 lakhs Company money
(C) Rs 400 lakhs either Government money or debentures

It was assumed that (C) would be divided into

(i) Rs 200 lakhs debentures
(ii) Rs 200 lakhs Government money[63]

Under the proposal of the promoter, if the line paid, on the whole, 2 per cent, or 27 lakhs "which may be taken as a certainty," the return would be thus distributed:

$3\frac{1}{2}$ per cent return on (A), Rs 7 lakhs
$3\frac{1}{2}$ per cent return on (B), Rs $17\frac{1}{2}$ lakhs

Government would get the balance of Rs $2\frac{1}{2}$ lakhs as its interest and return on its Rs 650 lakh contribution, i.e. being about 4/10 of one per cent. To Westland this was "only another name for a direct guarantee; only, whereas the company would hardly dare to ask for a direct guarantee of over 3 per cent, they can, by wrapping it up in words in this fashion, ask for $3\frac{1}{2}$."[64] And he further stressed, "we need not attempt to shut our eyes to the fact; and the first lesson to be drawn from it I take to be this—that it is far better that the guarantee should be a straight and simple one than that it should be wrapped up in roundabout methods."[65] Private enterprise, as understood in England, did not then exist in India, so far as railways were concerned. Elgin had rightly stated that genuine selfreliant Indian railways were few and far between. The schemes laid before Government as coming from private enterprise were usually only "promoter schemes, where the real interest was to float the company and little else."[66]

In addition to this, the offer of rebate failed to act as an inducement. C.H.T. Crosthwaite, the Member-in-Charge of Public Works in the Secretary of State's Council, opined, "I believe the offer of a rebate even with higher interest will rarely

# Railways

be taken."[67] "Experience has shown that no response will be made," stated Gen. H. Strachey, "on any appreciable scale of magnitude, to invitations to capitalists to undertake railways in India at their own risk, such as have been ineffectually made by the Government during a long series of years."[68]

Though construction by the State was considered to be the best and the cheapest way of extending the Indian railway system, this method suffered on account of lack of continuity. During famine and war, Government's resources had to be diverted. If railway development was to be continuous, it was essential that the money flow should be regular. In this context, only private companies could be useful. "The debt of India is really increased," argued Crosthwaite, "just as much by indirect borrowing as by direct loans. But the effect on the credit of the Government may not be the same. By raising money through a company the loan is marked off distinctly as raised for railway construction and is separated from the general unproductive debt of the country. For this advantage, such as it is, a heavier rate of interest will have to be paid."[69] Hence the need for a guarantee.

In the final analysis, it is clear that the whole thinking in Government and outside was obsessed with the guarantee system. The 1903 report of Thomas Robertson on Indian railways upheld the principle and stated that "unguaranteed enterprise have always been unpopular."[70] The Mackay Report of 1908 stressed even more the need for encouragement of private enterprise.[71] The Acworth Committee of 1921 was equally in favour of private enterprise.[72]

In formulating his policy, Elgin was primarily influenced by the falling exchange rate and the chequered history of private enterprise in Indian railway construction. He was convinced that the only solution lay in offering a "plain guarantee." Though he was conscious of the need, not to increase sterling liabilities, he was not prepared to curtail railway expansion on the ground of an adverse exchange situation. "I cannot help thinking that the indirect advantages of the railway extension go far to counterbalance even the loss on remittance."[73] Elgin firmly believed that, without railway expansion, the financial condition of India could not improve and for this expansion he was prepared to pay the price. In doing so, he had acknowledged the need for accepting the facts. He had also recognised that railway policy and railway expansion, without a system of proper control, a planned programme and efficient organisation, could never succeed in India. He set out to establish these as well.

Systematic planning was required for various reasons. One was that, if private enterprise was given some special facilities, it needed to be controlled as well, particularly when there were hardly any "genuine self-reliant Indian Railways."[74] The Government was determined to end the old situation in which profits went to private companies and losses to Government. Government was nevertheless interested in giving full scope to private enterprise in an organised way. "I see no way in which," admitted Elgin, "the railways of India can be wholly divorced from state control, the prejudice thus created can be avoided, except by the Government taking up the perfectly rational position that it does not throw the whole of India open to the company promoter, but will give free scope to private enterprise, the more genuine the better, by placing before the public the real requirements of the country."[75]

For the systematic growth of railways, it was essential to regulate the railway programme and maintain coordination between the Public Works Departments in London and India. The inconsistency of approach of the two was actually exploited by the promoters. Whenever they wanted to circumvent the Indian Government they went to the India Office and succeeded in getting done against the wishes of the Indian Government.[76] The grant of a $3\frac{1}{2}$ per cent Sterling guarantee to the Assam-Bengal Railways in 1892 by the Secretary of State in total disregard of the advice of the Indian Government was one such case. Another occurred as late as October 1895, when Hamilton announced, to the very great surprise of many, the sanction of a $3\frac{1}{2}$ per cent guarantee to the promoters of the Bhagalpur-Bansi branch line, without consulting the Indian Government, and this when a systematic policy in this behalf was being evolved.[77] "All I have to say is that, unless we do something of the kind, it is futile to ask us to pursue a consistent policy, because every forecast that we make is at any moment liable to be upset by the introduction of new and, possibly incompatible item."[78] Elgin's main desire was to shut all avenues which a speculative promoter tended to exploit.[79] He believed that uniformity of policy and approach was a prerequisite to a sound policy. The control of the programme was, therefore, a "far more important part of the new policy than any particular rate of interest or rebate."[80]

In order to attract genuine investors it was as important to check "speculative jobbers" as it was to avoid delays. At times, departmental delays were appalling and in some cases it took more than three years to start a project sanctioned by the Secretary of State.[81] These delays were caused primarily by the rivalry between the Finance Department and the Public Works Department, with each encroaching on the territory of the other.[82] To Elgin it was "labour in vain." Elgin felt that the most important need was to amend the departmental procedure and to lay down certain general lines of policy affecting the railways which could help to promote harmonious action by smoothening the differences in advance.[83]

This was achieved by establishing a committee of experts, comprising officials of the Public Works and Finance Departments and presided over by the Viceroy. The main business of the committee was to organise the working of the railways on a planned basis—to examine the schemes, select the best according to needs and implement them as quickly as possible.

The committee first met on 16 September 1896. At the outset, Elgin proposed the holding of an annual railway conference.[84] The deliberations of the first conference were sent to the Secretary of State in November 1896. In this despatch, the Government's policy concerning railway construction was recorded. It also underlined their reasons for preferring particular schemes to others.[85] As a first step, the conference had obtained reports from several local governments regarding their railway requirements.[86] After full consideration the conference divided railway construction schemes into four classes:[87]

*Class A*  Urgent lines sub-divided into (*i*) immediate, and (*ii*) early.
*Class B*  Lines not urgent sub-divided into (*i*) ready, and (*ii*) incomplete.
*Class C*  Lines set aside sub-divided into (*i*) postponed for further consideration, and (*ii*) rejected.

*Class D* Lines to be made without State assistance subdivided into (*i*) Native State Lines, and (*ii*) lines to be undertaken by private enterprise.

This classification was entirely Elgin's idea. "I say I have done so, for the whole thing was so much of a child of my own that I found it necessary to rewrite a good deal of the despatch."[88] This classification was put forward as an original piece just to avoid obstruction, confusion and unwarranted discussion which normally occurred in conferences.

Paragraph 14 of the Indian Government despatch of November 1896 was the most important one as it indicated, generally, the various factors the Government had taken into account in formulating its scheme. The distribution of railway lines on the basis of provincial divisions was deliberately avoided, for it could lead to provincial rivalries. It would have been equally impracticable to base it on the administrative areas of the railway companies since the railway lines passed from one into the another. Elgin therefore decided to set out the classification and distribution in more general terms, in the light of the importance of each case and each area.

Elgin decided that the annual railway conference should be a small one. In this he differed with Hamilton, who was keen to crowd it with representatives of local Governments and of large railway companies. "I should keep the shifting of schemes to a smaller official body," Elgin wrote.[89] The first of May each year was fixed as the date up to which recommendations from local Governments and Administrations could be considered.[90]

The annual railway conference, was the first consultative body of its type a precursor to the Railway Board and organised planning in general. For the first time, schemes and proposals for railway expansion, with adequate explanations attached to individual schemes, were presented, discussed and decided upon promptly. It was no surprise that Hamilton paid glowing tributes to Elgin on organising the railway on new and scientific lines. He considered Elgin's system of classification as "excellent." He fully agreed with Elgin's arguments against a classification by provinces, seaboards or companies, and considered them as conclusive. He agreed with the Viceroy that any

# Railways

such division could provoke and aggravate rivalry and controversy.[91]

Elgin was deeply gratified at the acceptance of his scheme. With characteristic modesty he wrote to Hamilton, "so far as I am concerned, it is a sort of work that interests me so much that I need no incentive."[92]

The success of railway policy and planning depended largely upon sound financial arrangements. Before 1896, estimates used to be prepared but were seldom adhered to. On the initiative of Lord Elgin, in 1896, the Government decided to set aside a definite sum for a planned period of three years. The purpose of this three-year plan was to secure regular growth and save the Government the embarrassment normally caused on account of shifting and changes of schemes. The Secretary of State accepted the idea and sanctioned Rs 27 crores for a three year programme.[93]

Though Rs 27 crores was fixed as a "standard" for three years, the Public Works Department distributed Rs 10 crores each for the first two years and the remaining Rs 7 crores in the third year. The purpose of this arrangement was, if Rs 10 crores were spent in one year, to ask for the third year's allotment, i.e., for 1898-99, be increased from Rs 7 to Rs 10 crores or to demand an increase in the total outlay. Westland correctly pressed the Viceroy to limit railway expenditure and argued that railway construction should be undertaken keeping in view the financial prospects of the country.[94] The Government also demanded a further sum of Rs 1,66,50,00 which they estimated would be spent by old guaranteed companies beyond the limit of Rs 28 crores. The Indian Government had understood the financial despatch of 2 April from the Secretary of State as entitling them to treat capital expenditure by the three old guaranteed railway companies as outside this limit.[96] The total sum combined with expenditure on lines already in progress, made up a grand total of Rs 29,66,50,000 to be spent in three years, from April 1896 to March 1899. This was, by any standard, a very ambitious scheme, particularly considering the impending famine. The Secretary of State approvingly stated that "The care evidently bestowed upon the schemes, and the strong personal interest you (Elgin) were taking in them, counterbalanced the arguments of famine and financial difficulties."[97]

By the middle of 1896, famine and plague had gained a strong foothold in India, but Elgin's enthusiasm was still high. The Indian Government inquired whether it was the Secretary of State's intention to permit the construction of branch lines under the guarantee alternative of their Resolution of 17 April 1896, irrespective of the limitation of the Rs $29\frac{2}{3}$ crore programme.[98] The majority in the Viceroy's Executive Council held that allotments for construction of branch lines were not included in this total outlay. In their evidence, they referred to the Secretary of State's railway despatch of 28 January 1897, which completely excluded the branch lines from this limit.[99] But both Westland[100] and Waterfield[101] strongly urged that the outlay on branch lines should be accommodated within the limit of Rs $29\frac{2}{3}$ crores. C.S. Colvin in his departmental minute also sided with Westland. The Joint Public Works and Finance Committee also endorsed his view.[102] But Hamilton did not agree with the interpretation of his Committee and opined that paragraphs 10, 13 and 14 of the Secretary of State's despatch of 28 January 1897 "specifically state that these branch lines are outside the 29 crore limit."[103] But he further added that, under the "present circumstances," "no new construction"[104] was found necessary.

It was in July 1897 that the Government was obliged to consider their finances in the face of demands for famine relief, anti-plague measures and military operations on the North West frontiers. These came upon the Government at a most trying time of the year so far as the supply of the funds was concerned, for under ordinary circumstances, Government cash receipts, including loans, ran down throughout the five months of July through November. In view of this, the Government was obliged to ask the Secretary of State to greatly reduce his drawings, and as the military operations became more extensive, he not only had stopped them altogether but remitted back to the Government Rs 1 crore out of the amount that he had already drawn.[105] In this situation, the demand was mounting from Westland and members of the Legislative Council that railway expenditure be curtailed.[106] Elgin and the Public Works Department reluctantly agreed to reduce railway expenditure in 1897 by Rs 1 crore.[107]

Out of the controversy, one important development took

place. Originally the railway programme was intended to include the State railways and construction by companies, out of the funds raised or advanced by them, but now the Rs 29⅔ crores allotted also included construction by branch line companies and old guaranteed companies. The whole question of financing railways was henceforward looked on as one of ways and means, and all expenditure for which Government had financial responsibility was included in the programme. Though the companies were permitted to continue sterling borrowings on their own account, they ceased to have the same freedom as before.[108]

With hindsight, we can now say that Elgin's three-year railway plans and projections were unduly optimistic. But in the process of formulation they had good reason to believe that, with the rising exchange and the end of the Chitral crisis, the financial position of India would improve. They could not have anticipated that the improvement in the exchange rate would be counteracted by an increase in the drawings of the Secretary of State and in turn, deplete the cash balances from which, in past years, such large railway advances had been drawn. Nor could they have visualised that 1896-7 would witness famine, plague and tribal risings. In the circumstances of these events, the administration had to yield and curtail railway expenditure. Construction of many lines sanctioned by the administration, like the Muthra-Nagda railway (354 miles) was postponed. The planned outlay for the three years, 1899-1902 was reduced to Rs 20.3 crores.[109]

To complement the activities of the consultative body he set up to regulate railway expansion, Elgin undertook a reorganisation of the Public Works (Railway Branch) Department. Both Fowler and Elgin thought that the railway department was not working well. There were inordinate delays; files did not move. Sir Charles Pritchard had lost the confidence of the department. There was acute rivalry between O'Callaghan, the Public Works Secretary, and the Member-in-Charge.[110] As a part of the preliminary reorganisation, Elgin took Pritchard into confidence and appointed Lt. Col. Bisset as Public Works Secretary on the retirement of O'Callaghan and also appointed a Director-General and a consulting Engineer for railways, initially for one year, pending final changes.[111]

The need for the reorganisation of the department was again felt by 1896, when the railway programme was classified.[112] The Secretary of State and his Council wanted decentralisation so that private enterprise could be speedily utilised. The setting up of a separate office of Director General of Railways, outside the Secretariat, and bringing in a person from England, like the English general manager of railway, was considered. But both A.C. Trevor (Public Works Member) and Elgin were not enthusiastic. Elgin wrote: "I doubt very much (the possibility of) any man accustomed to the independence and authority of a General Manager of a railway company in England ever consenting to such a position. The Secretary of the Department he might tolerate as it is possible though not pleasant, to tolerate a thorn in the flesh; but the civilian member, with little or no technical knowledge, but insisting, in accordance with tradition, that his orders are the orders of the Government of India over-ruled by Viceroy or Council, would I am sure fatally interfere with his usefulness."[113] For the same reasons, he was not enthusiastic about setting up a Railway Board which, without "full financial independence," he felt would be incompatible with the whole structure.[114]

Actually, Elgin was not against any progressive suggestion. But he believed that until and unless the whole structure of railways was modified, the appointment of a Railway Manager and the establishment of a Railway Board would be ineffective. When, on his arrival in 1894, Lord Reay, the Parliamentary Under-Secretary of State for India, wrote that opinion in the India Office was in favour of sending out a person from England who had experience of railway management,[115] Elgin pronounced his judgement very judiciously: "Any one who has had to do with Railways at home, as I have had, knows that in projects for new lines the General Manager meets face to face with the promoters and the bargain is struck. I am aware that such a course out here might be inconsistent with your financial control, unless limited in some way; but I am confident that such an experienced Railway Manager would be fish out of water unless he had some freedom of action in making bargains."[116] In this context, Elgin anticipated the criticism of the Mackay Committee that the friction between the Government of India (through the Member-in-Charge) and the Railway Board was because the latter lacked powers of financial control with which it should have been vested.[117] It is greatly to his credit that Elgin diagnosed the disease ten years in advance.

In the same context, Elgin had made another carefully considered suggestion, viz. that the Member-in-Charge of Railways should not be an official, "but one of shrewd practical sensce... devoted for years to railway working, combining it perhaps with a seat in Parliament."[118] Here again, it is significant that nearly twenty-five years later, the Acworth Committee had this to say about the Member-in-Charge: "If a man could be found to combine the qualifications of a capable administrator, parliamentarian and railway expert, he would be an ideal selection for the post."[119] Elgin was, thus, fully conscious in matters of railway organisation and administration, and his lack of enthusiasm for a Railway Manager and a Railway Board was not due to any aversion to professional management, but because it did not fit in the existing set-up. Yet, in more than one way, his reforms were forerunners of later developments in the railway department.

Before the reorganisation was undertaken by Lord Elgin's administration, the Public Works Department consisted of a Secretary who was responsible both for the Railway and Public Works departments; a Director-General of Railways who was the head of the railway administration and, as a Deputy Secretary, exercised general control over both companies and State lines; and a Consulting Engineer who was an adviser without executive responsibilities.[120]

The Government made the following recommendations:[121]

(1) The Public Works Department should have two branches —a railway branch to be under the Secretary to the Government of India in the Railway Department and a works branch, including all accounts, organisation and establishment cases, other than those relating to railways, under a Joint Secretary.

(2) The office of the Director-General should be abolished and its functions transferred to that of the Secretary to the Government in the Railway Department.

(3) The office of the Consulting Engineer should be abolished and it functions combined with those of the office of the Chief Engineer and Deputy Secretary in the Railway Department

whose designations should be Director (Railway Construction) and Deputy Secretary, Railways.

(4) A new post of Second Deputy Secretary with the designation, Director of Traffic, should be created and filled by an office especially selected for his qualifications as a traffic expert.

There were three reasons for disposing of the establishments of the Director General and Consulting Engineer. The first was to economise and avoid duplication of work. The second was that three top officers of the railways, the Secretary, the Director-General and the Consulting Engineer, were all selected from the same cadre. They had probably been rivals throughout their careers and had succeeded each other in the several steps. If any one of them was placed in a position of independence outside the Department or Secretariat, it could lead to bitter jealousies.[122] Thirdly, it was considered desirable, in the interest of efficiency, to decentralised the functions and responsibilities attached to the position of the Director-General as administrative head of the State railways and to devolve them upon the Managers and Engineers-in-Chief of the several lines.[123] "... it is an accepted policy of the Government of India," Elgin wrote, "that we should as far as we can see our way from time to time entrust the management and working of the larger system to the Companies"[124] He further stressed: "If we were to re-establish an independent Director-General of Railways, we shall have an official with a staff who would naturally oppose any curtailment of their sphere of influence, and whom it would be difficult to adjust to any reductions we thought fit to introduce."[125]

These proposals were accepted by the Secretary of State. He wrote: "They [the proposals] make a decided advance in the direction of decentralisation, in as much as they enable us at once to devolve on the managers of lines executive functions and responsibilities now centred in the Director of Railways and in the future to adopt further measures of decentralisation."[126]

After laying down the essentials of railway policy for rapid expansion, Elgin devoted his energy to its implementation. As it is not possible to deal with each and every case of railway construction, discussion will be confined to a few important projects in various parts of the country.[127]

One of the first important lines to be constructed was the Wazirabad-Lyallpur-Khanewal branch of the North Western

State Railway. This scheme was carried out in two stages. First, in October 1894, a line from Wazirabad to Lyallpur, traversing a total of 96 miles was started at the estimated cost of Rs 33,803 per mile.[128] The second phase was started in 1896, extending the line from Lyallpur to Khanewal, a distance of 84 miles.[129] The construction of this line was significant, for it tapped the fertile Chenab colony in Rachna Doab[130] and connected the colony with Karachi port via Multan. Combined with a canal, this railway revolutionised the region, the former enabling production of wheat on a vast scale and the latter conveying it to the market. The rail link not only facilitated cheap movement of surplus food but enormously relieved the pressure of population in the congested districts of the Punjab. This vast area was until 1892 sparsely populated, (the census of 1891 recorded a population of 70,000). In 1901 the census showed that immigrants numbered 539,493.[131]

Another line started early in 1895 and completed by November 1897 was the Delhi-Samasata Railway or South Punjab Railway. It was a branch of the North-West Railway and was financed by private capital raised on the terms of the branch line resolution of 1895. The line passed through Rohtak, Jindh, Tohana, Bhatinda to Samasata, a distance of 400 miles.[132] This provided the shortest route from Delhi to Karachi and was of immense commercial importance. Also, the line provided an alternative route to the Punjab and therefore, militarily and politically, was equally advantageous.

Yet another line to be constructed as a part of the North Western State Railway was the Rohri-Kotri line covering a distance of 206 miles, with a bridge over the Indus at Kotri. This line was laid primarily to safeguard communications between Karachi and Quetta, because the existing line used to get inundated during the monsoon.

All these lines had one thing in common. They greatly enhanced the importance to the port of Karachi and in each case they were the shortest routes. For instance, the Wazirabad-Kehanewal line provided the direct and shortest route from Karachi to Jammu. Similarly, the Delhi-Samasata route provided not only the shortest route to Karachi but formed the shortest rail route from Calcutta to Karachi. The Rohri-Kotri line, which was primarily constructed for military reasons also provided an alternative route to Karachi from Rohri to cope with heavy traffic.

One of the most important questions regarding the railway expansion related to the "linking up case"—the inter-linking of the metre gauge lines in northern, central and western India. There were four different and disconnected system of metre gauge lines which had drawn closer over the years due to the railway expansion but were separated from each other by a few miles only. The four systems were:

(1) The northern system (comprising the Bengal and North Western Railway, the Tirhoot Railway, the North-Bengal and the Assam-Bihar Railway) which had a total length of 1,173 miles.

(2) The Rohilkhund-Kumaon Railway and the Lucknow and Bareily Railway with a total mileage of 275 miles.

(3) The Rajputana-Malwa Railway which had a total length of 1900 miles.

(4) The Kathiawar Railway or the southern most system which was 333 miles long.

The first was 40 miles away from the second and the second was separated by 45 miles from the third and the third was within 40 miles of fourth. These gaps were crossed by sections of two railways on another gauge. A section of the Oudh and Rohilkhund broad gauge railway, not more than 85 miles in length, separated the first three metre gauge systems mentioned. The South-West end of Rajputana-Malwa system of the Kathiawar Railway was separated from it by 39 miles of broad gauge line belonging to the Bombay, Baroda and Central India Railway. Thus several thousands of miles of railway of identical gauge constituted were split into four systems separated by a distance of about 120 miles of railway of another gauge.[133]

In June 1892, Lord Cross realised the immense value of inter-linking the system and asked the Indian Government to take the necessary steps. Two considerations impelled Lord Cross to make this suggestion: an unbroken link would be advantageous for internal trade, for it would facilitate the conveyance and distribution of salt from Rajputana without a break and would promote at the same time the export of the northern produce in exchange; and unbroken lines of communication across India were desirable "upon military and political grounds."[134]

Unfortunately, till the middle of 1894, there was no agreement concerning the alignment of the lines required for the linking up of the northern system. Two opposite views were taken by the experts on the railways. Pritchard and Westland proposed that the linking up should take place via Bareily and Soron, because this link would be favourable to the development of the Oudh and Rohilkhand State Railway.[135] As the Oudh and Rohilkhand Railway ran from Lucknow to Bareily, any link on that line would naturally increase its traffic and enhance its importance. However, O'Callaghan, Crosthwaite and Elgin, supported by trading interests, wanted the link via Cawnpore (Kanpur)—Lucknow. This would obviously be beneficial to the Bengal and North-Western Railway. These differing views resulted in a deadlock. To expedite the matter, Elgin appointed a committee of experts.[136] Ultimately Government proposed that the linking up should be effected by

(1) a separate metre gauge track between Cawnpore (Kanpur) and Lucknow (running along the broad gauge track) constructed by the State as a part of the Oudh and Rohilkhand State Railway;

(2) the section from Lucknow to Bahramghat also being constructed as an integral part of the Oudh and Rohilkhand Railway;

(3) the bridge over the Gogra and the approaches to the bridge up to Bahramghat being constructed by the Bengal and North-Western Railway; and

(4) the construction by the State of a new metre gauge line connecting Bareily with Soron, so as to join the metre gauge system administered by the Rohilkhand-Kumaon Railway Company with the Cawnpore (Kanpur)—Achnera Railway.[137] This last was by way of compromise.

The Secretary of State accepted the first three recommendations but not the fourth. In doing so, he commented that the double links, one at Soron and another at Cawnpore (Kanpur), were "unnecessarily expensive," particularly when the purpose could be served with one only.[138] In November 1894, work was started on the Cawnpore (Kanpur)—Gogra metre gauge link. This link was no doubt important from trade point of view, but the maximum advantage went to the Bengal and North Western line at the cost of the State line. In approving this, the Government had an ulterior motive: they wanted the Bengal and North Western Railway Company to construct metre gauge lines south of Gogra from Bhatni (east of Gorakhpur) to Azimgarh and Banares with a branch to Ballia, in all about 210 miles. The principal purpose of these lines was political.[139] Actually, in 1893, when Hindu-Muslim riots took place, the Government had difficulty in sending troops to the trouble spots. To avoid any risk of repetition, the Government wanted to have an unbroken link in and around the area. Secondly, the construction would protect the eastern districts of Gogra-Ganges-Doab against famine and facilitate interchange of produce between the sub-Himalayan districts of the Gogra and Rajputana, Patna, Gazipur and Banaras.[140]

However, at that stage the Public Works Committee declined to sanction the construction of metre gauge lines in the Ganges-Gogra area and recommended instead that the East Indian Railway Company construct a board gauge line in district.[141] Though C.S. Colvin, Godley and Fowler were all inclined favourably towards the Indian Government, strong opposition from J. Strachey and R. Hardie, members of the Indian council, prevented the proposals from getting through.[142] For the time being the decision of the Secretary of State was reserved.[143]

There was, however, still sufficient scope for the company and the Indian Government to exert pressure. The Indian Government again addressed the Secretary of State on the issue, pressing for the acceptance of the Bengal and North-Western Railway Company's proposal, which they said was most favourable to the Government.[144] Under their proposal, the company was to raise their own funds, thereby avoiding pressure on Government's finances. Besides, the company, while in submitting the proposal, had added another project—one for extension of the Tirhoot system with a line from Hajipur to Katihar (162 miles in all) with a bridge over the Kosi.[145] A.C. Lyall once again supported the proposal[146] and Hardie again dissented.[147] Hamilton accepted the Indian Government's plea and the Joint Public Works and Finance Committee approved it on 20 December, and the Secretary of State finally permitted the Bengal and North Western Railway to go ahead with the construction.[148] The Company thus gained a significant contract for the construction of 373 miles of railway.[149]

There were important consequences of the alignment chosen. A continuous link was established from north to central India and from there to western India, which was of immense political, economic and commercial value. It was clearly demonstrated that utilisation and encouragement of private enterprise provided a means of expanding the system beyond what was possible on the basis of government borrowing. By giving concessions to private enterprise in the form of reasonable freedom to select avenues of alignment of lines, so that more construction could take place. The substitution of metre gauge link lines for broad gauge, in the areas otherwise earmarked for broad gauge, was a realistic and a purposeful step towards cheaper railway construction and smooth and efficient communication.

It was branch line construction which received the most notable attention from Elgin's administration. For the rapid construction of the feeders, the administration had not only amended the resolution of 1893 but also introduced a new resolution in 1896. The purpose of feeder line construction was twofold: to create passenger and goods traffic and to open up the interior for the development of local produce. The construction of these lines proved as useful in enriching the areas as to protect them against scarcity. Unfortunately construction was not as rapid as the administration had hoped. This was not because of diversion of financial resources for famine relief, anti plague measures and frontier wars. Nevertheless, many branch lines were constructed under the terms of the Resolution of 1896.

Bengal took a lead.[150] One such line was the Mymensingh-Jamalpur-Subhankhali (metre gauge) line, 63 miles in length. The line traversed mostly the jute districts of northern and eastern Bengal, centres of valuable and extensive trade.[151] Similarly, another branch line, Sultanpur-Bogra-Kalinganj, was opened to the jute interests from Rungpore district and tea interests in Assam. Another metre gauge branch line was opened from Segowli to Ruksaul. At Segowli it left the Partabgunj branch of the Tirhoot State Railway and ran up to the Nepal frontiers near Ruksaul. It was constructed as much for political reasons as to encourage trade between Nepal and India.

At the recommendation of the Bombay Chamber of Commerce and the Bombay government an important branch line connecting Surat-Nandurbar-Amalner-Jalgaon was laid. The line was purely commercial, for it brought the Central Provinces in direct communication with Gujarat.[152] The particular significance of the line lay in the fact that the whole of the capital for it was raised locally, in rupees. This was a new and satisfactory development. It was considered so important that Elgin himself went to turn the first sod for the line.[153] Another branch line for which the capital was successfully raised in India was opened between Ahmedabad and Prantij.[154]

In the Central Provinces, a branch line of 2'-6" gauge and 60 miles long was constructed between Raipur-Dhanti-Rajjim. This connected Raipur with the Bengal-Nagpur Railway and passed through the rich rice producing district of Chattisgarh. It provided the shortest route between this district and the famine districts of the Deccan.[155] A very important "famine line" was constructed in the Central Provinces running from Katri to Sauger. It passed through scarcity areas and for it had been laid by labour employed as a part of famine relief.

Briefly, it was in the jute, tea and cotton areas that branch line construction was concentrated. In their construction, full scope was given to private enterprise, which resulted in speedier railway expansion and opening up of the country than would have been possible with government resources exclusively.

Though the branch lines were substantially expanded, the expansion during the period of broad gauge lines was even greater. Lord Elgin sanctioned "far more standard gauge lines than any Viceroy did before or since."[156] The most useful of such commercial lines laid during this period were Madras to Bezwada, Cuttack to Midnapur and Sini and Midnapur and Howrah. This completed the northern end of the East Railway and linked on one side Madras, Cuttack and Calcutta and at the same time provided an alternative means of approaching Calcutta from the West, thereby bringing Bombay-Sini-Calcutta into one line. These lines played an immensely important role in developing the trade and industrial potentialities of the various areas they touched. Probably the most important achievement was that Calcutta was now linked directly with Madras, Bombay and Karachi and, in many cases, not only by the shortest route but by alternative routes as well. Dalhousie's dream was at last fulfilled.

The Assam-Bengal railway (742 miles long), which was primarily started to serve the tea plantations, saw some more expansion during the period. Though the Indian Government was as reluctant to proceed further on the northern section of the line as they were when it was first sanctioned, the Secretary of State persisted in its completion. Another large line sanctioned and started was the Mandalay-Kunlon metre gauge line (270 miles in length) at an estimated cost of Rs 225 lakhs.[157] It was constructed entirely for political and military reasons, in spite of the fact that the Government was facing financial difficulties.[158]

It is indeed very difficult to assess the motives for railway expansion. Was the expansion motivated by political-cum-military or commercial-cum-economic reasons or both? It may be stated at the outset that no imperial and colonial Government initiates a policy, much less a railway policy, which does not bring it political advantages. Therefore, all railway construction in India was influenced by that consideration. In some cases, railway lines were made exclusively for political and military reasons, like the Mandalay-Kunlon and the Rohri-Kotri lines; in others, for both political and commercial reasons, which benefited the economy of India, if not immediately then ultimately, if not directly then indirectly. It is true that only a few lines were built exclusively as famine lines, like the Saugaur-Katri line, though many of the lines constructed served to carry grain to tracts liable to famine in years of drought.

No doubt, much expansion in the last decade of the nineteenth centuary concentrated on serving tea plantations and jute and cotton interests, but surley they proved great foreign exchange earners for India. Though such rapid railway expansion was probably beyond the financial ability of India, the railways helped develop hitherto under-developed areas like Assam and Rachna Doab.[159] It is true that railway expansion benefited investors, bankers, iron and coal mine owners, but it also acted positively as an important ingredient or adjunct in the growth and ramification of modern commerce—both internal and external. There is no doubt that railway investment did not pay till 1899 and there were annual losses, but it is equally certain that, but for railway expansion, the financial position of India would have been worse. The system of guarantees came back and the guarantee of 3 per cent[160] on Sterling borrowing was fairly high, but that was the only convenient means of raising Sterling fund for rapid railway construction in India.

Though the expansion of railways during this period of study was to a large extent motivated by political and extra-commercial reasons, yet Elgin's personal intention was to see greater expansion in the more productive avenues, as in tea, cotton and coal areas. He was personally not in favour of the construction of the Mandalay-Kunlon railway; he discouraged the construction of the northern section of the Assam-Bengal railway, and was vehemently against the idea of extending railways beyond India's frontiers in the North-West. When military pressure was exerted on him to sanction a railway line beyond Khyber, he wrote: "For my part I must say at once that I cannot regard a policy of this kind as either desirable or necessary... I am not prepared to initiate a procedure which would mean the immediate locking up of a large sum in unproductive works...."[161] It was largely owing to Elgin's insistence that no railway line was laid beyond Khyber in the tribal areas.

Elgin devoted considerable attention to the expansion of railways in India and worked feverishly to formulate and implement a pragmatic policy. More than 4000 miles of railways were constructed during Elgin's five year tenure. Never before had so much railway track been laid in a five year period. 1899 saw the maximum amount of construction (1484 miles) and all these lines were sanctioned by Elgin's administration.[162] The special features of Elgin's railway policy were the encouragement he gave to branch line construction and the utilisation, to some extent, of rupee capital for this purpose in India. This earned the praise of the Acworth Committee, which recorded: "It (the Branch line resolution of 1896) has enabled lines to be built which would otherwise not have been built and thereby helped considerably to develop the country."[163] Another outstanding feature of the railway administration under Elgin was the laying down of a planned programme, without which it was impossible to pursue any policy, however well considered and accepted, either as a method of providing capital or the agency to be used in construction. The establishment of an annual railway conference was probably his greatest contribution. Hamilton was right when he commended Elgin saying, "There are a few things you [Elgin] have done in your Viceroyalty which will be of greater benefit to India than the establishment of the Conference."[164]

Railway construction was a passion with Elgin. He genuinely felt that it was through this method that the Government could substantially improve the condition of the vast population of India. While addressing the Legislative Council in 1896, he expressed his belief that the great railway system of India could be made "an all powerful agent in the promotion of the material and social advancement and the political tranquillity of the people."[165] Elgin might not have been a Dalhousie but, for his enthusiasm, railway expansion till the end of the nineteenth century would have been relatively insignificant.

### NOTES

[1] Elgin to Westland, 8 July 1895, E.P., vol. 67. In the same letter he wrote, "For myself, it is a branch of which my own inclination and previous training predisposed me."

[2] Parl. Papers, 1899, vol. 1 xvi, Appendix A.

[3] Sir Theodore C. Hope, in his paper, "The Rationale of Railways in India," eulogized Dalhousie for raising the question of railways from the 'theoretical and pedantic plane to the higher plane of political, military and commercial expediency, tempered by common sense. *Journal of the Society of Arts*, 1890, vol. xxxviii, p. 708. (Hereafter cited as *J.S.A.*).

[4] W.W. Hunter, *The Marquess of Dalhousie*, Oxford, 1895, pp. 193-4. See also L.H. Jenks, *The Migration of British Capital to 1875*, New York, 1927, p. 212.

[5] Quoted in J.M. Maclean, "The State Monopoly of Railways in India," *J.S.A.*, 1884, xxxii, p. 262.

[6] Daniel Thorner has discussed in detail the role of English financiers and promoters and the reason for, and the nature and extent of, the pressure they had applied on the East India Company. *Investment in the Empire, 1825-49*, Philadelphia, 1950, Chapters i and vi.

[7] H.M. Jagtiani, *The Role of the State in the Provision of Railways*, London, 1924, pp. 94-6.

[8] D.H. Buchanan, *The Development of Capitalist Enterprise in India*, New York, 1934, p. 183. L.H. Jenks states that the cost of railways per mile in India was as high as £18,000, whereas some of the railways in the United States were built, including the cost of the land, for only

£2,000 per mile. *The Migration of British Capital to 1875, op. cit.,* p. 222.

[9] So long as the British capitalist was assured of 5 per cent on the security of the revenues of India, "it was immaterial to him whether the funds that he lent were thrown into the Hooghly or converted into brick and mortar." W.N. Massey's evidence before the *Select Committee of the House of Commons,* Q. 8867, quoted by C.N. Vakil, *Financial Development in Modern India,* p. 195.

[10] *Imperial Gazetteer,* vol. iii, p. 368.

[11] Quoted by Horace Bell, *Railway Policy in India,* London, 1894, p. 94.

[12] H.M. Jagtiani, *The Rule of the State in Provision of Railways, op. cit.,* p. 115.

[13] It has been argued by many scholars like N. Sanyal and H.M. Jagtiani that there was nothing wrong with State construction and the slow rate of expansion was a result of the limitation which was imposed upon the Government of India by the Select Committees of 1871-4 and 1878-9 which laid down that no more than £2½ million a year out of the borrowed capital be devoted to productive public works. *Op. cit.,* p. 84 and p. 128 respectively.

[14] *Report of the Famine Commission, 1880,* Parl, Papers, vol. lii, (C. 2591), pp. 170-88.

[15] H. Bell, "The Recent Railway Policy in India," *J.S.A.* 1898, vol. xlvi, p. 532.

[16] The word assisted seemed in fact to have been "invented" in order to screen the facts that such companies were guaranteed. H. Bell, "The Recent Railway Policy in India," p. 532.

[17] For detail, see A. Prasad, *The Indian Railways,* Bombay, pp. 59-60.

[18] Indian Government to S.S., L. No. 23 (Ry.), Railway and Telegraph Letters from India, vol. 35. Enclosed with it was the draft of the Resolution. (Hereafter cited as R.L.I.).

[19] The "rebate" was a payment to a branch line by the parent line from the earnings of latter from traffic interchanged with the branch. It was limited to (1) a specific proportion of those earnings, and (2) the amount which, when added to the net earnings of the branch, made up a certain fixed dividend on the capital of the branch.

[20] Note by Offg. Director-General of Railways, Lt. Col. W.S.S. Bisset, 24 January 1894, Para 8, E.P., 132 (S), ix.

[21] H. Bell, *J.S.A.* 1898, *op. cit.,* p. 533.

[22] Elgin to Fowler, 1 May 1894, E.P., vol. 12.

[23] Fowler to Elgin, 9 November 1894, *ibid.*

[24] P.W.D. (R.C.) Proc., vol. 4787, No. 84 and 86, October 1895.

[25] *Ibid.*

[26] W. Shelford's Note on Extension of Railways in India, *ibid.,* No. 88, October 1895.

[27] P.W. 1071/94, vol. 412.

[28] *Ibid.*

*Railways* 99

<sup>29</sup>S.S. to Indian Government, Despatch No. 62 (Ry.), 2 August 1894, Para 6, R.D.I. vol. 14.

<sup>30</sup>Telegram Viceroy to S.S. P.W.D. (R.C.) Proc., vol. 4787, No. 95, October 1895.

<sup>31</sup>Telegram S.S. to Viceroy P.W. 358/95, attached to P.W. 760/95, vol. 436.

<sup>32</sup>Telegram, Viceroy to S.S., 1 March 1895, *ibid.*

<sup>33</sup>*Ibid.*

<sup>34</sup>Elgin to Fowler, 6 March 1895, E.P., vol. 13.

<sup>35</sup>*Ibid.*

<sup>36</sup>Telegram Viceroy to S.S., 1 March 1895, *op. cit.*

<sup>37</sup>Note, 31 December 1894, p. 6, *op. cit.*

<sup>38</sup>Elgin to Fowler, 13 February 1895 and 6 March 1895, E.P., vol. 13.

<sup>39</sup>Telegram S.S. to Viceroy, 12 March 1895, P.W.D. (R.C.) Proc., vol. 4787, No. 99, October 1895.

<sup>40</sup>Telegram Viceroy to S.S., 23 March 1895, P.W.D. (R.C.) Proc., vol. 4787, No. 100, October 1895.

<sup>41</sup>Telegram Viceroy to S.S., 27 March 1895, P.W. 492/95 attached to P.W. 760/95, vol. 436.

<sup>42</sup>Res. P.W.D. on "Extension of Railways by Private Agency," Parl. Papers, 1897, vol. 1 xv (88), pp. 14-15, Sect. 3(i) and ii.

<sup>43</sup>Extracts from *Bombay Gazette*, 1 July 1895; *Statesman*, 11 July 1895; *The Times* 14 and 17 September and 4 and 10 September 1895, Register No. 463, Private Secretary's Correspondence, E.P., vol. 96.

<sup>44</sup>Bombay Chamber of Commerce to Indian Government, 20 May 1895, P.W.D. (R.C.) Proc., vol. 4787, No. 276, November 1895.

<sup>45</sup>Elgin's Note on Railways, 27 July 1895, p. 1, Enc. Elgin to Hamilton, 9 October 1895, H.C., MSS. Eur. D. 509/1.

<sup>46</sup>Elgin's Note on Railways, 27 July 1895, pp. 2-3. Enc. Elgin to Hamilton, 9 October 1895, H.C., MSS. Eur. D. 509/1.

<sup>47</sup>Parl. Papers, 1897, vol. lxv, (88), pp. 15-18.

<sup>48</sup>*Ibid.*

<sup>49</sup>Indian Government to S.S., L. No. 78 (Ry.), 9 October 1895, Para 12, R.L.I., vol. 37.

<sup>50</sup>They were: (1) Mymensingh-Jamalpore, (2) Sultan Pur-Bogra-Kaliganj, (3) Bhagalpur-Bansi-Badyanath, (4) Gogri-Baptiahi with branch, (5) Segowli-Ruksaul, (6) Surat-Nandurbar-Amalner, (7) Amalner-Jalgaon. See Indian Government to S.S., L. No. 76 (Ry.), 4 November 1896, Para 12, R.L.I., Vol. 36.

<sup>51</sup>See Elgin's Note on Railway Policy, 27 July 1895, p. 2, *op. cit.*

<sup>52</sup>Elgin's Note on Railways, 31 December 1894, pp. 3-4, *ibid.*

<sup>53</sup>Fowler to Elgin, 16 May 1895, E.P., vol 13.

<sup>54</sup>Hamilton to Elgin, 31 October 1895, *ibid.*

<sup>55</sup>Elgin's Memorandum on Railway Policy, 9 October 1895, p. 1.

<sup>56</sup>Indian Government to S.S. L. No. 78 (Ry.), 9 October 1895, Paras 9-10, *op. cit.*

⁵⁷Railway Minute, P.W. 1880/95, vol. 447 of Indian Govt. L. No. 78 (Ry.) of 9 October 1895, Paras 9-11.
⁵⁸Railway Minute, P.W. 1880/95, vol. 447.
⁵⁹*Ibid.*
⁶⁰S.S. to Indian Government, Despatch No. 9, (Ry.), 6 February 1896, R.D.I., vol. 16.
⁶¹In 1896, the Government had to supplement the net earnings of this company by giving it an annual subsidy to enable it to secure $3\frac{1}{4}$ per cent dividend to the shareholders after payment of debenture interest. H. Bell, "The Recent Railway Policy," *J.S.A.*, 1898, p. 533.
⁶²J. Westland's Note on Railways and Railway Finance, 16 February 1895, E.P., vol. 132 (S).
⁶³As Government would actually have invested Rs 450 lakhs under A, this assumption was a reasonable one.
⁶⁴J. Westland's Note, 16 February 1895, Para 6, *op. cit.*
⁶⁵*Ibid.*, Para 9.
⁶⁶Elgin's Memorandum on Railway Policy, 9 October 1895, p.1, *op. cit.*
⁶⁷C.H.T. Crosthwaite's Memorandum on the Railway Policy, 24 December 1894, p. 1, P.W. 1880/95, vol. 447.
⁶⁸Minute by Gen. R. Strachey, Enc. S.S. to India Government, Despatch No. 69 (Ry.), 6 September 1894, R.D.I. vol. 14.
⁶⁹C.H.T. Crosthwaite's Memorandum on Railway Policy, 24 December 1895, *op. cit.*, p. 1.
⁷⁰*Report on the Administration and Working of Indian Railways*, 1903, Parl. Papers, vol. xlvii, (Cd. 1713), Para 117. See also Paras 129-132.
⁷¹*Report of the Committee on Indian Railway Finance and Administration*, 1908, Parl, Papers, vol. 75, (Cd. 4111), Para 8.
⁷²*Railway Committee Report*, 1921, Parl, Papers, vol. x, (Cd. 1512), chap. vii, (Summary of the Report), pp. 86-89.
⁷³Elgin to Hamilton, 19 February 1896, E.P., vol. 14.
⁷⁴Letter to the Editor, *The Times*, 10 September 1895.
⁷⁵Elgin's Memorandum on Railway Policy, 9 October, *op. cit.*, p. 2.
⁷⁶Crosthwaite to Elgin, 4 April 1895, E.P., vol. 30.
⁷⁷W.S.S. Bisset to H.B. Smith, 19 October 1895, E.P., vol. 67.
⁷⁸Elgin's Memorandum, 9 October 1894, *op. cit.*, p. 2.
⁷⁹Elgin wrote to Lord Reay, the Under Secretary of State, "I would very much like to get past the promoter and deal with bona fide investors." 22 October 1894, E.P., vol. 29.
⁸⁰Elgin's Memorandum, 9 October 1895, *op. cit.*, p. 2.
⁸¹See pp.
⁸²For detail see Elgin to Westland, 8 July, Westland to Elgin, 11 July 1895, E.P., vol. 67.
⁸³Elgin to Westland, 8 July 1895, *ibid.*
⁸⁴Elgin to Hamilton, 2 November 1896, *ibid.*, vol. 14.
⁸⁵Indian Government to S.S., L. No. 76, 4 November 1896, P.W. 2109/96, vol. 475.

[86]See P.W.D. (R.C.) Proc., vol. 4786, Nos. 339-43, August 1895. See P.W.D. (R.C.) Proc., vol. 5001, Nos. 183-241, March 1896. See P.W.D. (R.C.) Proc., vol. 5003, Nos. 211-222, July 1896.
[87]Indian Government to S.S., L. No. 76 (Ry.), 4 November 1896, Para 7, *op. cit.*
[88]Elgin to Hamilton, 2 November 1896, E.P., vol. 14.
[89]*Ibid*. The first railway conference was composed of Elgin, J. Westland, A.C. Trevor (P.W. Member), Col. Bisset (P.W.D. Secy), Col. Gracy (Dir. Gen. of Rys), J. Finley (Fin. Secy.), Col. I.S.M. Hamilton (off. Quarter Master General), A.R. Besher, (off. Accountant General P.W.D.) and Secretary of the Conference, F.B. Herbert.
[90]Indian Government to S.S., L. No. 76 (Ry.), 4 November 1896, *op. cit.*
[91]Hamilton to Elgin, 4 December 1896, E.P., vol. 14.
[92]Elgin to Hamilton, 23 December 1896, *ibid.*
[93]S.S. to Indian Government Despatch No. 59 (Fin.), 2 April 1896, Para 5, F.D.I., vol. 16.
[94]Westland to Elgin, 25 August 1896, *ibid.*, vol. 69.
[95]Elgin to Hamilton, 2 November 1896, *ibid.*, vol. 14.
[96]In addition to the imperial expenditure (Rs 28 crores), the Indian Government anticipated that some 2,763 miles of line would be constructed or commenced, at a cost of Rs 17,85,40,000, before 31 March 1899 by the following agencies: (1) The old guaranteed companies (The Great Indian Peninsular Co., The Bombay, Baroda and Central Indian Rly.; The Madras Rly.); (2) Native States; (3) branch line companies; and (4) assisted companies. Indian Government to S.S., L. No. 76 (Ry.), 4 November 1896, Para 10-13, *op. cit.* The details of railway construction to be undertaken by Companies and Native States (outside the Rs 28 crores limit) will be found in Enclosure No. 3, and the details of the imperial outlay during the 3 years in Enclosure No. 2, of the Indian Government Despatch No. 76 of 4 November, 1896.
[97]Hamilton to Elgin, 11 December 1896, E.P., vol. 14.
[98]Indian Government to S.S., L. No. 72 (Ry.), 29 June 1897, Para 1, R.L.I., vol. 39.
[99]Despatch No. 8 (Ry.), Para 10, R.D.I., vol. 17. But in the Financial Despatch No. 59 of 2 April 1896, Para 5 and, No. 1 of 7 January 1897, Para 9, it was clearly stated that railways whose capital was raised under a direct guarantee were included within the limit.
[100]Views of Westland were given in para 4 of the Indian Government, L. No. 72 (Ry.), 29 June 1897, R.L.I., vol. 39.
[101]H. Waterfield's Note, 26 July 1897, P.W. 1330/97, vol. 489.
[102]Joint Minute of P.W. and Fin. Committee, 2 September 1897, *ibid.*
[103]Hamilton's Minute, 20 September 1897, *ibid.*
[104]S.S. to Indian Government Despatch No. 106 (Ry.), 4 November 1897; Para 2, R.D.I., vol. 17. See also Hamilton to Elgin, 16 October 1897, (appendix), E.P., vol. 15.

[105] Financial Statement, 1898-99, Para 37, see also Para 59.

[106] Westland was the most ardent critic of railway expenditure. It was he who relentlessly took pains to see that the expenditure was curtailed. As a matter of fact, he had never accepted Elgin's railway policy. "Your Lordship is aware," he wrote, "that I have never accepted the Railway Policy, except in the sense that, having done my best to state the financial side of the question, I accepted the orders which the Secretary of State passed on the subject." Westland to Elgin, 1 November 1897. For details, see Westland to Waterfield, 22 June 1897, Enc. Westland to Elgin, 26 June 1897 (appendix), E.P., vol. 70.

[107] Elgin to Hamilton, 29 June (appendix), 23 September and 21 October 1897, E.P., vol. 15.

[108] For detail see Elgin to Fowler, 16 October 1894, E.P., vol. 12.

[109] See Elgin to Hamilton, 15 September 1898, vol. 16. Hamilton to Elgin, 24 August 1898, *ibid.*

[110] Pritchard had at one stage framed a charge sheet against O'Callaghan. Elgin had to intervene because of O'Callaghan's impending retirement and fear of publicity. Ultimately, Pritchard agreed to burn the papers relating to the case.

[111] Elgin to Fowler, 29 May and 3 July 1894, *ibid.*, vol. 12.

[112] Indian Government to S.S., L. No. 31 (Ry.), 14 October 1896, P.W. 1942/96, vol. 38.

[113] Elgin to Hamilton, 4 August 1897, E.P., vol. 15.

[114] The establishment of the Railway Board in 1905 did not mean that the entire control of railways came under it. The Board remained under the Member-in-Charge. Its main duties included the preparation of the annual programme of railway expenditure, the control of the State lines, the supervision of company lines and many cognate duties.

[115] Lord Reay to Elgin, 20 April 1894, E.P., vol. 29.

[116] Elgin to Fowler, 29 May 1894, *ibid.*, vol. 12.

[117] Mackay Committee Rep. 1908, p. 25, *op. cit.*

[118] Elgin to Hamilton, 4 August 1897, E.P., vol. 15.

[119] Acworth Committee Report, 1921, p. 25, *op. cit.*

[120] Indian Government to S.S., 11 August 1897, L. No. 219 (Fin. and Com.), P.W.D. (Gen.) Proc., vol. 5224, No. 88, August 1897.

[121] *Ibid.*, Paras 10-16.

[122] Elgin to Hamilton, 4 August 1897, E.P., vol. 15.

[123] Indian Government to S.S., L. No. 219 (Fin. and Com.), 11 August 1897, Paras 14-15, *op. cit.*

[124] Elgin to Trevor, 12 July 1897, *op. cit.*

[125] Elgin to Hamilton, 4 August 1897, *op. cit.*

[126] S.S. to Ind. Govt. Despatch No. 29 (P.W.), 14 October 1897, Para 16, P.W. 1627/97, vol. 492.

[127] The administration of Elgin sanctioned construction of the following mileage by the State and private companies on both broad and metre gauge railways.

(a) In 1894-5, 651 miles. *Administrative Report of the Railway in India*.

Parl, Papers, 1895, vol. lxxiii, (C. 7845), Para 5, p. 16. (Hereafter cited as A R.R.I.).

(b) 1895-6, 2394 miles, A.R.R.I., Parl, Papers, 1897, vol. lxv, (C) 8518), Para 3, p. 2.

After 1897, very few miles of railways were sanctioned because of the famine and plague.

[128] Indian Government to S.S., L. No. (Ry.), 10 October 1894, Paras 4-7, R.L.I., vol. 36. See also Telegram, Viceroy to S.S., 3 October 1894, E P., vol. 17. S.S. to Indian Government. Despatch No. 63 (Ry.), 6. December 1894, R.D.I., vol. 14.

[129] Indian Government to S.S. L. No. 76 (Ry.), 4 November 1896, Enc. No. 1, Statement No. 1, p. 47, E.P., vol. 135 (h).

[130] The area lying between the Chenab and the Ravi and irrigated by the lower Chenab canal was called Chenab colony. This was once a waste and desolate area, unpeopled except for a race of pastoral nomads known as "Janglis." This wasteland was called "Sandal Bar" which was situated in the districts of Jhang, Lyallpur, portion of districts Montegomery and Lahore and Tehsil, Kanghah Dogron and Hafizabad of district Gujranwala. It was in 1889 that a perennial canal of the first magnitude was opened. The headworks of the canal are at Khanki, a village near Gujranwala (now in West Pakistan). The total area watered by the canal at the end of 1903-4 was 5, 255 sq. miles. This area became so fertile that it soon earned the reputation of being the granary of the Punjab.

For details see *Imperial Gazetteer*, Provincial Series, Calcutta 1908, Punjab, vol. I, pp. 208-10, and vol. II, pp. 211-21.

[131] *Imperial Gazetteer*, Provincial Series, Punjab, vol. 11, p. 221. Most of the immigrants came from the following districts:

(a) Sialkot (103,000), Amritsar (68,000), Jullundur (57,000), Gurdaspur (44,000), Hoshiarpur (35,000), Lahore, (29,000), Gujarat (25,000), Ludhiana (18,000), Shahpur (16,000) and Ferozepur (15,000).

[132] A.R.R.I., 1895-6, Parl, Papers, 1896, vol. ixii, (C. 8136), Para 5, p. 14.

A.R.R.I. 1897-8, Parl. Papers, 1898, vol. lxiv, (C. 8921), Para 7, p. 5.

[133] S.S. to Indian Government, Despatch No. 61 (Ry.), 23 June 1892. Paras 2-3, Enc. Indian Government to S.S., L. No. 10, 15 February 1893, P.W D. (R.C.), Proc. No. 482 of 1892, P.W. 392/93, vol. 375.

[134] *Ibid.*, Paras 5-10.

[135] Pritchard to Elgin, 21 March, 1 May and 24 May 1894, E.P., vol. 14, Westland's Minute, Para 1-6 and Para 11, Enc. Indian Government to S.S., L. No. 34 (Ry.), 5 June 1894, P.W. 1286/94, vol. 415.

[136] The Committee, of experts consisted of Callaghan (P.W. Secy.), Col. Bisset (Dir. Gen.), and Col. Gracey (Consulting Engineer). Report of the Committee, 24 April 1894, P.W. 1093/94, attached to P.W. 1286/94, vol. 415.

[137] Indian Government to S.S., L. No. 34 (Ry.), 5 June 1894, Para 17-21, *op. cit.*

[138] S.S. to Indian Government, Despatch No. 77 (Ry.), 25 October 1894, Paras 8-9, R.D.I., vol. 14.

[139] Report of the Committee of Experts, Paras 25-26, op. cit.

[140] Indian Government to S.S., L. No. 76 (Ry.), 4 November 1896, Encl. No. 1, Statement No. 1, p. 25, E.P., vol. 135 (b). Actually, during the famine of 1896-97, the Ganges-Gogra Doab lines were utilised for laying earthworks as part of famine relief.

[141] Minute by F.W. Committee, 30 August 1894, P.W. 1383/94 attached to P.W./2005/94, vol. 426.

[142] J. Strachey, Minute, 22 November 1894, ibid.

[143] Telegram, S.S. to Indian Government, 17 December 1894, P.W. 2005/94, vol. 426.

[144] Indian Government to S.S., L. No. 80 (Ry.), 16 October 1895; Enc. No. 3, Memorandum by Mr Izat, Agent and Chief Engineer, Bengal and North-Western Railway, 5 July 1895, P.W. 1938/95, vol. 448.

[145] The company agreed that capital spent on Tirhoot extensions was to be treated as capital of that railway and that spent on the Doab lines as capital of the company, for the purpose of the division of the residue of the net earnings. The two amounts were to be equal, viz. Tirhoot capital Rs 1,24,75,000 and the company's capital Rs 1,25,50,000. The company were prepared themselves to raise the whole amount by either sterling or rupee debentures. Indian Government to S.S., L. No. 80, (Ry.), 16 October 1865, Paras 6-7, P.W.1 938/95, vol. 448.

[146] A.C. Lyall's Note, 20 December 1895, P.W. 1938/95, vol. 448.

[147] R. Mardie's Note, 14 December, ibid.

[148] Walpole (Under Secy. of State) to Secy. Bengal and North Western Ry., 23 December 1895, ibid.

[149] A.R.R.I. 1895-9, Parl, Papers, 1896, vol. lxii, (C. 8136), Para 5, p. 14. The division of the line was as follows: (a) The construction in the Ganges-Gogra Doab (211 miles) was to be undertaken by the Bengal and North Western Railway (Company section), and (b) the Tirhoot extension was to be part of the Tirhoot State Railway (162 miles). See S.S. to Indian Government, Despatch No. 71 (Ry.), 27 August 1896, R.D.I., vol. 16.

[150] For the lines recommended by the Bengal Government. see P.W.D. (R.C.), Proc., vol. 50001, Nos. 217-219, 231-232, March 1896.

[151] Indian Government to S.S., L. No. 76, (Ry.), 4 November 1896, Enc. No. 1, Section No. 2, pp. 2-4, E.P., vol. 135 (h).

[152] Indian Government to S.S., L. No. 76, (Ry.), 4 November 1896, Enc. No. 1, Sect. No. ii, pp. 31-32, op. cit.

[153] *The Times*, 3 December 1896.

[154] Indian Government to S.S., L. No. 76, 4 November 1896, Para 10, op. cit.

[155] Enc. No. 1, Sect. ii, to Indian Government letter of November 1896, pp. 35-36, op. cit.

[156] Lovat Frazer, *India Under Curzon and After*, London, 1911, p. 309.

[157] Railway Minute, undated, P.W. 135/96, attached with P.W. 357/96, vol. 455.

[158] Capt. Bower, an intelligence officer of the area, to whose recommendation this line owed its origin had revealed that "although the Chinese Empire is effete and corrupt to an almost inconceivable extent, it has its uses to us....We cannot be blind to the fact that two aggressive nations, one on the North (Russia) and one on the South (France) are working in harmony...." Indian Government to S.S., L. No. 155 (Pol., 30 July 1895, Enc. No. 1, Capt. H. Bower to Asst. Quarter Master General, Intelligence Branch (Conf.), 22 June 1895, P.W. 1493/95 attached with P.W. 1839/95, vol. 447.

[159] There was a great growth of the immigrant population to Assam since 1881. Between 1881-1891, the population increased by more than 11 per cent and another 12 per cent by 1901. *Imperial Gazetteer of India* (Provincial Series) Eastern Bengal and Assam, 1909. Col, pp. 43-4. Volume of tea production also increased immensely. The following figures give some idea.

|  |  | Production | Exported |
|---|---|---|---|
| 1885-89 | (average of 4 years) | 910 lakhs lbs | 870 lakhs lbs |
| 1890-94 | ,, ,, | 1250 lakhs lbs | 1190 ,, ,, |
| 1895-99 | ,, ,, | 1580 lakhs lbs | 1540 ,, ,, |

B. Prasad *Effects of Improved Transport upon the Distribution of Industry and Population*, unpublished, London University, M. Sc. Thesis, 1954 p. 133.

[160] Actually Elgin had proposed a $2\frac{1}{2}$ per cent guarantee on money borrowed in London (Elgin's Note, 27 July 1895, p. 3, *op. cit.*) but the Public Works Committee and the Secretary of State were unanimous in giving a sterling guarantee of 3 per cent. (Godley to Elgin, 9/10 January 1896), E.P., vol. 31.

[161] Elgin's Note on the Construction of Railway (Military) in the North-Western Frontier, 15 August 1898, Enc. Elgin to Hamilton, 15 September 1898, N.C., MSS. Eur. D 509/12.

[162] N. Sanyal, *Development of Railways in India*, p. 143.

[163] Acworth Committee Report on Railways, 1921, Para 177, *op. cit.*

[164] Hamilton to Elgin, 7 September 1898, E.P., vol. 16.

[165] *Proc. of the Council of the Governor-General in India*, 1896, vol. xxxv, p. 345.

CHAPTER IV

# THE FAMINE OF 1896-97

Indian famines have been a recurring feature since time immemorial.[1] Whenever the seasonal rainfall, which plays a crucial role in determining crop yields, failed, a large part of India was subjected to famine. In earlier times, a failure of food crops meant absolute want of food in the areas affected, due largely to the lack of communications. The scope for offering relief was thus very limited. During the Company's rule, hardly any attempt was made to organise measures to meet the challenge of famine.[2] Systematic and effectual planning to prevent suffering and mortality incidental to famine belongs to the later period of British rule in India.

In the middle and the later part of the nineteenth century, a great change took place in the very nature of Indian famines. Thanks to improved means of transport, famine no longer meant "an absolute dearth of food." It now implied a severe and widely prevalent distress among the population caused by a failure of crops over a large area which at once diminished local food supplies and deprived the great majority of the people of their means of livelihood. It was no longer a question of lack of food supplies but want of money to buy food.[3]

The first systematic effort by the Government to deal with famine was made in 1860, when the Government organised large scale relief works to provide employment to persons affected by the failure of the autumn crop. In 1865, the Government received a rude shock, when more than a million people died in Orissa for want of effective relief. As a result, Sir George Campbell conducted a thorough enquiry and this led to a decision by the Indian Government to undertake more resolute steps in future. This resolve was soon put to the test. In 1873, the autumn rains failed in Bengal and Bihar. The Government under Lord Northbrook at once organised extensive relief. The determination of the Government to save every life, whatever the cost, "was for the first time translated into action."[4] Unfortunately, this famine was followed by another in 1877-8 in which the loss of life and cattle was enormous.

In 1880, the Indian Government appointed a Commission to evolve a system to meet the challenge of famine in India. This Famine Commission recommended a twofold famine policy—first, measures to be instituted before and during an impending famine; and second, long term steps to minimise the effects of future famines.[5] In the former category they recommended the establishment of certain rules or codes for famine relief works.

On the basis of the recommendations, such rules or codes were formulated by each Province for the first time in June 1883. These were revised in August 1893. All provincial codes[6] emphasised three points: (1) the civil officers were to keep watch on any signs of scarcity and rise in the prices of foodgrain in their areas; (2) the officials were required to keep in reserve certain schemes under which people in distress could be employed for productive purposes as relief works (this principle of relief work was actually the most important feature of all the provincial famine codes); and (3) the ratio between labour and wage was to be so regulated as to prevent the relief work looking light or unduly attractive, for this might induce those who were not in distress to seek employment in the relief work.[7] The relief labourers were classified under various heads, according to the specific kind of work performed, depending on the ability and the capacity of the labourer. They were divided into four classes:

*Class A:* professional labourers
*Class B:* non-professional labourers
*Class C:* able bodied, but not labourers
*Class D:* weak, fit only for light employment

As regards protective and preventive measures, the Famine Commissioners urged more rapid extension of railway lines to the extent of 20,000 miles. They also recommended the creation of a famine fund as an insurance against natural disaster.

Fortunately, the period 1880-95 was "comparatively" free from any major agricultural calamity. There were, however, minor scarcities necessitating relief but none of them was very serious. By 1896, over 20,000 miles of railways had been constructed—an accomplishment in which Elgin's administration played no small role.

At the end of 1895, scarcity appeared in the four districts of Banda, Hamirpur, Jhansi and Jalaun in Allahabad Division. This was the result of a deficient south-west monsoon and the failure of the winter rains of 1895-6. Already, because of the prolonged drought since 1892, the stock of the grain in the province was very low.[8] Due to the repeated failure of rains, not more than a fourth of the average yield was expected in 1896.[9] By the beginning of the year, the prices of the foodgrains rose and the area of the Allahabad Division was suddenly in the grip of a famine.

Immediately, test works were started; executive staff was strengthened; relief circles were formed; sites were selected for the poor-houses; and Government forests were opened to cattle. In many cases, the Government suspended collection of the autumn instalments of the land revenue in the areas affected. The local government also advanced loans to the land owning and cultivating classes.[10] Though the relief was organised effectively and promptly, the process of phasing out the works were started prematurely, in anticipation of the monsoons, the failure of which caused a lot of hardship to the people.

The rains did not come. There was practically no rainfall during July, a little in August, and by September the monsoon had disappeared. The month of October closed with "the entire Indian Continent face to face with the most widespread... and the gravest impending famine of the century."[11] Starting from the North-Western Provinces and Oudh, this "grim spectre" stalked towards South Punjab, the Central Provinces, Central India, Bengal and spread over several parts of Bombay, stretching southwards on the borders of Madras Presidency. About 225,000 square miles and more than 62 million people were affected in British India.[12]

The gradual transformation of a local into an all-India famine was first indicated by the government of the North-Western Provinces on 30 September 1896 when it reported total damage to the *kharif* crop and doubtful prospects for the *rabi* crop. It therefore proposed launching relief on a large scale.[13] Soon the government of Bengal reported the failure of the vital rice crop. Lieutenant-Governor Mackenzie feared "acute distress in the part of Bihar and considerable pressure in many parts of the country."[14] Similar reports poured in from other provinces. Elgin said with grief: "It is not only that this will be a bad reason, but that it follows other bad ones, and the people have nothing to fall back upon. Burma, Madras, Bengal, Mysore and Coorg are, I believe, looked upon as safe; but if we have distress in all the remaining provinces, it will be an area terribly larger than anything that is commonly affected at one and the same time."[15] Taking the price index of foodgrains as the barometer of the intensity of the famines, Elgin's concern seemed to be justified. The prices of foodgrains had, within three months, shot up by 50 to 100 per cent throughout the country.[16] The situation took a grave turn when grain riots took place in Delhi, Agra, Nagpur, Muzaffarnagar, Mhow and Bombay.[17]

The Government of India undertook some prompt measures. They immediately appealed to the Secretary of State to stop drawings of council bills, to which he agreed.[18] Secondly, the Central Government restored the cut that had been made in the famine insurance grant in 1894 on account of continuous deficits in the budget. In 1896, the grant, which had been reduced to Rs 1 crore in 1894, was restored to its original value of Rs $1\frac{1}{2}$ crores. The provincial balances which had partially been absorbed earlier were also restored to the Provinces. Thirdly, an extensive railway programme was initiated in most affected areas. Elgin privately got some railway line sanctioned by the Secretary of State, notably in the Azamgarh district of the North-Western Provinces and the Oudh and the Saugor-Katni railway in the Central Provinces to serve as relief works.[19] There were areas that were particularly badly affected in the beginning. By the end of 1896, 28 large relief works (each employing 5000 workers) were in operation in the Punjab, 64 in the North Western Provinces, 67 in Bengal and 80 in Bombay. On the relief works in general, the Government was already spending at the rate of Rs 1,00,000 per day.[20] In addition to this, the Government halved the railway freight for foodgrains.[21] The main features of the Government famine policy in 1896 were: (1) to discourage panic; (2) to leave the supply of foodgrains in the hands of private trade; and (3) to leave the execution of famine relief work in the hands of the Provincial governments.

To avoid panic and undue alarm, the Government refrained

from making public references to the famine and relief works. This silence was misunderstood by the public. The Indian press, whick kept a close watch on the pulse of the people, felt agitated over the alleged indifferent attitude of the Government. They asserted that famine conditions had been prevalent ever since the beginning of the year, yet the Government had not officially recognised the fact. They questioned the right of the Government to take so "sanguine" a view of so emergent an event. The Indian newspapers described the miserable conditions of the people who were "selling off their movables and cattle to buy rice." Many starved for two or three days, after which they could manage one meal.[22] The Government's indifference was severely assailed.[23] The newspapers proclaimed the right of the people to know what steps the Government were contemplating to save them from the impending widespread scarcity.[24] They repeatedly reminded the Government that famine was prevalent everywhere. *The Bangawasi* wrote, "So great is the prevailing scarcity that even mothers have forgot [sic] their love for their dear ones. A few days ago three girls were sold to prostitutes by their mothers."[25]

The wisdom of keeping silent over the famine was questioned even by men like Mackenzie, the Lieutenant Governor of Bengal and J. Woodburn, the Executive Member-in-Charge of Famine. The Lieutenant Governor warned Elgin that if there was no rain in November, the *rabi* crop would be damaged beyond repair and that, "coming on the top of four bad harvests this means for Bihar, and probably for many other places, black famine... We have not declared famine or serious distress yet anywhere but the wolf is at the door."[26]

The "indifferent attitude" of the Government towards the famine was further criticised, when Elgin did not cancel his autumn tour of the princely states. There was hardly any influential Indian newspaper which did not urge the Viceroy to cancel the tour.[27] Elgin was repeatedly asked to emulate the good example of Northbrook and stay on at Calcutta. Many reminded him of the sympathetic attitude of Ripon.[28] Many newspapers poured out their emotions in very strong words, *The Bangawasi* wrote: "There is no ignoring the prevailing scarcity—no minimising the widespread nature of the impending calamity. It is, therefore, a matter of regret that the Viceroy should at the present moment be touring about to the disappointment of the distressed people who cannot be reassured by the optimistic utterances made by His Excellency."[29] Another influential paper, *The Hitavedi* commented: "There are on one side the wails of poor, miserable famine-stricken people, and on the other the sound of noisy festivities. You hear on one side a cry of hungry people for food, and on the other the sound of revelry in stately edifices, on the eve of tiger hunt, the preparation of which are all complete."[30]

There was some truth in the charges levelled against Elgin and his administration. The earlier attitude of the Government definitely misled the people. But in fact the Government was quite alive to the grave situation. As early as January 1896, when famine conditions were noticed, Elgin showed great concern. He desired that he should be regularly informed about agricultural conditions and about any possible signs of distress At one time he pulled up the North Western Provinces government for not showing proper vigilence. He asked Babington Smith, his Private Secretary, to write to MacDonnell that "It seems that this is not the first time that the officers responsible for the preparation of these reports have omitted to give notice of distress until it has been brought before the Government of India in some other way." He insisted that the Indian Government be promptly informed, "so that they are in a position to deal more rapidly and effectively with any application for sanction to special measures."[31] In turn, the district officers were asked to send in reports of distress without delay. By June, the Indian Government was fully alive to the "strains" of famine.[32] In a private letter to Hamilton in September, Elgin, in fact, admitted that famine conditions had emerged.[33] He further informed him that the relief machinery was being organised throughout the country.[34] J. Woodburn, the Member-in-Charge of Famine, made a statement in the Legislative Assembly on 15 October about the agricultural prospects. He affirmed the determination of the Government to meet the challenge.[35] Elgin went to the extent of pledging financial help to the local governments (particularly the most affected ones like North Western Provinces and Oudh and Central Provinces) for relief works. He believed in the need for scrupulous economy in general measures, but for the famine he was prepared to spend any amount. A little later he wrote to

Lyall that for the relief works which related to the famine, he was prepared to pledge any amount of financial aid.[36]

If Elgin was so ready and prompt about the measures, why did he not publicly say so? There was only one reason for this. He did not want to cause any undue concern or alarm in the minds of the public till he was sure about the intensity and seriousness of the famine. He firmly believed that great administrative success lay in maintaining high spirits both among the people and the officials. This principle guided Elgin in all his decisions about the famine.

He lamented that "the Native papers show their invincible tendency to exaggerate, and my humble efforts to keep up people's spirits are not at all to their liking."[37] All his endeavours were directed towards avoiding panic. It was for this very reason that he personally redrafted John Woodburn's official statement about the famine which was delivered in the Assembly on 7 January 1897. The original statement appeared rather "gloomy" to Elgin.[38] This action was deliberately planned by Elgin to keep the morale of the public high. Besides this, he kept the spirits of his officials alive by constantly lending them his valuable encouragement. When Lyall's administration was assailed by the press and the Secretary of State for want of proper vigilance in matters of famine in the Central Provinces, Elgin singly and publicly supported him.[39]

This partly explains why Elgin did not cancel his autumn tour of the princely states. However, his not cancelling the tour was probably a tactical mistake. It certainly cast doubts on the intentions of the Viceroy. Though the utility of a cancellation of the tour might be doubted, the psychological and political gain from the gesture would have been immense.[40] Another consideration which perhaps influenced Elgin not to cancel that tour was that it would have been mistaken as an interference in the administration of the relief works in the provinces. He explained this point in great details to MacDonnell: "I am sure you do not sympathise with the silly notion that I ought to run about the country poking my head into all sorts of places, and interfering with business that is much better done by others. But on the other hand, I hope you all know well that I meant what I said when I promised that if I was ever wanted anywhere I would present myself."[41]

Unfortunately, another controversial point in the earlier

stages of the famine policy was the question of an appeal to the public for contributions to a relief fund. It had been usual in times of such calamaties for the better-off sections of the public to come to the aid of the suffering and the needy. The English people in particular had in the past shown considerable generosity during famines. In 1877-8, private charity from England alone amounted to $700,000. It was but natural that during this year of calamity a timely appeal should be made. The question of the establishment of a charitable fund and making an appeal to England was for the first time raised by John Woodburn who wrote to Elgin that "a movement of the kind would be quite right and proper and would have a good political effect both in India and England. I am, therefore, inclined to say that I should, under the circumstances, give it my best support."[42]

In November the Government considered the question of an appeal at the repeated request of George Hamilton.[43] In the same month also, India had substantial rainfall. This made the Government optimistic about the prospects of the *rabi* crop. They thought that the danger of a grave famine had receded and therefore decided to defer for some time the launching of an appeal for charity.[44] In the meantime Elgin took counsel with his colleagues and invited their opinions. A.P. MacDonnell, the Lieutenant-Governor of the North Western Provinces and Oudh, whose knowledge and experience of Indian famines was widely respected, stated that "if the decision has to be taken on North Western Provinces figures alone, then I think the necessity or expediency of making the appeal is now at least doubtful."[45] Most of the other local governments also suggested postponement until Christmas. The Executive Council was also unanimous in holding this view. Elgin personally considered that it would be "premature" to appeal at this time.[46] Mackenzie, in India, was the lone official voice to advise that an appeal for public charity be made immediately. He wrote. "It seems to me, however, that Government need not run counter to the public conscience or throw cold water on offers of subscriptions, especially when these come from outside India."[47] Similar advice poured in from the India Office. Hamilton again wrote, "Politically I think such subscription will be beneficial, and tend to soften any feeling which may still exist in connection with the cotton tariff."[48] *The Times* also counselled likewise and warned the Viceroy against taking "so sanguine a view."[49] Yet Elgin decided to defer the appeal and Hamilton reluctantly agreed.

This decision added fuel to the fire. It was taken to mean that the Indian Government did not recognise the existence of famine. *The Charu Mihir* wrote, "he [Elgin] declines to accept England's aid, simply to avoid the humiliating admission that there is famine in India."[50] *The Indian Spectator* and *The Voice of India* questioned: "Are Government determined to show to the world that they can manage a vast national calamity with their own unaided resources?"[51] Another paper of north India wrote, "Perhaps they will not recognise the existence of the famine until one-third of the population was [sic] succumbed to starvation."[52] For the first time the Anglo-Indian press joined in criticising the Government. *The Times of India* commented:

> Such a step as the Government of India has taken at this juncture is on the face of it hurtful and impolitic, and one that should never have been resorted to . . . . People who are hoping against hope that Lord Elgin may be able to vindicate the course that is being followed are amazed at the silence of the Government on the subject, and are asking how much longer the faction who think ill of all the measures of men in authority are to have their case made out from them by the Government itself. It becomes more difficult every day to resist the conclusion that the Supreme Government is allowing itself to be lulled into the belief that a famine is a mere episode, which will be enacted upon a very limited area, and which may easily be coped with by the unaided resources of the state.[53]

Criticism in England mounted too. Dadabhai Naoroji, Wedderburn and Hydaman held many meetings in London. Hamilton admitted to Elgin that public pressure was very great and the Indian National Congress had been very active. He asked the Viceroy to start a fund immediately as he did not want that agitators should get credit for having forced the hands of the Government.[54] By then it had also become very clear that the rains in November were hardly sufficient to ward off the famine. On 14 January 1897, a simultaneous appeal for charity was launched in Calcutta and London by the Indian Government and the Secretary of State.⁵⁵ The response to it was immediate and very enthusiastic.⁵⁶

The Government attitude towards famine was not at all surprising as from the very beginning, it intended to be cautious and avoid hasty steps. They certainly wanted to be on firm ground before launching an appeal. Though the Government never altogether ruled out an appeal to private charity, its postponement in the given circumstances was certainly impolitic. If it had acted earlier, without much effort, it would, have earned the manifold sympathies of millions.

The second and the most important aspect of the Government's famine policy relates to the question of the supply of food. Under the traditional British policy of *laissez faire*, the generally recognised practice of the Indian Government was to rely on the ordinary operations of trade to meet the food needs of the country even during famine. This policy had been implemented during the famine of 1877-8 and was endorsed by the First Famine Commission.⁵⁷

Whenever prices of food rose to a high level, it was feared that food supplies might totally fail. In the famine of 1896 also prices rose suddenly and sharply. For example, the Kanpur wheat which was being sold at 16 seers per rupee in early 1896, shot up to 8 seers a rupee in October 1896.⁵⁸

The attention of the Government was drawn to the rise in prices of food by the vernacular press. They forewarned that a country like India where there was "always a chronic food scarcity" and where rice was always in short supply, the Government should take steps to stop its export.⁵⁹ *The Bangawasi* reported that it was beyond the ability of the poor to buy rice at 7 or 8 rupees per maund, whereas a short while ago it was sold for 2 or 3 rupees a maund.⁶⁰ It was urged that the "only means now of saving the people from starvation and death is to stop the export of corn."⁶¹ In its next issue the paper went further and stressed that the Government should import food grains on its own account,⁶² and urged that it follow the liberal policy of Lord Northbrook—when on Government account food was imported into the country—and not the dangerous policy of Lytton (when no food was imported by the Government).⁶³ *The Bombay Gazette* asked the Indian Government to give up the policy of non-intervention. It wrote that "adhering to principles of free trade is advantageous [only] in some cases and on some occasions."[64]

The Poona Sarvajanak Sabha sent a memorial to the Government urging the stoppage of exports and the import of food into India.[65] Some others reminded the Government of the need to keep a vigilant eye on the *baniah* who might hoard and further aggravate the situation.[66] Some suggested that Government should open fair-price shops to check the rise in prices.[67] Sayani, the President of the twelfth session of the Indian National Congress, told the Government that the most pressing problem of the hour was not irrigation or railways but the stock of food in the country. If need be, he said, the Government must import from Persia, Russia and America.[68]

The early criticism of the press did not make any impact. The Indian Government instructed all the local governments to refrain from interference with private enterprise in the matter of purchasing or importing grain for famine relief.[69] When the Bengal government for the first time raised the question of food supply, the situation took a different turn. The actual start of the controversy was provided by Bourdillion, Commissioner of the Patna Division. After making a detailed survey of the Division, taking into account the three harvests of the year together with stocks in hand (assumed to be equal to three months supply), he came to the conclusion that there would be an estimated shortage of 550,000 tons.[70] Commenting on the report, the Bengal Government doubted the ability of the private trade to meet so huge a deficit and expressed the opinion "that little reliance can be placed on supplies from within the province."[71] The Lieutenant-Governor went on to say that "It is necessary to report that, in view of the unparalleled highness of prices and of the extent of the area over which there has been shortage of crops throughout India, the situation as regards the food supply is not free, even in Bengal, from elements of doubts and anxiety."[72] The Lieutenant-Governor came to the conclusion that there must be some intervention. His resolve was further strengthened by the outcome of his meeting with officials and public men held at Sonepur on 20 November 1896. Everyone was convinced that the only way out of the difficulty was to increase the stock of food by imports.[73] The Bengal Government, therefore, requested the Indian Government to authorise them to advance money to the traders and other persons in Bihar so they could import or purchase foodgrains.[74] In making this request, the Bengal Government assumed that the question would appear "to be more one of finance than of interference with trade."[75]

This caused quite a stir in Government circles. Elgin, whose adherence to the principles of free trade was amply known at once retorted: "I am sure we shall not agree to anything of this kind."[76] Earlier, he reiterated to the Secretary of State: "Any interference with trade, either in way of prohibiting exports, or promoting imports, would be a very extreme measure, for which there is certainly no justification."[77] He believed that private trade was resourceful enough and was already providing the supplies by importing surplus rice from Burma.[78] But the question of food supply was too vital to be brushed aside by mere assurances. As the question was of all India importance, Elgin immediately went into the merit of the case. He consulted the members of his Executive. The Executive Council unanimously approved the principle of non-intervention. Their views were best summarised by Westland who opposed the suggestion of the Bengal government on three grounds: (1) that such a scheme would create a bigger administrative problem of supervision and control and subsequently cause greater confusion; (2) the scheme would be expensive and would tend to increase the dependence of the people on the exchequer; and (3) there was yet no reason for taking such an extreme measure.[79] Besides, O'Conor, the Director-General of Statistics and Trade, assured Elgin that there was "more than sufficient" food stock for another three months.[80] Elgin was favourably influenced by the advice of MacDonnell, who officially stated his strong aversion "to departure from the principles of non-intervention."[81] MacDonnell was very confident of the *baniah* and the private trade. This support from MacDonnell must have strengthened Elgin in the policy of absolute non-intervention. Elgin decided to over-rule the Bengal Government. He went even a step further. He dealt with the question in great detail and published the Indian Government's reply in the Gazette of India.[82] The main reason for doing this was to remove fear from the minds of the private traders that the Government ever intended to come into the market.

The Indian Government reiterated their confidence in the efficacy of the private trade. "The Governor-General-in-Council," their reply read, "believes that the intervention of Government as a purchaser or importer would do infinitely more harm than good, as it would cripple and discourage the agency which is best able to gauge the need, which is impelled by self interest to anticipate it and which alone is best able to supply it effectively." "The fact that there are hungry men in a district," the despatch emphasised, "is not in itself sufficient to induce a flow of food towards that district in the ordinary course of trade, there must also be money available with which the hungry may pay for it. And this guarantee Government provides by undertaking (as it does) to find work for all who are in danger of starvation, and to pay them at rates which will suffice to buy them a subsistence ration at whatever prices may, from time to time, be locally current."[83] Another argument they advanced was that the Bengal scheme would be tantamount to giving "a blank cheque," the effect of which on other provincial administrations was bound to be serious. The Government thus rejected the Bengal Government's appeal on the ground that it could not be granted without interference, "or at any rate without bearing the appearance of intervention, for such a case would be almost worse than the reality, since, while producing all its evils, it could carry with it none of its advantages."[84] This decision of the Indian Government was approved by George Hamilton who wrote: "I am sure the less you interfere with private trade, the better, for any dislocation of so ubiquitous an instrument might lead to a wholesale disorder, for the consequences of which you should be held responsible."[85]

Thus there were two main reasons why the Government of India overruled the Bengal Government. First, their firm belief in private trade, aided by the conviction that any alternative to this would lead to confusion. In order to seek maximum cooperation from private trade the Government intended to give it all conceivable help.[86] Elgin and his advisers were sure that even minor restrictions would draw the private trade into hoarding. Secondly, some rains in the months of November and December had brought a fresh wave of optimism in the mind of the Indian Government and a hope that the *rabi* crop would be two-third of the normal.

But the winter rains stopped all of a sudden. The intensity of the scarcity deepened. The danger to the *rabi* crop became real. More starvation deaths were reported. There was a repeated

## The Famine of 1896-97    119

attack on the Government's famine policy in the British Press with many English newspapers publishing pictures of hungry and dying men.[87] This criticism alarmed Hamilton who confessed that he had never visualised that famine would be so widespread.[88] On 29 January Hamilton wrote to Elgin for the first time asking him to consider the ways and means in advance, "if due to emergency" the Government had to import food. He advanced three suggestions: direct purchase of food stock by the Government; purchase of food stock indirectly by giving advances (same as the earlier suggestion of Mackenzie): and encouraging imports by bonus. Of the three, he personally favoured the first and went on to say, "I do not want to unduly press you, but summing up the situation, I should say that we ought to err on the side of over-precaution rather than on that of risk or chance."[89]

Members of the India Council, particularly Hardie and Crosthwaite,[90] were even more agitated. They pressed the Indian Government to regulate the food supply on their own account. In a special note on the question of food supply Hardie criticised the Government and commented that, "the famine policy of the Government is based on economic theory that the Government should not interfere with private trade, a policy which is in effect little else than that the Government should do nothing at all."[91] He submitted that private trade under this grave emergency could not provide the relief required for the population for two reasons: First, the machinery of private trade did not exist in the interior of India to the extent necessary to secure the object in view; secondly, it was hampered by the limited supply of money available in India on account of the currency legislation. According to him, the prices of food stuff had risen and the scarcity had been intensified because foodgrains tended to move into the Government relief centres, creating hardship for the majority of the people who did not come to the relief works. He, therefore, strongly felt that if the Government imported or purchased food for their relief works "only" then the pressure could be largely eased on the bulk of the population, who did not come to the relief centres.[92] This system, as Godley said, in a way would not have been new because the Government already purchased for the army and the goals.[93] Crosthwaite also argued on the same lines as Hardie.[94] Even Queen Victoria urged the purchase of foodgrains on Government account.[95] In addition to this, it may be stated that the very success of the relief system depended upon food being purchasable everywhere by the persons relieved. Supposing the monsoon again failed, and the dealers refused to sell grains, the whole system would collapse. Therefore, the protagonists for the intervention urged the Government to hold a reserve stock of foodgrains to feed the population on relief for two or three months in the event of sudden collapse of private trade.

Elgin vehemently denied that the food stock had been or was likely to be exhausted in the near future. He saw a downward trend in their prices, particularly in the Punjab, where the fall was 15 per cent, and the Government decided to adhere to their earlier stand.[96] But before doing so, they extensively examined the position of food stocks *vis-a-vis* private trade.

The Central Government soon realised that the problem of estimating the total food stocks in the country was an immensely difficult one. Nevertheless, they were satisfied, after their enquiries from the local administrations, that food stocks in hand were adequate to meet the demand till the next crop. Punjab, they believed, possessed enough stock not only for local consumption but also for some export to other Provinces.[97] Similarly, the position of the North Western Provinces was not considered as bad as it had been in the beginning of the year. There also existed a considerable stock with the grain dealers and agriculturists.[98] Although the Central Provinces' stock was very low, some reserve still existed in the richer districts. The Province, as a whole, the Government believed, was fairly well provided. In Madras and Bombay, the crop failure was limited to the Carnatic and Deccan districts where the population was sparse. Elsewhere in Bombay and in the southern districts of Madras, there was a good harvest. In Bengal, there was a great loss of the rice crop, but the depleted stock was supplemented by the inflow of Burma rice, where there was a surplus of $1\frac{1}{2}$ million tons.[99] The Indian Government therefore contended that the general indications regarding the position of the stock of food were good, the prices were stable and the markets were not excited.

The Government had no complaint against the private traders concerning hoarding and unwillingness to sell. They also asserted "that export of foodgrains from India to foreign countries has for months past virtually ceased, and that great economy is every-

## The Famine of 1896-97

where excercised under pressure of high prices by nine-tenths of the population."[100] The Government believed that even in the contingency of the failure or delay of the monsoon, they would have enough for at least two months' consumption throughout the country. In case the monsoon failed, there would be at least the possibility of reaping a 4 anna crop over the whole country (which was actually a much lower average than that of 1896) and if this were added to what remained from the older stocks, a supply equivalent to perhaps two months could be held in reserve. So it seemed to the Government hardly possible that in the worst event, the "failure of supplies" would come upon them so suddenly that foreign supplies could not be brought into the country in the ordinary course of trade.[101] Only in the final eventuality—the failure of the 1897 monsoons—the Government might have to intervene.[102]

Elgin said that it was "mischievous" to say that private trade had failed. Private trade, he maintained, had, in fact, been active in placing food at the disposal of the public through the means of the railways. For example, it was private trade that imported rice from Burma on their own resources. Already, as much as 300,000 tons of rice had been imported and another 600,000 tons were available in the market. This, Elgin believed, was sufficient to feed the entire army of relief workers in the province of Bengal and the North Western Provinces.[103] Elgin did not agree with Hardie that the Government should import food for its relief works and leave private trade undisturbed to supply the rest of the population from local supplies. In countering this view he wrote:

> The private trade of a district exists for the supply of the people within it, and to suddenly restrict its operations where perhaps 20 per cent of the population on relief works, would so absolutely dislocate it that I am convinced that, far from lowering the prices to those outside the Government works, it would be much more likely to run them up. I do not think Mr. Hardie has allowed enough for the manner in which the improvement of railway communication has equalised prices all over India. There is no longer the sharp division between local and external stocks in any particular area.[104]

As to the suggestion that the Government should buy food stocks in advance for the relief workers against the eventuality of the failure of the monsoon, the Indian Government raised objection on two grounds. First, the purchase of so large a stock would block about Rs two crores. If the contingency feared did not arise, the Government would have to dispose of the stock at low prices and lose about half the money spent. This, the Indian Government nevertheless felt, was not an insuperable objection where the lives of millions were involved. Their, second, and more serious objection was that Government purchases would, by introducing "an unknown element" into its calculations and by creating an artificial level of prices, make the trading class distrustful of the Government. "However clearly we defined our intentions," the Indian Government wrote, "the trade would be always apprehensive that the Government reserve would be poured into the market, or that the Government would be driven to extend its operation."[105] And finally, the Government closed the discussion by emphasising that they "are strongly and deliberately of the opinion that, even in the worst conceivable emergency, so long as trade is free to follow its normal course, we should do far more harm than good by attempting to interfere."[106]

This attitude of the Government has led B.M. Bhatia to believe that the policy of non-intervention was carried out to the "absurd limit."[107] He supports his charge by stating that where the loss of crop in the year was estimated at one-third of the average annual production or "18 or 19 million tons," the total imports against this (all from Burma only) during the same period amounted to only 6 lakh tons.[108] To him this is a sufficient indication of the failure of the Government's food policy. Unfortunately, Bhatia does not amplify his argument and errs on the side of over-simplification.

The key to the understanding of the Government's food policy lies in correctly answering two questions: (1) If the loss was one-third of the total foodgrains in India, as claimed, then what was the total production? Did India produce surplus food? Or was there some accumulated surplus of stock? (2) Did the imports increase and exports decrease correspondingly to the loss of the produce—say to the extent of one-third during this crisis? To find the answer to the first question is indeed very difficult—for total grain production in British India cannot be accurately assessed. The Famine Commissioners in 1880, after careful inquiry, had come to the conclusion that India produced a surplus of 5,165,000 tons over total consumption. This surplus was available for export or storage.[109] T.W. Holderness, the Special Officer during the 1897 famine, calculated that, since the writing of the report, the population of the same area had risen by 17 per cent and, in comparison, the area under foodgrains had risen by only 8 per cent. On this basis, the available surplus of the foodgrains could not remain as high as 5,165,000 tons and probably was only 1,700,000 tons.[110] But the information supplied by the local governments to the Famine Commission of 1898 showed a surplus of 9.5 million tons.[111] This contradiction is inexplicable. Coming from Government sources within a span of one year it only shows that exact information was not attainable. It would be safe to assume that, in any case, the surplus could not be as high as 9.5 million tons and might not be as low as 1,700,000 tons. But certainly it could not be more than what was estimated in 1880. Secondly, the food to the estimated surplus of 1,700,000 tons in 1897 must have been gradual, the fall varying with the annual rise in the area under cultivation and the simultaneous rise in the population. One tends to agree with the Famine Commissioners that there must have been some surplus "in ordinary years."[112] But this could not be gauged accurately. Even if we accept Holderness's estimate, there was some surplus left after internal consumption and export. For example, in the ten years before 1896, the export of foodgrains from British India averaged 1.25 million tons to 1 million tons in the five years preceding the famine.[113] In 1897, though the scarcity was extremely acute, "the stock at the end did not seem to have been close on exhaustion."[114] But the availability of food stocks did not in any case indicate abundance or prosperity; nor did it mean that the people did not die of starvation. They died, not because there was absolutely no food (of course during famine the normal supply was thoroughly dislocated), but because they were unable to purchase food even when it was available. It was primarily the lack of purchasing power which proved fatal. Invariably the surplus of production over consumption was the result of lack of purchasing power. Had there been full consumption of food according to the needs, could the surpluses have been so high? The poverty of India was amply visible even in ordinary times, but during famine it was much more so. Certainly the large dislocations of normal availability to the extent of 18 or 19 million tons must have greatly aggravated the "normal" hardship and the scarcity must certainly have further been enhanced by hoarding by private traders and farmers.

Another significant point regarding the availability of food stocks in India emerges on analysing the nature of the movement of food stocks internally. There was a large export from comparatively surplus districts to the more distressed areas. The table shows the movement of foodgrains between January 1897 to September 1897.[115]

| Districts | Import (tons) | Export (tons) | Districts | Import (tons) | Export (tons) |
|---|---|---|---|---|---|
| *Bengal* | | | *North Western Provinces and Oudh* | | |
| Patna | +14,620 | | Banda | +23,573 | |
| Darhanga | +44,141 | | Allahabad | +45,529 | |
| Monghair | | —31,055 | Bullandshahar | | —28,017 |
| Bhagalpur | | —27,554 | Aligarh | | —26,482 |
| *Central Provinces* | | | *Bombay* | | |
| Jubbulpur | +12,065 | | Poona | +38,672 | |
| Nagpur | +17,365 | | Bijapur | +25,512 | |
| Raipur | | —14,337 | Panch Mahal | | —23,339 |
| Sambalpur | | —22,599 | Shakurpur | | —75,414 |
| *Punjab* | | | *Madras* | | |
| Hissar | +35,985 | | Malabar | +32,539 | |
| Jullundur | | —30,138 | Godavari | | —52,976 |

These figures do not present fully the incoming and outgoing traffic of food stocks from one district to another in the same province. They serve only as a pointer to the fact that food stocks were being moved from some surplus areas to deficit areas. These movements took place under the auspicious of the private trade, whose confidence and energy was boosted by the encouragement it received from the Government and the provision of railway facilities.

In the examination of the second question regarding the rise and fall of imports and exports, we find that in 1893-4, the import of foodgrains into India was 341,750 cwt; in 1894-5, 483,523 cwt; in 1895-6, 306,333 cwt; and in the famine year of 1896-7 (it increased threefold) 1,080,602 cwt. Imports continued on the same

## The Famine of 1896-97

scale in 1897-8, when the import was 1,073,415.[116] Foodgrain exports from British India declined even more drastically. Whereas in 1894-5, the export of grain was 48,864,395 cwt; in 1895-6, 48,332,973; in the famine year it fell to 32,420,134 cwt. The downward trend continued in 1897-8 when the total export was 30,890,379 cwt. The most interesting feature was the manifold decline in the export of wheat in the famine year. Whereas in 1895-6, the export of wheat amounted to 10,002,912 cwt, in 1897-8, it came down to 1,910,553 cwt.[117] These figures show that when food production declined exports correspondingly showed a downward trend. Besides, this very scarcity also affected the rate of food consumption.

If it is presumed that food was available, though in a very limited quantity, then the question arises as to what was the best means of distribution. Was it necessary to regulate the supply? The ideal answer would be that the State should have organised and regulated the food supply, particularly when there was so much poverty. But was that practicable in the given circumstances? And was such a regulation consistent with the spirit of the time?

The policy of intervention and State control was not feasible for various reasons. The civil administration was fully occupied with famine relief operations and plague control. Further, in 1897, the Indian army was occupied in the North Western frontier wars. In such circumstances, the regulation of food supply would have been extremely difficult, if not impossible particularly because of the lack of trained and experienced staff. Ineffective control could have proved more dangerous than no control. Besides, the principle of intervention was not popular with the thinking of the age. Even "enlightened" Indians did not approve of State control. The Indian National Congress never boldly suggested State intervention. S.N. Banerjee's influential newspaper, *The Bengalee*, too, did not come out in support of Government intervention in food trade. In his very forceful speech at the Congress Session of 1896, Banerjee discreetly omitted any reference to the food policy.[118]

It is possible that there was some tendency on the part of the private traders to make maximum profits during the crisis, but the Government failed to find any evidence of a general combination among dealers to keep up the prices. MacDonnell, who investigated the question in detail in his Province, did not find any proof to that effect.[119] It was, therefore politic and wise to solicit the cooperation of private trade to the maximum limit. Keeping this in view, the Government reduced railway freight and provided regular information about the course of the grain trade to the dealers. Arrangements were made in each district under which the district officer, at the end of each week, received a weekly return from each railway station in his district of the imports and exports of grain, so that a grain dealer could readily despatch grain to places where it was most required.[120] Each local government maintained personal contact with the important grain dealers for food requirements of the markets.[121] The Government believed that minimisation of administrative problems would leave more time to the officers to concentrate on relief works.

Apart from administrative convenience, the policy of non-intervention had some other advantages. The money supply situation was tight. No trader could afford to tie up large sums of money in grain hoarded in anticipation of high prices. This checked speculation. Similarly, the uniformity of prices throughout India also acted as a deterrent to speculators. While the universal prevalence of high prices must have caused acute suffering, specially amongst the poorer classes, control and regulation of the import and export trade would have created suspicion among the traders, and induced them to hoard. This could have caused enormous suffering to the people before the Government could take effective counter action. It thus appears that Government's decision was wise. Before upholding the policy of non-intervention, they had twice given it a very careful consideration and examined the issue in detail. In deciding to do so the Government had never been more unanimous. Nor was the Government's attitude rigid. In exceptional cases, where private trade did not serve effectively, the Government did intervene. For instance, the Government imported grain in Palamau District in Bengal, in Bhadrachalam Taluk of Godavari District in Madras, in Setphal relief work in Poona District in Bombay, and in Mandla and Balaghat in Central Provinces.[122]

A major reason for the bitterness of the controversy seems to have been the unfavourable comparison with the famine policy of Lord Northbrook. Howsoever liberal Northbrook's policy was, it could hardly have worked during 1896-97. The famine of

1873-4 was limited to a small area in Bengal and it was therefore not difficult to supervise and regulate the import of grain. Yet even Northbrook did not fully control the food trade. Exports continued unchecked. Sometimes, the same ships which brought Burma rice to Calcutta, carried Bengal rice to Burma.[123] Besides, it was probably imperative at Northbrook's time to purchase rice on Government account in view of the then lack of railway communication. In 1873-4, there was only one railway in Bihar (the area of famine), and that ran through the two southern district of Patna and Shahabad. In 1896, there was at least one line in each district, and in the Patna division alone there were 589 miles of railway. In 1873-4, the Sone canals had also been opened. In 1896 these provided communication for many miles.[124] By 1896, relief work had also been streamlined and well regulated. Thus, the administration in 1896 was much better equipped to follow a policy of non-intervention and was certainly well advised to follow it. Even Lord Northbrook whole-heartedly supported Elgin's policy.[125] From the practical point of view, the policy pursued was the only feasible one.

The third feature of the famine strategy was that the administration of the relief works was left in the hands of the Provincial Governments. Lord Elgin believed that relief work must be left to the local governments. He gave expression to his belief while addressing the Legislative Assembly in October 1896: "It is upon the local governments that, whatever happens, we must rely to carry out the measures that may become necessary. . . .We are justified I think in our belief that the work will be done, and will be done well." He added, "as to the share of the Government of India, it is not for us ourselves to enter into the arena and to take charge of the operations. We should hamper the proper authorities, and not assist them. Our duty is to devise means for helping the local governments with the wider knowledge of the whole circumstances available to us and to supply the sinews of war where required."[126] Thus the success of the relief measures depended largely upon the efforts, planning and efficiency of the respective provincial administrations.

The North Western Provinces and Oudh were the first area to be afflicted, and it was here that famine relief measures were first undertaken. The Provinces were specially fortunate in having A.P. MacDonnell, who had wide experience of famine work ever since 1874, at the helm of the affairs.[127] The basic features of his administration were efficiency and economy. To achieve these, he introduced innovations in the field of relief organisation and relief distribution. Firstly, the government departed from the policy laid down in the code of small relief works and introduced a system of large relief works managed by the Public Works Department. The main reason for laying stress on large relief works was to increase returns from them.[128] With the widespread activity in connection with the expansion of railways it was not difficult to organise large works.

The small works were executed locally by giving advances to zamindars and landlords. This system had been tried earlier during the Bundelkhand famine of early 1896 and had proved a success. It was more fully developed in January 1897. The rules provided for the execution of small works of "village utility" by village landlords. The landlords were under an obligation to employ village labour and to pay certain rate of wages out of the loans advanced to them. When the work was duly completed, one-fourth to one-half of the advance, as agreed, was remitted back to Government, the balance was to be refunded in periodical instalments. In case some landlords could not undertake or were unwilling to bear the cost, the collector could execute the work either directly or through the zamindar acting as an agent.[129] Under this scheme, the Government gave loans and advances to the extent of Rs 42,13,831.[130] The government of the North Western Provinces and Oudh was the only one "which used to any extent the system of partly recoverable advances." This system offered a substantial inducement to the landlords to undertake works of general village utility, and it was also more economical to the State than village works at its sole cost.[131] The advances given for developing local resources indeed proved very useful. For example, 550,759 temporary wells were constructed in the years of famine. The number of masonry wells constructed was 4,227, and many others were repaired and improved. Irrigation facilities such as embankments and tanks, were largely extended. It was calculated that the additions made to various sources of irrigation were sufficient to protect 1,381,494 acres and produce 465,000 tons of food.[132]

In December 1896, the government of the North Western Province and Oudh introduced an important change in the

## The Famine of 1896-97

organisation of famine relief. It abolished the fourfold classification of the relief workers. In its place, it introduced a twofold classification—diggers and carriers. The motive for this change was economic. Wages (A) and (C) of the Code were abolished. Wage (B) and the lowest wage (D) were now awarded respectively to diggers and the carriers. The table shows the difference between the grain equivalent wage and dependents dole by the Code and by the Resolution of 5 December 1896 which introduced the change.[133]

| By the Code of 1895 | | | By Resolution of 5 December 1896 | | |
|---|---|---|---|---|---|
| | Males Chattacks | Females Chattacks | | Males Chattacks | Females Chattacks |
| Class A Professional labourers | 21 | 19 | | | |
| Class B Labourers not Professional | 19 | 17 | Diggers | 19 | 16 |
| Class C Able bodied not Labourers | 16 | 15 | | | |
| Class D Weakly, fit for light employment | 14 | 13 | Carrier Class | 14 | 13 |
| Adult dependent | 14 | 13 | Adult dependent | 12 | 10 |
| Children under 14 years of age from 3/4 to 1/4 of the adult male wage (i.e. from about 14 to 5 *chattacks*) according to the age and requirements | | | Working children above 12 and under 16 years | *Chattacks* 10 | |
| | | | Working children over 7 and under 12 | 6 | |
| | | | Not in arms and under 7 years infants in arms extra pie to the mother | | |

In justification of this change it was said that a full days work on relief operations was done only by a minority of the workers employed as "diggers" and that the majority, whether ablebodied or not, consisted chiefly of women and children who worked as "carriers." It was also stated by the local government that, as the people came in family groups to the works, the joint earnings of the family "ought to be so restricted as to be sufficient only for its subsistence, and that for this purpose the minimum code wage for the majority was enough."[134]

This was a drastic change. It was criticised by the Famine Commission of 1898. In the important matter of periodical conversion of the grain wages into cash wages with reference to prevailing prices, the Commission commented that the new rules were harsher for the labourer than provided in the Provincial Codes, because fluctuations of less than 10 per cent in the price of grain were ignored. Between the rate fixed and actual prices, there was often a considerable difference. For example, in Allahabad District the conversion rate remained at 10 seers a rupee from March to July 1897, but the grain was as dear as $8\frac{1}{2}$ seers a rupee.[135] This necessarily imposed extra hardship on the people and there was a general complaint that the daily wage paid were not sufficient to "allow them to satisfy their hunger."[136] There was reason to believe that many people must have been "severely pinched," particularly in June and July when "a considerable number of incapable people failed to get the relief that was desirable."[137]

But the Government believed that stringent measures could be redeemed by efficient and prompt decisions. In this sphere, the local government showed extra care and the Lieutenant-Governor personally supervised famine relief measures. For this untiring effort, he was complimented by the Viceroy, the Secretary of State and the Queen.[138] The two leading vernacular weeklies of the Province, *Ams-i-Hind* (Urdu), and *Hindustan* (Hindi), commended the famine administration.[139] The Famine Commission also singled out MacDonnell's administration for incessant activity and watchfulness for their "constant grasp of the situation, skill in combining all forms of relief, and a great power of enlisting the services of the leaders of the native society. . . . We agree in the general verdict that the result was a conspicuous success and a great administrative feat."[140]

At one time, more than one and a half million people were on direct relief in the North West Provinces and Oudh. The direct expenditure on relief, excluding establishment and incidental charges, came to Rs 1,67,15,147. The money spent on loans and advances was Rs 42,13,831; that against revenue suspension

## The Famine of 1896-97

Rs 1,44,64,875 and revenue remission Rs 65,19,100; Rs 48,87,527 of the Indian Charitable Fund was also appropriately utilised.[141]

Similar relief measures were taken in the state of Bengal where the relief organisation had come into full operation by the end of November 1896. The distressed tracts were blocked out into relief charges and relief circles. A charge comprised an area with a population of about 250,000 persons. A relief circle comprised an area of about 30 to 40 square miles with a population of about 25,000 to 30,000.[142] In its main features of relief operations followed the North Western Provinces and Oudh system of recognising only two main classes of workers, the diggers and the carriers, with their wage scales.[143] As in the North Western Provinces and Oudh, hardships arising out of the stringent measure were felt in Bengal also. The Bengal Government was equally meticulous in enforcing completion of the work allotted and often resorted to fining. As the ordinary wage for the majority of the workers corresponded to the minimum wage of the provincial code, it was found that workers fined for short work were left with very little which caused extra hardship.

While the administration of relief works was unduly stringent, gratuitous village relief was liberally provided in Bengal. The number of persons in receipt of gratuitous relief in the province were always more than those on relief works. In May 1897, the number stood at 414,324 and on works at 376,295; in June 459,000 and 360,698; in July 423,186 and 218,181; in August 316,424 and 109,402; and in September 108,148 and 35,426 respectively.[144] The reason why so much of gratuitous relief was given was the general poverty of the people and the density of the population in the affected areas.

As regards the nature of relief works, the Bengal government followed a different policy from the government of North Western Provinces and Oudh. Whereas in the North Western Provinces the backbone of the system was the large relief works, in the case of Bengal, with few exceptions, small works remained, throughout, the basis of relief. There were two reasons for this. First, the great mass of the labouring and cultivating population was believed to be greatly averse to seeking work at a distance from their homes. Secondly, there were very few large works ready for execution. Construction and deepening of village tanks were considered to be more useful than building roads.

In Madras Presidency, the need for relief was confined to four districts of the Deccan and to the two northern districts of Ganjan and Vizagapatam.[145] Early and prompt measures were taken. In marked contrast to the famine organisations of the other governments, the Madras government deviated from the code in the direction of liberality. Acting on the advice of the Sanitary Commissioner of the Madras Province, the government recommended the abolition of the two lowest classifications of labourers from the Code.[146] It was decided that all relief workers should be placed in one or other of the two highest classes and given (A) or (B) wages. The task of each gang of relief workers was closely adapted to their working capacity. Fining below the lowest wage level was prohibited.[147] The basic reason for taking such a humane view was that even the existing level of wages for the relief worker was not considered adequate.[148] Due to this consideration, the labour test was "less severe in Madras than elsewhere, while the average wage paid to relief workers was higher, and . . . throughout the greater part of the relief operations, the tendency was to relax provisions of the code in favour of workers, not to tighten them as in other provinces."[149]

Havelock, the Governor of Madras, proudly wrote to Elgin: "We might have erred on the side of indulgence, but perhaps this is safer than to err on the side of severity."[150] The liberal policy did have a substantial effect in keeping down the mortality rate to 4 per cent of the normal rate.[151]

Other local governments like Bombay, Punjab and Berar also executed prompt and extensive relief works, and were distinctly successful both as regards the saving of human life and mitigation of distress.[152]

It was only the government of the Central Provinces which failed in organising relief works promptly and efficiently. The province had unfortunately suffered from famine conditions ever since 1894, particularly in the three districts of Saguar, Damoh and Jubbulpur. But, strangely, the first direct relief measures were taken up only in December 1896.[153] This lack of vigilance on the part of the Central Provinces government was specifically criticised by the Famine Commission of 1898. They wrote: "It seems to us that dangerously little was done by Government in all three districts in 1894-95, and that the theory that though privation prevailed among the poor classes it was

## The Famine of 1896-97

not too acute, was too sanguine."[154] They further charged the government with staking too much on the hope or chance of better harvests in the future.[155]

After having realised the gravity of the situation, though late, the government organised extensive relief. C.J. Lyall, the Commissioner, toured the whole Province.[156] Following the example of the North Western Provinces and Oudh, large relief works under the Public Works Department were opened. Subsidiary to these large works, small works of local utility were also started.[157] But by then enough damage had already been done. The death rate rose above the normal. From the average of 33.76 (per mile, per year) it increased to 49.31 in 1896 and to 69.34 in 1897.[158] According to the official report of the Central Provinces, 91,397 people died of famine.[159] But this figure appears to be low and was doubted by the Famine Commission of 1898.[160] Many of the starvation deaths were attributed to lack of proper and timely appreciation of the situation. In passing its judgement on local governments, the report said: "We regret to have to express the opinion that the degree of success in the saving of life and relief of the distress was not all that it should or might have been."[161]

The public criticism had its effect. For showing lack of proper vigilance, C.J. Lyall was duly reprimanded. He was immediately transferred from his post, much to his regret, and sent to the India Office as Revenue Secretary. This ended his Indian career (which should have taken him very high in the executive hierarchy). Secondly, the tragedy of 1896-7 taught a lesson to the local government to start relief in time. During the famine of 1899, the Government showed extra care and prompted immediate measures. Of the total famine units (1135 million) given as relief in 1899 famine, nearly 50 per cent (555.8 million) were in the Central Provinces.[162]

It is thus clear that the relief administered through the local governments was extensive, though varying and at times insufficient, depending on the efficiency and effectiveness of the provincial government. The government of North Western Provinces and Oudh showed as much awareness of the urgent needs of the people as of the need for efficiency and economy. The Madras Government gave top priority to the saving of human life by giving generous relief. Only the Central Province administration was unable to grasp the gravity of the situation and was therefore found wanting.

To sum up, it may be said that large scale government relief was undertaken actually "far greater than any that has yet been recorded."[163] In the beginning of the famine, in October 1896, there were only 50,000 persons on relief; in time of acute distress, in April 1897, their number rose to 33 million. In all, the number of units relieved was 821 million,[164] each at a cost of 1.42 annas a day per person. This was equivalent to an average of 2,220,000 persons relieved day by day for a period of one year, at the rate of Rs 32.7 per head per annum.[165] The total relief expenditure in the famine of 1896-97 was as follows:[166]

| | |
|---|---|
| Direct expenditure on relief | Rs 6,22,64,970 |
| Loans and advances | Rs 1,84,11,519 |
| Suspension of Land revenue | Rs 2,10,73,135 |
| Remission of Land revenue | Rs 1,17,90,898 |
| Indian charitable fund | Rs 1,49,04,571 |
| Total | Rs 12,84,45,093 |

If the loss of revenue under salt, excise, customs and the loss of railway freight is added, the grand total comes to more than Rs 17 crores. This was the largest single expenditure on any famine in the nineteenth century—it was higher than that during the much publicised famine of 1899, when the total expenditure, including from private charity, totalled Rs 16.5 crores.[167]

Finally, the Indian Government appointed a commission to examine the measures taken and suggest recommendations for future guidance.[168] The Commission was headed by Sir J.B. Lyall[169] and included an Indian, Rai Bahadur B.K. Bose, an advocate from Nagpur.[170]

The Commission made a useful and exhaustive survey of the whole situation. In their findings and recommendations, by and large, they agreed with the "principles" as laid down by the Commission of 1880. In some avenues, the report made valuable suggestions.[171] First, they accepted the innovation of the North Western Provinces and Oudh government regarding the twofold classification of relief workers—the diggers and the carriers, as convenient and desirable.[172] But they did not agree to its wage scale and instead adhered to the original full ration

# The Famine of 1896-97

of wage (A) for the diggers. For the other class (carriers) they recommended that the wage scale should be 75 per cent of the first.[173] They also suggested that all relief works should be classed in the programmes under either the heads of "public works" or "village works" and devoted mostly to the development of irrigation projects. And, finally, regarding the policy of contracting ordinary public works in time of famine, they suggested that, so far as Imperial or Provintial finances and establishments could possibly permit, they should be fully maintained or expanded in districts not recognised as actually distressed but in which there was reason to suppose the existence of an exceptional demand for labour.[174]

The famine of 1896-7 came at a time when the cotton duty controversy was still fresh and currency changes were just beginning to take effect. It was accompanied by war on the North Western frontiers of India and plague. But Elgin's administration did not lose its nerve. Although in dealing with the famine he never innovated—the policy as laid in 1880 was followed in all its detail, he led his team through difficult period without chaos or confusion. He neither had any conflict with local administrations, as Lytton had had, nor did he overextend himself as Northbrook did. The relief measures were not extravagant but were exacting. In his famine administration he was his own master and showed neither subservience nor deliberate obstinacy. The Secretary of State fully supported him and his colleagues and his subordinates cooperated with him. His energetic railway policy, which resulted in adding nearly 5,000 miles of railway lines, proved a useful asset in the utilisation of relief works.

The most important outcome of the famine of 1896-7 and the one that followed close on its heels in 1899 was that the economic aspects of British rule became the most important target of attack for Indian nationalists. Famine, it was urged by leaders like Dadabhai Naoroji,[175] R.C. Dutt,[176] D.E. Wacha,[177] William Digby[178] and others, was the result of India's poverty. It was the question of poverty—the root cause of all suffering which attracted most attention. They urged economic changes and better utilisation of India's resources.[179] It was during this period that the "drain theory" become a catchword with the nationalists.

The Government also began to realise the need for a change in their attitude towards the people. This and the change in the attitude of the Government towards the subject of the prevention of famine were among the most important developments of the period. It was in this context that the Punjab Alienation Act was passed on 19 October 1900.[180] Actually, the work in connection with alienation of land on account of unchecked borrowing had been in progress for some time previously.[181] On 26 October 1895, Denzil Ibbetson, officiating Revenue and Agriculture Secretary to the Indian Government, invited the views and proposals of local administrations on the problem of land transfers. Ibbetson remarked that the gift of the free power of transfer was an "evil" and a "positive political danger."[182] Unfortunately, owing to many other pressing problems, nothing much could be achieved except that a useful attempt to "advance its discussion" was made.[183] Another preventive measure was taken in the beginning of the twentieth century: the Government devoted considerable attention to the development of irrigation so as to reduce dependence on the vagaries of seasonal rainfall. A Rs 44-crore plan for the next twenty years was drawn up in 1905.[184]

The Nineteenth century was thus unceremoniously closed with two ghastly famines and a dastardly plague. Politically the very occurrence of famine was a stigma which convinced most Indian National leaders that the effects of the British rule "on the prosperity of people were undoubtedly disappointing."[185]

## NOTES

[1] This is not a study of the general famine policy of the British in India. Nor does it deal with the economics of famine and the wider aspect of the question of poverty in India. Such an attempt is not possible when dealing with a specific period of administration. The policies of the Indian Government *vis-a-vis* economic conditions have been exhaustively made in a publication of B.M. Bhatia, *Famines in India, 1860-1945*, Bombay, 1963.

[2] For a synoptical view of famine chronology since 1769-1880, see *The Report of the Famine Commission*, 1880, Parl, Papers, vol. iii, (C. 2591), pp. 22-3. See also A. Loveday, *The History and Economics of Indian Famines*, London, 1914, pp. 29-43. See also *Report of the Indian Famine Commission*, 1901, p. 1.

[3] A.P. MacDonnell's remarks on the discussion on the paper presen-

ted by T.W. Holderness: "The Indian Famine of 1899 and the measures taken to meet it," *Journal of the Society of Arts*, 1902, p. 454.

[4] B.M. Bhatia, *Famines in India*, p. 86.

[5] *Report of the Famine Commission*, 1880, Para 112.

[6] See Memorandum on the Provincial Famine Codes, pp. 3-34. *Appendix to Report of the Famine Commission*, 1898, vol. ii, Parl, Papers, 1899, vol. 33, (C. 9258).

[7] *Report of the Famine Commission*, 1880, Para 131.

[8] *Narrative of North Western Provinces and Oudh Famine*, chapter ii, p. 9. Parl, Papers, 1898, (C. 8739).

[9] MacDonnell to Elgin, 18 March 1896, E.P., vol. 68.

[10] *Narrative of North Western Provinces and Oudh*, pp. 10-11, *op. cit.*

[11] Holderness *Narative of Famine 1896-7*, Para 3, Revenue and Agriculture (Famine) Proc., vol. 5209, No. 23, December, 1897. (Hereafter cited as Famine Proc.).

[12] *Report of the Famine Commission*, 1898, Para 339. The famine stretched over 504, 490 square miles comprising a population of 96,931,000 people. Holderness, *Narrative of Famine*, Para 10, *op. cit.*

[13] N.W.P. and O. Govt. to Indian Govt., Indian Famine Proc., vol. 4892, Nos. 1-2, November 1896.

[14] Mackenzie to Elgin, 10 October 1896, E.P., vol. 69.

[15] Elgin to Hamilton, 14 October 1896, E.P., vol. 14.

[16] Telegram Viceroy to S.S., 31 October 1896, *ibid.*, vol. 19.

[17] See Telegrams Viceroy to S.S., 3, 6, 15 and 31 October 1896, E.P., vol. 19.

[18] Hamilton to Elgin, 30 October 1896, *ibid.*, vol. 16.

[19] Elgin to MacDonnell, 10 February 1896, *ibid.*, vol. 68.

[20] Telegram Viceroy to S.S., 10 January 1897, E.P., vol. 20.

[21] *Report of the Famine Commission*, 1898, Para 589.

[22] *Sanjivani*, 1 August 1896, Bengal N.N.R., 1896.

[23] *Burdwan Sanjivani*, 18 August 1896, *ibid.* See also *Bengalee*, 17 October 1896.

[24] *Sanjivani*, 3 October 1896, Bengal N.N.R., 1896.

[25] 7 November 1896, *ibid.* See also *Mahratha*, 27 September, *Indu Prakash*, 28 September, *Kesari*, 29 September, Bomb. N.N.R., 1896.

[26] Mackenzie to Elgin, 2 November 1896, E.P., vol. 69.

[27] See *Mahratha*, 18 October, *Kesari*, 20 October 1896, Bomb. N.N.R., 1896. *Capital*, 7 October 1896, *ibid. Bengalee*, 17 October 1896.

[28] *Champion*, 13 December 1896, Bomb. N.N.R., 1896.

[29] 14 November 1896, Bengal N.N.R., 1896.

[30] 11 November 1896, Bengal N.N.R. 1896.

[31] H.B. Smith to A.P. MacDonnell, 4 January 1896, E.P., vol. 68.

[32] Elgin to Hamilton, 2 June 1895, *ibid.*, vol. 14.

[33] Eligin to Hamilton, 16 September 1896, E.P., vol. 14.

[34] Elgin to Hamilton, 30 September 1896, *ibid.*

[35] *Proc. of the Council of the Governor-General in India*, 1896, vol. xxxv, pp. 382-5,

[36]Elgin to Lyall, 22 January 1897, E.P., vol. 70.
[37]Elgin to Hamilton, 23 December 1896, E.P., vol. 14.
[38]Elgin to Woodburn, 5 January 1897, ibid., vol. 70.
[39]See Elgin to Hamilton, 17 February, 31 March 1897, ibid., vol. 15.

[40]When Northbrook cancelled his tour and personally supervised famine relief measures in Calcutta, he was acclaimed by everyone. But during this famine, neither Elgin nor his senior officials attached much importance to it. It is very interesting to note MacDonnell's reaction. He said, the staying back of Northbrook did no good that he knew came of it. "The machinery of the state went no better, while, as a wag said, the B (e) arings go heated," MacDonnell to Elgin, 4 March 1897, E.P., vol. 70.

[41]Elgin to MacDonnell, 28 February 1897, ibid.

Actually Elgin did visit some famine affected areas in C.P., N.W.P. and O. and Bihar.

[42]Woodburn to Elgin, 23 October 1896, E.P., vol. 69.

[43]Hamilton to Elgin, 9 and 20 November 1896, ibid., vol. 14. Also Telegram S.S. to Viceroy (Pr.), 16 November 1899, ibid., vol. 19. Hamilton wrote to Elgin stressing that the public in England was desirous of opening the fund earlier and both the Lord Mayor of London and the Lancashire Cotton and Spinning Association were very anxious to launch an appeal for charity to redress the Indian grievance about the cotton duty controversy.

[44]Telegram Viceroy to S.S. (Pr.), 24 November, E.P., vol. 19.

[45]MacDonnell to Elgin, 30 November 1896, Enc. Elgin to Hamilton, 3 December 1896, H.C, MSS. Eur. D 509/iii.

[46]Elgin to Hamilton, 7 December 1896, ibid.
[47]Mackenzie to Elgin, 8 December 1896, ibid., vol. 69.
[48]Hamilton to Elgin, 17 December 1896, ibid., vol. 14. See also Queen Victoria to Elgin, 27 November 1896. Family Collection, MSS.
[49]14 December 1896.
[50]22 December 1896, Bengal N.N.R., 1896.
[51]27 December 1896, Bomb, N.N.R., 1897.
[52]*Bharat Jiwan*, 4 (January 1897), N.W.P. and O. N.N.R., 1897.
[53]2 January 1897.
[54]Hamilton to Elgin, 31 December 1896, E.P., vol. 14.
[55]*Speeches by Earl of Elgin*, 1899-99, pp. 302-5.

[56]Up to 12 March 1898, the date of the dissolution of the Central Executive Committee of the Famine Fund, the total fund collected amounted to Rs 1,70,27, 540. *The Report of the Famine Commission*, 1898, Para 512.

[57]The Commissioners wrote: "We have no doubt that the true principle for the Government to adopt as its general rule of conduct in this famine matter is to leave the business of the supply and distribution of food to private trade; taking care that every possible facility is given for its free action, and that all obstacles material or fiscal are, as far as practicable, removed." *Report of the Famine Commission*, 1880, Para 153.

See also Resolution of the Govt. of India, 22 September 1869 on the policy of non-intervention in the operation of trade during famine. Quoted in C.H. Philips, *Select Documents on the History of India and Pakistan*, vol. iv, London, 1962, p. 668. See also Lytton's Minute on Famine Policy, 12 August 1877, *ibid.*, p. 670.

[58] Holderness, *Narrative of Famine. op. cit.*, Para 21.
[59] *Charu Mihir*, 20 July 1896, Bengal N.N.R., 1896.
[60] 12 September 1896, Bengal N.N.R., 1896.
[61] *Sulabh Dainik*, 3 October 1896, *ibid.*
[62] 3 November 1896, *ibid.*
[63] 9 November 1896, *ibid.*
[64] 19 October and 18 November 1896, E.P., vol. 77 (Newspapers Cuttings).
[65] Summarised in *India*, 16 January 1897.
[66] *Samachar*, 11 November 1896; *Bangavasi*, 14 November; *Dainik-e-Samachar*, 22 November 1896, Bengal, N.N.R., 1896.
[67] *Mahratha*, 18 October 1896, Bomb. N.N.R., 1896.
[68] *Report of the Indian National Congress*, 1896, pp. 57-8.
[69] Telegram Viceroy to S.S., 15 October 1896, E.P., vol. 19.
[70] Commissioner Patna Division to Bengal Govt., 11 November 1896, Paras 96-104 and 112, Enc., Bengal Govt. to Indian Govt., 18 November 1896, India Famine Proc., vol. 4982, No. 21, December 1896.
[71] Bengal Govt. to Indian Govt. 18 November 1896, Para 17, *ibid.*
[72] Para 19, *ibid.*
[73] Proceeding of the Conference, Enc. Bengal Govt. to Indian Govt., 26 November 1896, *ibid.*, No. 22, December, 1896.
[74] Bengal Govt. to Indian Govt., 12 December 1896, Para 4, India Famine Proc., vol. 5203, No. 71, January 1897.
[75] Bengal Govt.'s Resolution, No. 5133, 10 December 1896, Para 13, India Finance Proc., vol. 4982, No. 25, December, 1896.
[76] Elgin to Hamilton, 3 December 1896, E.P., vol. 14.
[77] Elgin to Hamilton, 11 November 1896, *ibid.*
[78] Elgin to Hamilton, 19 November and 23 December 1896, *ibid.*
[79] Westland to Elgin, 21 December 1896, *ibid.*, vol. 69.
[80] Elgin to Hamilton, 6 January 1897, *ibid.*, vol. 15.
[81] N.W.P. and O. Govt. to Indian Govt., 23 November 1896, Para 16, Parl, Papers, 1897, vol. 64, C. 8302.
[82] Indian Govt. to Bengal Govt., 4 January 1897, India Famine Proc., vol. 5203, No. 74, January 1897.
[83] *Ibid.*, Para 6.
[84] *Ibid.*, Para 11.
[85] Hamilton to Elgin, 7 January 1897, E.P., vol. 15.
[86] So strong was the belief in the private trade that the Indian Government rejected the offer of shiploads of grain from Canada and the USA (as a part of charity) for the sake of avoiding suspicion in the minds of traders. Government preferred money to grain. See H.B. Smith to Col. J.W. Ottley (Secy. Indian Fam. Charitable Relief Fund, 29

January 1897, E.P., vol. 70.) A similar offer was made by Russia and was rejected on a slightly different ground. The best explanation of this is found in MacDonnell's letter to Elgin: "Bulky gifts attract attention and out of their distribution political capital can be made. Besides, there is nothing we are more criticised for by natives of all classes than our refusal to import grain, and thus pull down the market rate....We can easily decline all gifts of grain on the ground that we do not interfere with the private trade in grain. If Russia gives help it must be by money contributions to the English or Indian fund. The money is not earmarked." MacDonnell to Elgin, 30 November 1896, Enc. Elgin to MacDonnell 3 December 1896, H.C., MSS. Eur. D 509/iii.

[87] Hamilton to Elgin, 26 February 1897. To Elgin, such press criticism appeared as "scandalous and mischievous." Elgin to Hamilton, 17 February 1897, E.P., vol. 15. The Secretary of State also feared the increasing criticism of "Naoroji and Co." The socialists led by Hyndaman held a meeting in St. James Hall and made "virulent" attack on the Government. This incidently was given wide publicity. Hamilton to Elgin, 12 February 1897, E.P., vol. 15.

[88] Elgin to Hamilton, 15 January 1897, E.P., vol. 15.

[89] Hamilton to Elgin, 5 February 1897, E.P., vol. 15.

[90] Chairman Finance Committee and Chairman Public Works Committee respectively.

[91] Hardie's Note on Food Supply, 9 February 1897. Enc. Hamilton to Elgin, 12 February 1897, E.P., vol. 15.

[92] *Ibid.*

[93] Godley to Elgin, 12 February 1896, E.P., vol. 136.

[94] Crosthwaite to Elgin, 10 February 1896. Family Collection.

[95] Queen Victoria to Elgin, 5 February 1896, unpublished letters, Family Collection.

[96] Telegram, Viceroy to S.S., 6 February and 22 February 1897, E.P., vol. 20.

[97] Indian Govt. to S.S., L. No. 33 (Fam.), 10 May 1897, Para 4, Revenue and Agriculture Letters from India, vol. 18.

[98] MacDonnell to Elgin, 4 March 1897. E.P., vol. 70.

[99] Indian Govt. to S.S., L. No. 33 (Fam.), 10 May 1897, Para 6-10, *op. cit.*

[100] *Ibid.*, Para 11.

[101] *Ibid.*, Para 12.

[102] It was Lord Northbrook who suggested to Elgin that if the monsoon again failed or withdrew earlier than usual, the Government must resort to import so. Otherwise, he fully appreciated Elgin's food policy. Lord Northbrook to Elgin, 19 March 1897, Family Collection.

[103] Elgin to Hamilton, 10 February, 24 February and 10 March 1897, E.P., vol. 15.

[104] Elgin to Hamilton, 3 March 1897, E.P., vol. 15.

[105] Indian Govt. to S.S., L. No. 33 (Fam.), *op. cit.*, Para 13.

[105] *Ibid.*, Para 14.

[107] *Famines in India, op. cit.*, p. 240.

[108] *Report of the Indian Famine Commission*, 1898, Para 585.
Shortage of crop during famine, 1896-7, was as follows:

| | | | | | | | |
|---|---|---|---|---|---|---|---|
| Punjab | —25 per cent of the total yield | | | | | | |
| N.W.P. & O | —40 | ,, | ,, | ,, | ,, | ,, | ,, |
| C.P. | —50 | ,, | ,, | ,, | ,, | ,, | ,, |
| Bombay | —35 | ,, | ,, | ,, | ,, | ,, | ,, |
| Bengal | —33 | ,, | ,, | ,, | ,, | ,, | ,, |
| Madras | —20 | ,, | ,, | ,, | ,, | ,, | ,, |

Holderness's *Narrative*, Para 27, *op. cit.*
[109] Para 156.
[110] Holderness's *Narrative*, Para 24, *op. cit.*
[111] *Report of the Famine Commission*, 1898, Para 587.
In 1902, the Government estimates showed a surplus of 6.1 million tons, or, excluding Burma, Assam and Coorg, 4.5 million tons. Quoted in B.M. Bhatia, *Famines in India*, p. 236.
[112] *Ibid.*
[113] Holderness's *Narrative*, Para 24, *op. cit.*
See also *The Trade Review* of the relevant years of British India.
[114] *Report of the Famine Commission*, 1898, Para 588.
[115] Holderness's *Narrative*, Appendix vii, *op. cit.*
[116] Tables relating to Trade of British India, 1893-4 to 1897-8, Parl, Papers, 1899, vol. ixvi, part 1, C. 9120, p. 8. A cwt is one hundredweight =112 lb, 20 hundredweight=1 ton or 2240 lb.
[117] *Ibid.*, p. 22.
[118] *Bengalee*, 9 January, 1897.
The Bengal National Chamber of Commerce, in a special memorandum of 15 December 1896, urged the Government not to interfere in the private trade. They wrote that any attempt by the government to act as a purchaser or importer would be "mischievous," Encl. Bengal Govt. to Indian Govt., 22 December 1896, India Famine Proc., vol. 5203, No. 50, January 1897.
[119] MacDonnell to Elgin, 4 March 1897, *op. cit.*
[120] Holderness's *Narrative*, Para 100, *op. cit.*
[121] Elgin to Hamilton, 31 March 1897, E.P., vol. 15.
[122] *Report of the Famine Commission*, 1898, Para 585.
[123] George Campbell, *Memoirs of my Indian Career*, vol. 11, p. 324.
[124] Holderness's *Narratives*, Para 32, *op. cit.*
[125] Lord Northbrook's speech in the House of Lords reported in *The Times*, 2 February 1897. "Speaking generally there could be no doubt whatever that the more trade was left untrammelled the greater was the possibility of meeting the demand for grain or any other article that was necessary."
[126] *Proc. of the Council of the Governor-General in India*, 1896, vol. xxxv, p. 389.
[127] MacDonnell was well known for his report on the Food Supply and his Statistical Review of the Relief Operations in the distressed districts of Bihar and Bengal during the famine of 1873-4.

[128]N.W.P. and O. Govt. to Indian Govt., 23 November 1896, Para 20, Parl, Papers, 1897, vol. 64. C. 8302.
[129]*Report of the Famine Commission*, 1898, Para 101.
[130]*Ibid.*, Para 349.
[131]*Ibid.*, Para 101.
[132]*Narrative of North Western Provinces and Oudh Famine*, p. 24 op. cit.
[133]*Report of the Famine Commission*, 1898, Para 100.
[134]*Ibid.*
[135]*Ibid.*
[136]*Ibid.*, Para 246.
[137]*Ibid.*, Para 249.
[138]In recognition of his famine services he was awarded the G.C.I.E.
[139]See the issues from August 1896 to September 1897, N.W.P. and O., N.N.R., 1896 and 1897.
[140]*Report of the Famine Commission*, 1898, Para 147.
[141]*Ibid.*, Para 349.
[142]Resolution, Bengal Govt., 10 December 1896, Para 2, *op. cit.*
[143]*Report of the Famine Commission*, 1898, Para 108.
[144]*Ibid.*, Para 110.
[145]At the time of the greatest pressure, in June 1897, the total area of the province declared to be affected covered 26,073 square miles with a population of 5,674,000 persons. *Report of the Famine Commission*, 1898, Para 301.
[146]Madras Govt. to Indian Govt., 4 May 1897, India Famine Proc., vol. 5206, Nos. 109-111, June 1897.
[157]*Ibid.*
[148]Madras Govt. Res. 18 February 1897, *ibid.*
[149]*Indian Famine Commission Report* (1898), Para 190.
[150]Havelock to Elgin, 11 May 1897, E.P., vol. 70. Actually when the order prohibiting fines was issued in March 1897, the total workers on relief were 81,000. It rose to 157,000 in April, 312,000 in May, 507,000 in June, and 773,000 in July 1897. *Report of the Famine Commission, 1898*, Para 131.
[151]*Ibid.*, Para 309.
[152]*Ibid.*, see Paras 319-31.
[153]See Report on Famine in Central Provinces, Paras 1-20, India Famine Proc., vol. 5207, No. 9, July 1898.
[154]*Report of the Famine Commission*, 1898, Para 271.
[155]*Ibid.*, Para 278.
[156]Lyall to Elgin, 25 December 1896, 12 February and 21 March 1897, E.P., vols. 69 and 70.
[157]*Report of the Famine Commission*, 1898, Para 114.
[158]*Ibid.*, 294.
[159]Report on Famine in Central Provinces, Para 22, *op. cit.*
[160]Para 298. The total mortality on account of this famine had been variously estimated. William Digby, puts the estimate of deaths at 4.5

## The Famine of 1896-97 143

million. *Prosperous British Rule in India*, p. 129. In an article "India under Elgin" the total deaths due to famine were estimated as 150,000. *Quarterly Review*, 1899, vol. 189, p. 325.

[161] *Report of the Famine Commission*, 1898, Para 299.
[162] B.M. Bhatia, *Famines in India*, p. 253.
[163] *Report of the Famine Commission*, 1898, Para 404.
[164] Out of which 479 million (58 per cent) were relieved on works and 342 million (42 per cent) gratuitously.
[165] *Report of the Famine Commission*, 1898, Para 339.
[166] *Ibid.*, Para 349.
[167] *Report of the Famine Commission*, 1901, Para 22.
[168] Resolution, Indian Govt. on Famine, 23 December 1897, Parl, Papers, C. 8737 1898, vol. 62, pp. 6-8.
[169] Earlier, C.A. Elliot was selected but on the advice of J. Woodburn, the Executive Councillor, who was at that time on leave in London, Lyall was appointed. It is not clear why this change was made. Probably it was feared that Elliot might be more critical. Woodburn to Elgin, 12 November 1897. Correspondence from Abroad, E.P., vol. 32.
[170] The other members of the Commission were Surgeon-Colonel J. Richardson, T.W. Holderness and T. Higham.
[171] See the summary of the recommendation, *Report of Indian Famine Commission*, 1898, pp. 319-325.
[172] *Indian Famine Commission Report*, 1898, Para 439.
[173] *Ibid.*, Para 452.
[174] *Ibid.*, Para 421.
[175] See "Causes and Cure of Famine," Speech delivered on 30 April 1901, in London, vide *Speeches and Writing*.
[176] *Economic History of India, op. cit.*, pp. vi-xix.
[177] Presidential Address to the Indian National Congress, 1901 Session. See also P.C. Ray, *Indian Famines: Their Causes and Remedies*, Calcutta, 1901.
[178] *The Prosperous British Rule*, London, 1901.
[179] The 1896 session of the Congress, Res. xii stressed the need for husbanding Indian resources.
[180] For the principal and features of the Act, see C.H. Philips, *Select Documents on the History of India and Pakistan*, iv, pp. 646-7, *op. cit.*
[181] See for detail S.S. Thorburn, *Mussalmans and Moneylenders in Punjab*, London, 1886.
S.S. Thorburn, *Report on Peasant Indebtedness and Land Alienation to Moneylenders in Parts of the Rawalpindi Division*, 1896.
S.S. Thorburn, *His Majesty's Greatest Subject*, London, 1897, p. 151.
M.L. Darling, *The Punjab Peasent in Prosperity and Debt*, London, 1932, chapters i, x and xi.
[182] Indian Govt. Confidential Circular to Local Govts., 2 October 1895, Enc. Indian Govt. to S.S. L. No. 58 (Rev), 30 October 1895, Revenue and Agriculture letters from India, vol. 16.

[183]Elgin's Minute, vide Summary of the Administration of Lord Elgin, Revenue and Agricultural Department, p. 45.
[184]*Report of the Irrigation Commission*, 1903, Para 114.
[185]Very Anstey, *Economic Development of Modern India*, p. 5.

CHAPTER V

# PLAGUE AND SEDITION

"For India, 1897 has been a year of calamities, famine, plague, earthquake, floods—offended Nature seems to have avenged herself, on the people and the rulers alike, with these and other afflictions."[1] This was how B.M. Malabari summarised the events of 1897. Added to these frowns of fortune were riots, murders, political trials and the change in sedition laws. Undoubtedly the last years of the viceroyalty could have been hardly more troublesome.

Of all the troubles, it was plague which gave the Government and the people by far the most anxious time. Although in real terms famine was a much greater social and economic evil, in combating the challenge the Government had evolved a long-term famine policy. In the case of plague there was neither any policy nor any systematic machinery to deal with it. In the first place, therefore, the steps taken to encounter the disease were experimental and often conceived in a spirit of alarm, fear and haste. When the trade of Bombay was seriously threatened with the outbreak of bubonic plague, the Government undertook some strong measures which came in conflict with the social and religious beliefs of the people, resulting in the outbreak of violence in various parts of the country. This necessarily assumed political importance and ultimately prompted the Indian Government and the Home Government to take stock of the wider issues of administrative policy towards India.

The presence of plague in the city of Bombay was officially recognised on 23 September 1896.[2] The responsibility to deal with plague was entrusted upon the municipal authorities. On 6 October 1896, the Bombay government gave special powers to the municipality to clean, disinfect, remove or destroy any insanitary property and take away the patient to the hospital or put him in isolation.[3] The provisions of this notification, particularly the removal of the sick from their homes to hospitals evoked great resentment of the public. People began to conceal cases. Many more migrated out of Bombay, completely dislocating the economic life of the city.[4] The public expressed their grievances by resorting to complete *hartal* throughout the city on 29 October. On the same day 1000 mill workers attacked a municipal hospital. The government apprehended serious violence. Gauging the emotions of the people, the Bombay government immediately issued a proclamation by which the earlier notification of 6 October was tacitly withdrawn. The public was assured that there would be no compulsion for the removal of the sick and no insistence for the evacuation of the infected houses.[5]

One important outcome of this development was that it became clear that the people would not tolerate anything infringing affecting their social and religious customs. Tact, persuation and skill were needed to evolve a plague policy with which the public could cooperate.

During the winter months, the epidemic assumed serious proportions. Mortality rate increased and Bombay's foreign trade declined. In the first six months of the outbreak more than 9000 deaths were recorded in the Bombay Presidency,[6] and during the financial year 1896-7, the aggregate value of the trade of the port of Bombay fell by 9 per cent.[7]

This fall in the trade was neither very extensive nor was it entirely due to plague. The overall foreign trade of India in the same year declined by 3.6 per cent from the preceding year.[8] Further, the shrinkage in the exports from Bombay and Karachi was largely due to famine, yet it was actively feared that western countries would object to carry on trade with India and that there would be a larger decline in trade unless more positive steps were taken to deal with plague.

The Indian Government and the Home Government both realised the gravity of the situation. Lord Elgin immediately dispatched Surgeon-General Dr Cleghorn of the Indian Medical Service to Bombay to report on the epidemic. He prepared a memorandum in which he expressed dissatisfaction with the Bombay government's handling of plague. He stated that plague was a disease of dirt and insanitary conditions and, therefore, needed thorough and strong sanitary measures. He recommended the evacuation and segregation of the sick and the destruction of unhygienic surroundings and dwellings.[9] The Home Government, particularly the Secretary of State, George Hamilton, who was frankly "more concerned about plague than famine" for the reason that a "market once lost, or even partially diverted is not easily regained," goaded the Government of India for still stronger action.[10] In addition to compulsory segregation and evacuation he asked for the closure of Indian ports to *Haj* pilgrims. Such an action, he believed, would please the European countries and thus act as a great deterrent against the possible loss of trade.

Elgin was more disposed to accept Cleghorn's recommendations. Unlike Hamilton, he was moved not only by economic considerations but was inclined to take stock of social and religious implications of any policy that might be introduced.[11] Before giving a final reply to the Secretary of State, the Viceroy decided to gauge the opinion of local governments, particularly the government of Bombay. The Bombay government agreed to close their port to pilgrim traffic.[12] Similarly other local governments, except the Bengal government, agreed that Bombay port should be closed but after observing quarantine rules and medical precautions, the pilgrims should be allowed to proceed from Calcutta and Madras.[13] It was the opinion of most of the senior officials that total prohibition of *Haj* would be "politically injurious." John Weodhurn, the Home Member, personally undertook a survey of the Muslim feelings and came to the conclusion that total prohibition would complicate rather than ease the situation.[14] Such was the opinion of MacDonnell also.[15] It might be further stressed that after 1 February 1897 no pilgrim ship had left Bombay. In response to the protection of trade and commerce the Indian Government had already instructed the Bombay government to adopt any measure to prevent the outbreak, including the stoppage of pilgrims and the checking of the railway passengers.[16]

In compliance with the wishes of Dr Cleghorn, the municipal organisations in Bombay, Madras, Bengal. Presidencies and the North Western Provinces and Oudh were provided with summary powers by the respective provincial governments to restrict abatement of overcrowding, evacuation and cleaning of the affected areas.[17] In so doing the Government not only took almost all precautionary measures but also retained their confidence in the municipalities which was a very important step in soliciting the cooperation of the public.

After taking into account all shades of opinion, Elgin forcefully reiterated his views against total prohibition of *Haj* pilgrimage. He wrote: "It was an axiom of Indian administration, established by teaching of bitter experience, that to enforce orders which the ignorant masses could regard as infringing religious privileges must be dangerous."[18] Elgin's view was supported by the majority of the Executive Council.[19]

But nothing short of total prohibition appealed to Hamilton. He over-ruled the Indian Government.[20] In doing so, Hamilton supported by Lord Salisbury, was merely motivated by imperial considerations and did not take into account the possible political implications. He himself confessed to Elgin, "I am always sorry from here to press you to do something, the benefit of which we feel in Europe and the danger and drawback of which you have to bear in India."[21]

From 20 February, from first time, the annual *Haj* pilgrimage was suspended,[22] obviously to the annoyance of Elgin, who recorded: "I must confess to some surprise that those whom you consulated were unanimous in recommending the step, but perhaps it is another illustration of the fact that it is the men who were actually concerned in the administration on the spot who were most keenly alive to the possible presence of waves of sentiment."[23]

This action of the Home Government was not an isolated one but was coupled with many other restrictive instructions to change the structure of plague administration in Bombay. Hamilton believed that it was beyond the powers of the municipal authority to shoulder so huge and onerous a responsibility. He considered it essential to substitute the municipal authority by an executive body of a few officials.[24] In the first instance, both Sandhurst, the Governor of Bombay and Elgin were not favourably disposed towards Hamilton's views.[25]

But soon the pressure of the English and the Anglo-Indian press incressed. The Government's plague policy was condemned as week, foolish, timid and obstinate.[26] Unfortunately, under the bellicose and hysterical attitude of the India Office and English press, the Bombay Government by March 1897, succumbed to their pressure and relieved the municipal authority of their plague duties, and appointed instead an executive committee of four under Surgeon Brigadier-General Gataere.[27] The Committee was given the widest possible powers. It was authorised to evacuate any building, destroy it, forcibly search private homes, segregate the patients and remove them to hospital.[28]

Search parties were deployed. They visited houses in order to detect the cases or insanitary surroundings and were supported by a cordon of soldiers to prevent the people from escaping.[29] These parties were not always sensitive to the feelings of the local people. An evidence of the reckless attitude of the search parties could be seen in the very words of a City Health Officer, who said "we treated houses practically as if they were on fire, discharging into them from steam engines and flushing pumps quantities of water charged with disinfectants."[30] The most intolerable feature of the search parties which were exclusively composed of the British officials related to their invasion of the privacy of an Indian house—for the Indian women, Hindus and Muslims alike practised *purdah*. Secondly, the behaviour of the British soldiers was not often up to the standard. Sandhurst himself was not too sure of the Tommies.[31]

This lack of concern for the private property and social customs excited distrust and alarm among people. The feelings of the people in Bombay ran high. By the end of March riots were only avoided by the timely withdrawal of all British search parties and by incorporating an Indian element into them.

These measures which were already exceedingly unpopular did not deter India Office from suggesting some more stringent steps, like corpse inspection and a system of land quarantine. The latest suggestions were made by Dr Lowson, the Medical Director-General at the India Office, who ardently believed in very vigorous and drastic measures. Hamilton and his special committee on Plague[32] recommended to despatch Dr Lowson and Dr Reade to India to carry out their schemes. Both of them, who had previous experience of plague in Hong Kong, arrived in Bombay on 1 March 1897. With their arrival a new phase in the anti-plague operation started.

No sooner did Dr Lowson land in Bombay than he started advocating land quarantine. He proposed a sort of sanitary cordon across the affected places in order to completely seal off the infected areas. He found a passionate supporter to the idea in the Lieutenant-Governor of Bengal, Mackenzie.[33] However, Elgin and his executive council generally with the exception of Collen, came out forcefully against land quarantine. The Indian Government rightly argued that land quarantine would be ineffective and could not be administratively feasible. It would give opportunities for "oppression and extortion" and quarantine stations could themselves become centres of serious outbreak. It was argued that any additional restriction on the movement of the people would be bitterly resented and might lead to disastrous consequences.[34]

The Bombay government could not, however, check Dr Lowson's measures for corpse inspection. Under the influence of the Secretary of State, Sandhurst agreed to put this into practice. The purpose of inspecting the dead was twofold: to ascertain the cause of death and to detect the suspected cases in the houses of the deceased.

Surely the examination of the corpse, particularly of the woman, was bound to excite the religious prejudices of the public without obvious post-mortem benefits. Elgin refused to take a hasty view of the situation. He termed Dr Lowson's opinion as "rash" "lacking in experience" and urged Hamilton not to commit the Government to more severe measures.[35] It was as much to Elgin's insistence as to Lord Sandhurst's concurrence with him, that Bombay city escaped the practice of corpse inspection. Poona and Karachi were less fortunate.

It was, therefore, not a matter of surprise that in June 1897 sharp violence broke out in Poona. Elgin had done his best to forewarn Hamilton. He discreetly wrote: "I am not sure that it would be safe to conclude that the Bombay Government were not well advised in feeling their way towards the very severe restrictions they now impose. For myself I shall wait till the history of this Plague is written."[36] In yet another letter he emphasised that "a very small spark might cause an explosion."[37]

Dr Lowson still insisted on corpse inspection. But the Bombay government was now no longer prepared to tolerate any rash measures for fear of open violence. They discreetly packed off Dr Lowson to Calcutta, where he and Mackenzie formed a formidable team.

The Lieutenant-Governor of Bengal, with the aid of Dr Lowson, revived the demand for land quarantine.[38] Elgin reacted swiftly and sharply. He wrote curtly to Mackenzie: "I will only say that no amount of protest from Dr Lowson will convince me that any responsible authority in India can shirk the consideration of the political dangers of forcing the people prematurely into methods repugnant to their ideas of right and wrong. Much can be done by kindly leading, much can be lost by rigid and unsympathetic attitudes."[39] He plainly told the Lieutenant-Governor that the system of land quarantine was not even favoured by Dr Cleghorn, the highest medical authority in India. Talking about Dr Lowson, he wrote: "I believe that the Home Department had no wish to enhance his (Dr Lowson) importance as an adviser, but felt bound to forward the Bombay recommendation. I sometime wonder if Bombay in their hearts wished to see his energies employed elsewhere."[40] Lest Elgin's weakness were over-emphasised, the Viceroy categorically told the Secretary of State that if Bengal government passed any legislation in favour of land quarantine, he would be constrained to overrule and disallow such an act.[41] Elgin at last succeeded in restricting the more ominous and vulnerable tendencies.

In the meantime plague restrictions began to bite. The Muslims showed strong resentment against the suspension of pilgrimage and compulsory removal of the sick. In the Muslim centres of the North Western Provinces and Oudh there were bitter feelings against the Government.[42] These restrictions were not only disliked by Muslims but were also hated by Hindus. There was a unanimity between the two communities in registering their condemnation of the Government measures. Indian newspapers, who really represented the feelings and reactions of the people were extremely critical of the government's handling of the plague. The *Hitavadi* observed that "the plague regulations have made the people more uneasy than the plague itself."[42]

The most despised regulation related to segregation and inspection of females. The *Hitavadi* commented that the "inspection is most offensive to female modesty, as it is made on a crowded platform by touching various parts of the body."[44] The executors of the Government policy were named as "brutes," "butchers," "barbarous" and "wild bulls."[45]

The final outcome of these emotions was open violence. Plague riots broke out in the Punjab, Mysore, Calcutta and Bombay and the most serious of all in Poona, where the restrictions were the severest.[46] On 22 June 1897, the chief plague officer W.C. Rand and Lieutenant C.E. Ayerst were fatally shot.[47] On the same evening Captain Ross was assassinated in Peshawar.[48] Almost simultaneously serious riots took place in Chitpur, Calcutta.[49] These riots coincided with the tribal rising, in the North Western frontier of India. Last but not the least, there was a great excitement in India on the Turkish victory over Greece in the Greeco-Turkish war, which gave stimulus to the Pan-Islam movement.[50]

Although circumstances and reason for these various disturbances were different, but all these events taken together became a source of great concern and suspicion to the large section of the Anglo-Indian community. Their fears were further aggravated when the real issues were confused with imaginary and alarming news published by the English press in India and outside India.

The *Pioneer* stated that there was a well-planned conspiracy throughout India and the Poona murders were deliberately planted to coincide with the Jubilee.[51] Echoing the same sentiment, the *Englishman* wrote that the commulative developments exhibited a large scale antipathy of the "natives" against the British.[52] The *Times of India* saw in the events a clear "sign of preparation and organisation."[53] Many others reported that there was a general unrest comparable with the rising of 1857. The *St. James Gazette* wrote that Chitpur and Poona riots and other accidents "bears too much resemblance to that which was allowed to be brought about in the parts of India. . . .Every sensible man is very well aware that the old antipathy of East to West was not ended—has not even, it may be really diminished. Sometimes it reaches a point at which the different sects will sink their mutual hatreds for a space to unite against the common enemy. They did so in the early days of mutiny."[54]

*The Times* specially took a conservative view. It repeatedly stressed that the events of the time represented a political danger to the Empire. Elucidating its point, *The Times* made a reference to an incident in the Punjab, that on the Jubilee day, a certain rowdy element (mostly children) disturbed the opening ceremony of the unveiling of the statue of Queen Victoria in Lahore. Commenting on this incident, which in any other circumstances would not have been worthwhile, *The Times* wrote: "And this happened, be it be remembered in the capital of the Punjab, the most loyal province of India, which turned back the tide of the Mutiny and stemmed the National Congress movement. If...such things are done there, what may not occur in Poona, Benares, and Calcutta, the head centres of Brahmin or Bengali disaffection."[55]

In view of the outcome *The Times* recommended the control of the vernacular press—the mouthpiece of sedition.[56] In a special article on Indian affairs,[57] *The Times* repeated its call to check the Indian press. It constantly drew attention to "a new danger from possible combinations by masses of ignorant men, accustomed to work together in their daily life, but totally ignorant of the motives and designs of those who would use them for their own ends."[58]

The following questions arise: Were these outrages the result of a calcutated political move against the British Raj? Was India inseminated with a wave of unrest and sedition? Was there any need of controlling the vernacular press?

Lord George Hamilton appeared convinced by the utterances of the English press. He felt certain that the "outrages" in Poona were not the outcome of personal revenge or religious fanaticism but the work of a critical hostile press which preached and sowed the seeds of sedition.[59] He assumed that the vernacular press offered a favourable medium to the Brahmins of Poona, "to fan the flame of ignorance and prejudice, and they have done so successfully."[60] He believed that the hostile Muslim feelings, the popularity of the Turkish victories and the rapprochement between Hindus and Muslims—all indicating a serious trend dangerous to the British Raj.

Hamilton suspected a definite connection between the Pan-Islamic movement and the tribal rising, which he surmised was fostered by the vernacular press.[61] He wrote, "It seems to me impossible that so widespread a combination of disturbance can be indigenous." Hamilton attributed this unpopularity to "the processes of education, of an unclicensed press, and the development of national feelings or religious enthusiasm which they (press) work to create, all tend to make the onslaught against our Government more powerful while the powers behind the authorities do not correspondingly multiply."[62] Speaking of the overall situation, Hamilton felt that "not since the Mutiny has there been much combination of difficulty inside India."[63] He feared that the "Native troops," who formed the main pillars of British imperialism in India were being gradually influenced and there appeared to him already some visible signs of unrest. He could think only of one remedy—the adoption of "exceptional measures" to control the Indian press.[64] He expressed similar views in the House of Commons on 1 July 1897.[65] On 10 July he telegraphed Elgin to bring a new Press Act and change the sedition laws immediately.[66]

Elgin, on the other hand, was sceptical of any such widespread danger which warranted so sweeping a treatment.[67] But it induced him to investigate. Accordingly Elgin wrote confidentially to MacDonnell, Mackworth Young, Lyall, and Sandhurst enquiring as to whether there was any visible element which lent support to the view that the Poona murder, the Peshawar outrage, the Calcutta riots and the Tochi rising were evidences of a general movement which was alleged to be taking place in India.[68]

Regarding the Poona murders it was evidently known that they took place as a reprisal against the plague measures which were exceedingly unpopular in Poona and other places.[69] Sandhurst and K.C. Ollivant, the Home Member of the Governor's Executive Council, were of the opinion that the murder of Rand was due to the personal vendetta against him.[70] C.S. Bayley, the superintendent of the department of *Thagi and Dakaiti* who carried out a thorough investigation, never found any semblance of evidence linking the Poona tragedy with anything else.[71] Nor has any evidence cropped up since then.

As to the murder of Captain Rose at Peshawar, the Punjab Government's enquiries revealed no clue or collaboration with any outside influence. It was merely an act of a Muslim fanatic.[72]

Nor was there any evidence available which could trace any bearing of Chitpur riots to any such general wave of unrest. Actually the trouble originated on a controversy over a plot of land belonging to Sir Jotendra Mohan Tagore which was wilfully occupied by a Muslim, Himmat Khan, who falsely alleged that the plot contained a mosque. On 30 June 1897, the police got possession of the land. Next day nearly 2000 Muslim assembled and again rebuilt the mosque. The police went and dispersed the crowd. To avoid trouble Sir Jotendra Nath agreed not to force the eviction. But the Bengal government thought it judicious to carry out the orders of the court. On 2 July 1897 the rioters attacked Tallah pumping station and also some Europeans. The police resorted to firing and some people were killed.[73]

On 6 July many mill hands in Barrackpore struck in sympathy with their cause. Many Europeans who feared an attack on mills fired indiscriminately till the mob was bogged down by the police. Many were killed and many more injured.[74] Stevens, the officiating Lieutenant-Governor of Bengal, believed that these riots were caused due to the Europeans taking a very alarmist and exaggerated view of the situation.[75] He said that the general behaviour of the English was panic-stricken and wrong. Reporting to the Indian Government, the Chief Secretary of Bengal wrote: "There has been much unreasonable excitement in Calcutta among the non-officials, and much foolish correspondence has been admitted into the paper?"[76] Stevens asserted, there was no doubt that Muslim feeling was agitated on account of the plague rules. It was in the same vogue that Pan-Islam movement in Bengal carried their sympathy. He was firmly of the opinion that the Chitpur riots were an isolated event which needed on overestimation.[77]

There was no foundation in the charge that the army was disaffected. The recent performance of both the Muslim and the Sikh Sepoys against the tribesmen had proved their loyalty to the Raj. There was no manifestation of any malevolent feeling on the part of the army, asserted Elgin and C.S. Bayley.[78] Similarly no proof was forthcoming indicating the Amir's connivance with either the tribes or the sepoys. Kabul and Constantinople were distinctly apart.[79]

On the whole, Assam, Burma, the Central Provinces, Berar and Madras were perfectly quite and "free from agitation and ill feelings."[80] In the North Western Provinces there was some excitement, particularly amongst the Muslims and some natural sympathy with Turkey but there were no indications of any sedition. MacDonnell reported that there was dissatisfaction with the existing orders of things on the part of the English-educated classes, but their purpose was not to destroy or supplant the British Government.[81] He, however, frankly confessed that much had been exaggerated by the "hysterical" English press and added, "Perhaps the *Pioneer* is doing more harm than any Native paper by its needlessly alarmist letters under the heading '*the signs of times*'."[82]

Bayley too was of the opinion that most of the European fears were exaggerated by the needlessly dismayed and panic-stricken Anglo-Indian press.[83] MacDonnell who had experience of the Home Office, considered it neither necessary nor desirable to remedy the situation by controlling the press. However, he did not object to taking judicial action against any patently seditious paper.[84]

C.J. Lyall, the Chief Commissioner of the Central Provinces and formerly Home Secretary to the Indian Government, also attached no political significances to the Calcutta or Poona riots. He agreed that the sympathy of the Muslims with Turkey was a disturbing factor but in no case was it dangerous. He said that though of late the vernacular press had become hostile, it had not "in any part of the empire, with which I am acquainted, gone the length of producing serious and active disaffection." He advised strongly against the resurrection of the Vernacular Press Act.[85] Such was also the opinion of both Stevens and Sandhurst.[86]

Macworth Young, the Lieutenant-Governor of the Punjab, on the other hand, discerned among some people a growing feeling of impatience with the authority. This feeling, he said, was more alive in the urbanised and educated section of the society and was encouraged by the newspaper editors, unsuccessful pleaders and disappointed aspirants for government jobs. He found the Indian press "scandalous" and largely responsible for the Poona riots. He personally favoured the re-arming of the Government with the "Lytton Act" but hastened to add "that the spirit of the times is against anything in the shape of the Press Act and the extension of the Criminal Law is the only practical method of dealing with such firebrands."[87]

From the evidence given it could be deduced that there was in India discontent but not disaffection, resentment but no sedition.

Much of the bitterness was due to the plague rules. The vernacular press was not outrageously scandalous. It was the Anglo-Indian press which was often irresponsible. Even in Bombay where the Indian press was deemed to be the fountainhead of sedition, the Government's annual report issued on 27 July 1897, found only 12 papers out of 200 using offensive language which could be "near the verge of seditious writing."[88] On the other hand, the press of Madras far from being hostile was distinctly friendly.[89]

Strengthened by the opinions of the officials, Elgin finally surmised that "if special executive powers against the press are intended we consider them undesirable."[90]

Elgin's opinion did not please Hamilton. In addition to the strengthening of the law against sedition by adopting procedure, he urged and repeated his preference for executive action to suppress the "Native press."[91]

Hamilton's latest communication upset Elgin, but he declined to hurriedly legislate at Simla and to revive Lytton's Press Act. He argued that any legislation produced under the pressure of panic would not be durable and, may even be dangerous. Secondly, the implementation of so strong and extreme measures "would do absolutely nothing to assist in the detection and punishment of those concerned in the recent outrages."[92] Therefore, he asserted, there was no justification in passing an Act of the kind at Simla. He then elucidated the point of difference between him and the Secretary of State: "In your telegrams you imply that, unless we are unanimously opposed to it, we ought still to consider the strengthening of the executive powers by which I suppose I am to understand some such powers as were conferred by Lord Lytton's Act. I am afraid that I would have to oppose that, whatever the opinion of the Council."[93]

Elgin knew that public opinion in England had been led astray by the gross misrepresentations of the Anglo-Indian correspondents. The Poona murders could have been serious at any time, but without the "scandalous exaggerations" from Calcutta there would have been nothing to suggest a widespread conspiracy throughout the Empire. Elgin urged that

> if, as a result of a deliberate and careful investigation, it is determined that the powers of the Government of India to deal with the Sedition are insufficient, I do not think it is likely I should refuse any support to proposals for amendment of the law, even if they go in a direction which I generally disapprove. But what I do not think I can fairly be asked to do

is to prejudge the case against my own side. If I stood alone, it might be different. The remedy then will be simply, for I could stand aside and let someone else play the part I refused. ... I must confess your yesterday's telegram has disturbed me and it may be well if I unfortunately am compelled to differ from you that you should know that I have not decided lightly.[94]

In this long letter Elgin made two things clear (1) that he was fundamentally against a Vernacular Press Act and would prefer to resign them to agree to, and (2) that he would resort to non-executive action against sedition but not without due consideration and deliberation.

This resolute stand of Elgin had the desired effect. Hamilton agreed, though reluctantly, to drop the demand for a Vernacular Press Act.[95] Perhaps the most significant outcome was that Calcutta regained the initiative once again in dealing with matters of vital administrative importance, which it had lost in connexion with the cotton duty controversy. Besides, Elgin had refused to be committed to any negative restrictions. Though his attitude might not be considered to be liberal, it was calm, cautious and calculating. But Hamilton's attitude in this whole affair deserves some explanation.

Hamilton knew and realised from the very outset that there was no general movement of any kind, but he found in the murder of Rand an excuse to crush the press. In the very first telegram after Rand's murder, Hamilton wrote to Sandhurst whether the outrages could be connected with the incidiary tone of the press.[96] The very next day he expressed the same sentiments to Elgin.[97] A little later he wrote to Elgin that both he and the Judicial and Public Committee[98] of his Council were strongly of the view that advantage should be taken at this juncture to legislate and restrict the vernacular press.[99] To make it sound more convincing he suggested to the Viceroy that the initiative must come from India and this, he wrote, "you have, especially if Rand's murder can be associated with his personal denunciation by the press."[100] He was obviously more insistent to do it quickly, lest the tempers might cool down and the opportunity slip.

Though Elgin refused to be hustled, Hamilton kept up the

pressure. Replying to Elgin's long letter of 20 July, Hamilton wrote:

> In my earlier telegrams I rather pressed the immediate alteration of the law, as I thought we could more easily carry public opinion with us in England, when the shock of the two murders at Poona had generally affected the public. It is really a question of tactics, and tactics depend on local considerations, and what may be judicious in England may have an opposite effect in India; but my own political experience is in favour of utilizing without hesitation for the accomplishment of a difficult but necessary task any unforeseen advantage an exceptional occurrence may give.[101]

In the same letter he again stressed:

> I dread the day when the northern or the fighting races, from whom we drew recruits, take to reading the vernacular press. Prevention rather than conviction should be our object. A summary executive power exercised without noise, or demonstration, is what oriental people appreciate. . . .

Hamilton was obviously more anxious about the future than about the present.[102] He wrote: "I am anxious to utilize the present opportunity, when we have a House of Commons ready to assent to anything the Government of India may demand, to try and put our house in order for future troubles."[103]

This illiberal view was not suddenly acquired by Hamilton. Ever since he became the Secretary of State for India he had been constantly pressing Elgin to pass some restrictive laws. There was onething which he feared most, it was the Indian press. Writing in September 1896, when no riots or any other trouble had taken place, he had dwelt on the danger of allowing the freedom of press. He could not trace in the papers he read any symptoms of loyalty to the British rule.[104] In another letter he observed: "I grant that Indian native press do not advocate the overthrow of our rule but their everlasting criticism and imputation of motives must ultimately make an impression just as a perpetual drop wears out the stone."[105] He added: "Every year we turn out more and more educated Natives, every year the press will increase, and become more powerful. Its circulation may now relatively be small, but it must continually increase, and, if there is nothing to counteract it, its effects must be yearly more and more pernicious."[106]

This was only one aspect of his concern. He also wanted to see the influence of the Indian National Congress decline by merely ignoring it.[107] He was equally determined to see that the Hindus and the Muslims remained disunited. He believed that when the Hindus and Muslims were disunited they were an administrative problem, but when they were united they would become a political problem and a political problem was worse than an admistrative problem.[108]

Elgin, on the other hand, thought precisely the opposite. First, he said, it would be as much wrong to set the clock back by bringing in Lytton's Act, as to look far ahead to the dangers of distant future. He wrote to Hamilton, "I feel the force of what you say of dangers that may arise in the future, the comparatively distant future. So far as we can, we must, I admit, frame our measures so as to guard against these dangers. But at the same time there is a danger in looking too far ahead, and not observing the rocks that may be under the bow."[109] Secondly, it was too much to except from a man belonging to Gladstone's and Ripon's party to enact a law already repealed. Even then Elgin was prepared to go far, if there was any apparent danger to the Empire. He approached the problems of India, not as Hamilton did—from narrow and limited view, nor also, as probably Ripon would do from a positively liberal point—but in a deliberately cautious and non-alarmist way.

Elgin was genuinely convinced that the "Native Press" was not hostile. Actually much of the muddle was created on account of the extra-suspicious attitude generally adopted by the European officials towards the Indian press.[110] His colleagues like Trevor and Westland entertained serious misgivings against the press and would welcome some means of repressing it. But Elgin was not influenced by them. Writing to the Home Member he said, "Personally I do not consider the Native Press to be either so seditious or so dangerous as I know some do. I doubt whether any amendment of the law relating to sedition is at this moment required, and if it is not required, it cannot be desirable."[111] He maintained that it was the Anglo-Indian press which excited racial feelings by publishing false and exaggerated stories.[112] He rightly calculated that it would be a political mistake of the first magnitude to enact extreme measures and decided to resist the demand for any such measures.

Elgin's approach towards the Indian press had been very consistent from the beginning. He had not found in the selections from the "Native Press" which he "conscientiously" studied, any trace of a design to "substitute for British authority a native, for less another foreign rule." Nor did he attach much importance to what he called the "vapouring of the papers" as some of the "thinskinned" bureaucrats did.[113] In fact Elgin, immediately after his arrival, was put to a very severe pressure from his colleagues to change the press laws This happened when in June 1894, Crosthwaite, then the Lieutenant-Governor of the North Western Provinces and Oudh considered prosecuting Bishan Naryan Dhar, the writer of an allegedly seditious pamphlet, which criticised the Government's pre-Muslim and anti-Hindu bias.[114] Elgin had written: "What I want to say now is that I think the majority of my Council are distinctly in favour of strong measures to put down 'false and seditious writings' . . . . I consider some (both vernacular and English) papers perfectly shameless, but I think it is impossible to exaggerate their importance, and that where 96 per cent of the population is illiterate, and secret agencies (for example tree smearing) can defy detection, it is better not to drive everything under surface."[115] It was on the strong insistence of Elgin that Crosthwaite reluctantly agreed not to prosecute Dhar.[116]

Elgin's attitude towards the Hindu-Muslim issue also differed considerably from that of the Secretary of State. He stressed the need to tackle any problem concerning the two communities with "absolute impartiality."[117] He even did not hesitate to impress this point on Queen Victoria, who was specially interested in placating the Muslims. In September 1894, when Hindu-Muslim riots took place in Poona, she wired, "Mohamedans should be protected, and their worship not disturbed. They are real supporters of British Government."[118] To this Elgin replied that his Government was committed to the policy of impartiality and informed the Queen that reasonable men existed on both sides.[119] As a matter of fact, Elgin had shown great interest in the Hindu-Muslim issue. On his arrival in India he undertook determined measures to avoid any clashes between the communities on *Id* festival in 1894.

Common dislike of the plague measures brought the Hindus and the Muslims closer together in 1897. This baffled and disturbed some. Many emphasised that the Muslim sympathies towards the British Raj had been sacrificed for small imperial reasons and they urged to take necessary steps to win back the Muslims. One of the ardent advocates of this approach was E.K.C. Ollivant. He wrote, "there is a common ground of discontent in reference to plague measures, but much more than this there can be no doubt that the recent unfortunately anti-Mohamedan attitude of English political parties and English public speakers has produced a great feeling of resentment. Those hostile of us are not slow to take advantage of this, and I should hail with delight any freedom from European political entanglement which would enable us once more to enlist the Indian Mohamedans cordially on our side."[120]

There were, on the other hand, influential officials like MacDonnell who pointed out that the successive British Governments had been so far showing partiality towards the Muslims, especially in the North Western Provinces and Oudh. This had, he believed, necessarily alienated the larger section, that is, the Hindus whom he considered more loyal. He informed that until now Muslims dominated in the subordinate executive and police services. For example, out of 240 Tehsildars, 140 were Muslims and there were 2,570 Muslim police officers against 2,120 Hindu officers; though the population ratio was 7 to 1 in favour of Hindus. He therefore proposed to win the support of Hindus by altering the ratio in course of time to 5 to 3 in favour of the Hindus for these jobs.[121]

It is doubtful to say as to how far this and other suggestions were given practical effect, but this sort of exhibition of personal likes and dislikes by the officials must have perpetuated the rift between the two communities. However, Elgin maintained an outward calm and did not express any preference for one to the other. But he felt constrained to explain to Hamilton that Muslims distrusted the clever Hindus and he did not apprehend any danger on that account.[122]

Elgin was also fundamentally at variance with Hamilton in dealing with the growing politically conscious and "discontented" elements in society. Elgin realised that Indian nationalism was bound to develop with the passing of time and British rule in India would "never be free from anxiety." He recognised that the danger in the present and the future was obvious in the movement that "they can no more stop than Canute could restrain the waves, the progress of education and the acquisition of knowledge."[123]

The Indians considered the English as alien and there was truth in what T.J.C. Plowden, the British Resident to the Court of the Nizam of Hyderabad stated, "I have been too long in India to have illusions to the real feelings of the Natives towards us."[124] But there was no such move to supplant the British Government. Nor was the Congress ready to usurp the reins. But lately discontentment and dissatisfaction with the British rule had grown. To some extent it was due to the spirit of the times and to the exceptionally hard time through which the people had passed in the years 1896 and 1897.

Elgin's diagnosis was essentially moderate and realistic. He fully recognised that it was difficult to concede the same amount of liberty of action in a country under a foreign rule but he equally realised the danger in annihilating "all right of free speech."[125] Total restriction could exacerbate the political situation rather than ease it. He desired to divert the growing political consciousness in India into constitutional channels and not to turn it into open hostility against British rule by trying to suppress it.[126] Secondly, he emphasised that it would be dangerous to exaggerate the potentiality of the discontented elements. Talking of the Indian National Congress, which was a "red rag" to the Secretary of State and many officials, he said that the Congress "not infrequently trespasses on the borderland of what is permissible and I dare say contains within its ranks men who would go much further if they dared, I doubt whether any responsible man would even propose to prohibit the congress."[127] Earlier he had written "Remember I do not myself admit that these men are disloyal. Some of them are discontented men, and discontent may of course verge on disloyalty, but I do not believe that a man like Mr Pheroz Mehta wishes to overthrow the British Government."[128] It was a fact that the Congress merely agitated "to improve the system of administration and not to abolish it."[129] It was in the context of these circumstances that the Viceroy desired to bring that element into the open. This attitude of Elgin is fully reflected in the stand he took in dealing with the question of Legislative Councils for the Punjab and Burma and bears a sound testimony to his administrative farsightedness.

The Punjab and Burma were two Provinces which were not given the Legislative Councils in 1892 because both were border states and needed a strong and powerful executive. Actually the retiring Lieutenant-Governor Sir J.B. Lyall had conceded the desirability of having a Legislative Council in the Punjab but the question was left to the discretion of the new Lieutenant-Governor.[130] The new Lieutenant-Governor, Fitzpatrick, vehemently opposed the idea and the matter was allowed to be dropped.[131] But when the question of raising the status of Burma from a Chief Commissionership to a Lieutenant-Governorship was mooted, Elgin took the opportunity of suggesting a Council for Burma as well as the Punjab.[132] Fitzpatrick opposed the move again and emphasised the uniqueness of the Punjab in being a border state, containing a turbulent people and rival religious sects which at all costs needed a strong executive.[133] To Elgin, Fitzpatrick's objections appeared rather flimsy. Commenting on his Note, Elgin said that if such objections were taken into account there would be no legislative council in any province. In his usual diplomatic way, Elgin decided to take advantage of Fitzpatrick's retirement and approached the Secretary of State for making an appointment of a new Lieutenant-Governor who necessarily would not stick to his predecessor's opinion.[134] Such a person Elgin found in Mackworth Young.

But Elgin's Executive Council was still opposed to his idea and he asked Hamilton to give him his positive support.[135] When the matter was finally put before the Executive Council, the majority agreed with Fitzpatrick's view and opined "it would be impolitic at present to establish a Legislative Council in the Punjab." Surprisingly a Legislative Council was approved for Burma by 5 to 2 and rejected for the Punjab by 5 to 2, Elgin and Woodburn dissenting.[136] Elgin's Minute is very revealing and significant and mirrors his basic approach to the political problems of the period. He wrote:

I affirm that to oppose the institution of Provincial Councils on the ground of the possibility of a recrudescence of sedition and disloyalty is to misunderstand the whole situation. No one can absolutely deny that hidden dangers may exist, or that the smouldering embers may some day be fanned into a flame. But if so, it will not be the open discussions of a council, but one of the mysterious agencies, which the "voiceless millions" of India know both how to use and how to conceal from our most careful scrutiny, that will once more imperil the existence of the Indian Empires .... How best to cope with the great silent, indefinite and implacable danger is a problem that has yet to be solved. Of one thing I am confident, and that is, that it will not be overcome by stifling criticism, but rather by inviting free discussion, whenever and wherever we can and by throwing open to the light of day and being prepared to justify every act of our administration and of the officers who carry out our orders.[137]

Elgin refuted the charge of those who said that the Act of 1892 was a "concession to political agitation" and urged Hamilton to extend the Constitution of 1892 to the Punjab as well.[138] In September the matter was referred to the Judicial and Public Committee of the Secretary of State's Council. Arthur Godley suggested a compromise that a Council might be created not on the basis of 1892 Constitution but on the 1861 Act.[139] Hamilton agreed.[140] The majority of the Councillors approved except A.C. Lyall who favoured extending the 1892 Act to the Punjab.[141]

With the best of intentions, Elgin did not entirely succeed, but he gained his point substantially. In December 1896 the Legislative Councils were granted to both Burma and the Punjab,[142] though many protested and agitated against restricting the scope of the new change to the 1861 Act.[143] It was a matter of regret that no elective element was introduced.[144]

This analysis of the two different approaches of the Secretary of State and the Viceroy is very revealing. First, we find that Hamilton's wit and judgement were obscured by his imperialist myopia and prejudice. Elgin, in contrast to him, appeared liberal and more pragmatic especially because he had to deal with a dominant Secretary of State, intellectually shrewd, constitutionally strong and politically conservative. The tension between the two accounted for a compromise in the context of the basic policies to be followed towards India. They were to be more cautious than liberal, more watchful than suspicious. This was the main significance.

Secondly, it also explodes the myth that Elgin was unduly subservient to either Witehall or the Indian bureaucracy. Nor did he lose his grip over the administration. He refused to take an alarmist view of the situation—a fact which Hamilton was constrained to admit. He wrote to Elgin: "whilst I differ from you as to the nature of weapons to be employed, it is most satisfactory to find that you hold such strong and non-alarmist view as to the general condition of India."[145]

On the main issue concerning sedition, Elgin agreed in principle to strengthen the existing law. But the nature of the change and the extent to which it would be strengthened were left to the deliberate and careful attention of the Indian Government.

In connection with the Poona riots, the Bombay government arrested some people under Section 124A of the Indian Penal Code for making seditious utterances, the most notable among them being B.G. Tilak, who was arrested on 27 July 1897.[146] Their trial, which ended in conviction, had the distinction of passing through three stages. There was a trial in the High Court, then the application for leave to appeal the Privy Council and finally the application before the Privy Council.

The charge against Tilak was that he made some provocative and irresponsible statements intended to cause disaffection. Tilak had written in the *Kesari* of 4 May 1897, that the Bombay government should not have entrusted the execution of objectionable plague orders to a "suspicious, sullen and tyrannical officer like Rand." On 12 June 1897 he addressed a Shivaji memorial meeting in which he justified the murder of Afzal Khan and reminded his audience that everything was permissible to attain national ends. He said, "do not circumscribe your vision like a frog in a well; get out of the penal code."[147]

Writing a week later in the same paper Tilak said, "to speak the truth, none can help thinking that this is surely not the proper time for celebrating the jubilee, at least not in India."[148] These statements were considered incendiary enough and he was brought to trial on 8 September 1897. A jury of six

Europeans found him guilty against three, two Hindus and one Parsi, and Tilak was convicted for eighteen months.[149] An appeal against the conviction and for leave to appeal to Privy Council was rejected by the full bench of the High Court on 24 September 1897.[150] This decision was finally upheld by the Privy Council.[151]

The significance of the trial was immense. Tilak at once became a national here. The *Bengalee* of 25 September appeared with black borders. In the Amraoti Congress that year, S.N. Banerjee said, "For Mr Tilak my heart is full of sympathy, my feelings go forth to him in his prison house. A nation is in tears."[152] Actually Tilak and many more were convinced that there was nothing seditious in what he had said or written and that he had no hand in the crime of 24 June.[153]

Sandhurst, the Governor of Bombay, did not find Tilak's speech particularly seditious. He wrote, "I have read a full translation of the Shivaji speech, but I can see nothing in it."[154] On the other hand it gave the Government some satisfaction that Section 124A was found workable. The Government was obviously pleased with Justice Strachey's interpretation of Section 124A, defining disaffection "as simply an absence of affection. It means hatred, enmity, dislike, hostility, contempt and every form of ill-will to the Government." He went on to add that, "the amount of intensity of the disaffection is absolutely immaterial, except perhaps in dealing with the question of punishment: if a man excites or attempts to excite feelings of disaffection, great or small, he is guilty under the section."[155]

In spite of the fact that three out of four sedition trials had succeeded and the adequacy of Section 124A had been proved, the Government decided to change some sections of the Indian Penal Code and the Criminal Procedure Code to make the judicial machinery flexible to deal with sedition effectively. After the trial of Tilak, Elgin wrote to Sandhurst, "Though it is satisfactory to have got a verdict against Tilak, it was only by a majority, and the result of the subsequent trial shows how the change of sides of the member of the jury might have prevented Tilak's conviction. It cannot be pleasant for either you or me, personally to be responsible for the proposals to set aside juries in these cases, but it is exceedingly difficult to see how we can avoid it."[156]

The amendment of the sedition laws was discussed by the executive Council on 3 October and it was decided that the changes should be of a non-executive and general nature.[157] The Indian Government also did not attempt to redefine Section 124A of the Indian Penal Code. Amendment of three sections of the Criminal Procedure Code and two sections of the Indian Penal Code was recommended.[158]

The suggested changes were as follows: First amendment concerned Section 107 of the Criminal Procedure Code to empower the Magistracy to demand security to keep the peace from a person who was likely to do any such wrongful act, not only as might probably occasion a breach of the peace, which was the existing law, but also as might probably disturb the public tranquillity.[159] Secondly a new clause was added to Section 109 of the Criminal Procedure Code, which would provide a summary method for stemping the dissemination of seditious or defamatory matter, written or spoken in cases which were not of sufficient importance to make it desirable to institute prosecutions under the Indian Penal Code.[160] Thirdly the amendment was to the Schedule II of the Criminal Procedure Code to enable trials under 124A, Indian Penal Code, to be held by a Presidency Magistrate and Magistrate First Class.[161] The two changes proposed in the Indian Penal Code related to Section 505 and 499. Section 505 pertained to false statement with intent to cause mutiny or commit offence against the public peace. The Government proposed to reword the explanation so as to leave the burden of proving it on the defence.[162] The accused under the changed clause would be liable to conviction in spite of his intentions or actual effect, if he could not prove that the statement he made was false and Section 499 related to the offence of defamation. The majority of the councillors favoured to add to the earlier explanation that it would be an offence to make imputation against one class or community of persons. The purpose of this addition was to restrict the embitterment between one sect and the other.[163] Woodburn supported by Elgin opposed this change because it could suggest to various sects or make it more easy for sects to bring charges of defamation against each other and could further inflame the class animosity. Elgin pointed out that already under Sections 107 and 109 of the Penal Code the executive possessed the exact authority, it seemed to need.[164]

With these recommendations, Elgin asked Hamilton to give their proposals a fair trial.[165]

Elgin also invited the opinions of the local governments on the nature and extent of the changes proposed in the despatch to the Secretary of State. All local governments agreed that there was no need for reviving the Vernacular Press Act, or changing the wording of Section 124A, except the government of Madras who wanted to amend it to make it clear to a layman.[166] Similarly most of the governments accepted the principle of amendment but Lyall, Stevens and MacDonnell felt that the wordings of some of the changes must be more sober.[167] It was Cotton, the Chief Commissioner of Assam who totally rejected the need for any change. He wrote: "I trust I may not be deemed to have exceeded my duties if I venture to offer you my most respectful warning against the trend of legislation it is proposed to undertake. It will certainly be received with tremendous opposition in India, and I anticipate that the embitterment of racial feelings which is continually growing will be augmented."[168] Besides Cotton, all approved of the changes in Sections 107 and 109 of the Criminal Procedure Code. Regarding Section 499 of the Indian Penal Code, all local heads except Havelock and Young supported John Woodburn.[169] Changes in Section 505 of the Indian Penal Code were opposed only by Cotton and Stevens who wanted that the burden of proving falsity should lie on the prosecution.[170]

After receiving their opinions Elgin was inclined to further soften down the wordings of certain clauses. He emphasised that there was a need for minimising the opposition, particularly by redrafting the wordings of Section 505 and completely dropping Section 499 of the Criminal Procedure Code. His inclination was to alter the new Section 505, by omitting the word "false" which was objected to, and make the explanation an exception. This he considered would be a distinct improvement, the effect of which would be that the prosecution could bring up against a man any statement, true or false, but the accused by proving its truth could escape. There would thus be shifting of the onus of proof, though the practical effect in working would be exactly the same under both forms of section.[171]

Elgin rightly feared that there would be bitter criticism at the hands of the public of the provision giving all powers to the

District Magistrates, the Presidency Magistrates and Magistrates First Class to try sedition cases and deprive the jury of the right to do so. He summed up his personal views by stating that "to be charged with introducing legislation restricting the right of free speech and free criticism and trial by jury is so unpalatable that nothing short of a feeling that it is a positive duty would induce me to support what is now proposed."[172]

While Elgin was trying to minimise the effect of the new changes, Hamilton was planning to further enhance its scope and extend the nature of the changes proposed. The recommendations of the Indian Government were presented to Wilson, the legal expert at the Indian Office. He opined in favour of the Indian Government and approved their suggestion not to redraft Section 124A of the Indian Penal Code. He also hinted that the Magistrates should not be given such wide powers.[173] Arthur Godley did not approve of the above opinion and forcefully suggested that Section 124A must be amended and the powers of the Magistrates need not be curtailed.[174] Hamilton agreed with Godley.[175] But the Judicial and Public Committee did not agree to amend Section 124A. However, it agreed to the amendment of Section 499 of the Indian Penal Code and also accepted the Secretary of State's suggestion to modify Section 505 which would make even a true statement which was "likely to cause offence" punishable.[176] Godley again sent a memorandum to Hamilton repeating his earlier views, in spite of the fact that the Privy Council had upheld the decision of John Strachey on 19 November. He also stated that he had obtained the concurrence of Wilson to the draft of his instructions.[177] On 4 December 1897, in accordance with the wishes of the Secretary of State, the Legal Committee approved his decision. In their minute the Legal Committee wrote, "It appears to us however open to question whether, after the recent favourable decision of the Privy Council, it is desirable to make any amendment of the section." Yet they hastened to add: "But as we understand that the Secretary of State considers the time opportune for a restatement of that law, we think it advisable to take advantage."[179]

On 7 December, Hamilton telegraphed his decision. In addition to the changes suggested in Section 505, he proposed to add the following new words to Section 124A: "hatred, contempt or disaffection, towards the Queen or Government or promote or attempt to promote feelings of ill will between different classes of the Queen's subject."[180] He also urged Elgin to push through both amendments in the Indian Penal Code and the Criminal Procedure Code together and quickly.[181]

Elgin accepted Hamilton's modifications, but refused to combine both bills together for want of proper deliberation and for reasons of political tactics.[182] He wrote, "It appeared to me that to make one Bill of these proposal would have the inevitable result of concentrating all attention on this Bill, and its attaining unenviable notoriety as the Press Legislation of Lord Elgin's Government."[183] After having secured the major point, Hamilton was prepared to leave to the Indian Government the discretion in the method of introduction.[184]

The question arises as to why Elgin agreed to change Section 124A of the Indian Penal Code? A simple answer to this query is rather difficult. It could perhaps be best rationalised with the surmise that in considering to agree to the concession he was striking a compromise with the Secretary of State. However, he attempted to minimise the impact of such a change.

Elgin informed Hamilton that all his proposals were adopted and on 21 December 1897 two separate Bills, one to amend the Indian Penal Code and the other, to amend the Criminal Procedure Code were introduced in the Legislative Council.

The changes in the Indian Penal Code were first discussed and were bitterly assailed by the non-official members of the Council.[185] Officials like Cotton protested against them.[187] There was a good deal of criticism outside the Council chamber all declaring that the new changes were uncalled for, restrictive and punitive. But Chalmers actually denied that any change in Section 124A was really contemplated. The Government was merely introducing a few words to make the clause more understandable.[188] But this was not true. Actually by choosing to change the explanations of Section 124A, the Government had the intention of arming itself with substantial executive powers.

So strong was the opposition to the Bill that Elgin had to reexamine the situation.[189] He telegraphed to Hamilton privately that the Select Committee on the Penal Code had proposed certain amendments and urged him to agree to it. The Committee believed that some degree of ill will was inseparable from criticism, however legitimate, and could be compatible with genuine loyalty. Accordingly the Commission suggested to drop a few words like, "or promotes or attempts to promote feelings of enmity or ill will between different classes of Her Majesty's subjects" from the text of the clause which were originally recommended by the Secretary of State in Council. They also proposed to drop the words, "ill will" from the explanation and defined disaffection to include "disloyalty and all feelings of enmity."[190] They also added another explanation stating that "comments expressing disapprobation of the administrative or other action of the Government without exciting or attempting to excite hatred, contempt or disaffection, do not constitute an offence under this section."[191]

A similar suggestion to tone down the element of harshness in Section 505 was also recommended. The committee forcefully pointed out that it was too much under the conditions of modern journalism to require persons publishing statements to prove its actual truth. Its proposed new explanation which read: "An offence within the meaning of this section when the person making, publishing or circulating any such statement, rumour or report has reasonable grounds for believing that such statement, rumour or report is true, and makes, publishes or circulates it without such intent as aforesaid."[192] The Secretary of State chose to accept the recommendations.[193] These changes were finally passed by the Select Committee on the Bill to amend the Indian Penal Code.[194] On 18 February the Bill was approved by the Legislative Council.

As a matter of fact, all these changes now approved were originally proposed by Elgin and Chalmers on 16 December 1897. But Westland and Trevor, the members of the Executive Council, had opposed the proposals and it was then decided that if the pressure mounted the concession could be given to render an appearance of amenability to the public opinion.[195]

The changes in the Bill to amend the Criminal Procedure Code were also hotly contested and concessions had to be made before they were enacted on 18 March 1898. The most important change actually pertained to the summary method of stopping sedition and its dissemination by giving powers to the Chief Presidency Magistrates and the Magistrates First Class to try the cases and also allowing them to take a security from the persons suspected of any such activities.

The alteration was criticised by almost all the Europeans and the Indians who submitted their criticism to the Government. The European and Anglo-Indian Defence Association asked that either the amendment be cancelled or the Magistrates should have a definite proof of a person's guilt before taking a security.[196] H.T. Princep, formerly the Judge of the Calcutta High Court and now the additional Member of the Viceroy's Council, also voiced his concern on the issue and wrote, "I am sorry that it has been settled to propose to give such power to magistrates both by lowering the jurisdiction in under Section 124A, Penal Code, and in security cases of this class. In neither case in my humble opinion, was it essential to enforcing the law, and I also think that it certainly is not worth the agitation that it will provoke in which Europeans will join the natives."[197]

Actually the main motive of the European agitation was that they did not approve of being equated with the "native" press. *The Pioneer* openly advocated to confine the restrictions to the "Vernacular papers" and often eulogised Lytton that his arrangements were "distinctly more convincing than those of Lord Elgin and Lord Chalmers."[198] The European critics were most interested in confining the jurisdiction of section 124A to the Presidency and the District Magistrates who were Europeans. They feared that in case of reducing the jurisdiction to Magistrates, there could be the possibility of a European being tried by a "native."[199] The motive behind their agitation was primarily racial. Sir C. Paul, the Advocate-General of Bengal, was openly carrying on propaganda in the Calcutta Bar.[200] The most fervent support to this idea came from G. Evans, a Member of the Legislative Council, and Mackenzie, the Lieutenant Governor of Bengal. The latter even threatened to move an amendment to that effect.[201] Elgin did not like this tendency of introducing any element of race distinction in the Code.[202]

The Indian press and the public were equally critical. They resented the abolition of the trial by jury. They wanted some safeguards and demanded the provision for review of cases by the High Court. In most cases they did not trust the young Magistrates. Rivaz, the new Home Member, and Chalmers were also now convinced that some changes in the proposed amendments were required. Similarly Elgin felt that the stringency of the law should be relaxed as far as it could be done safely.[203] Ultimately the Government made many changes. The Magistrates were now allowed to have sureties of good behaviour from the publisher and did not insist on securities. Secondly, all orders issued under Section 108 were subjected to the review of the High Court.[204] These recommendations were accepted by the Secretary of State and by March both the Indian Penal Code and the Criminal Procedure Code stood amended.

There is no doubt that but for the active opposition they aroused and the ready conciliation and moderation shown by Elgin, the sedition laws would have been very restrictive.

One important fact emerged from these changes. Political offenders could now be tried by the Presidency, the District and the First Class Magistrates without recourse to the jury. This meant wider and greater powers for the Government. By omitting the clause "which he knows to be false" from Section 505, it made impossible for the newspapers to publish and news regarding the action or intention of the Government.

During all this period of political difficulty, the Government did not ignore plague. The Government measures continued with almost unabated zeal. During the summer months there was a marked decline in the plague cases and fewer plague deaths were reported.[205] The decline in the outbreak of plague gave the impression to the Government that plague had been contained due to the implementation of strong measures. But by the beginning of monsoon and the coming of winter the plague reappeared with great virulence. Some thought that the large scale outbreak was again due to the relaxation of rules after the riots and other political disturbances. A cry was raised for more effective arrangements, which meant the revival of land quarantines and corpse inspection. Sandhurst and Elgin were not disposed to take steps in that direction.[206] But by December and January plague reached its peak and more cases than ever before were reported. Hamilton again feared the loss of trade. In December 1897 rules were once again issued for compulsory segregation and in January military search parties were employed to evacuate the sick in various parts of the Bombay Presidency.[207] In addition, the Bombay government voluntarily resorted to land quarantine.

On 3 February 1898 the Government of India issued a fresh resolution and tightened the plague rules. The segregation of the sick with the aid of search parties was its main measure; but the Government still refused to agree to any drastic measure like corpse inspection.[208] As it was, the situation was already explosive. In March 1898 it was rumoured that the government in Bombay was instituting corpse inspection. This was the proverbial last straw which broke the camel's back. Already in Bombay all British search parties were in use for plague purposes, and land quarantine, though officially prohibited was being regularly practised in Bombay.[209] On 9 March 1898 fierce riots borke out in Bombay. The disturbance was caused due to the attempted removal of a Muslim female plague patient to the hospital. There was complete *hartal* of the Bombay dock workers and cartmen which continued with varying success from 9 to 16 March 1898.[210]

This spontaneous outbreak forced the government to reconsider its policy. On 15 March 1898 the Bombay government announced the withdrawal of the military search parties. House visitation was restricted to voluntary groups composed of the local population.[211] MacDonnell and Macworth Young also sounded the note of caution and both urged that the responsibility of the plague administration should and must be given to the Indians and the local people.[212]

By now the medical and administrative authorities were coninvced that plague did not recede on account of stringent measures but increased and decreased in the winter and summer months respectively. Hamilton was also brought around and was finally convinced that extra-hard rules did not necessarily bring good results.[213] Local governments were given maximum discretion to apply rules according to the need and circumstances of the situation. Segregation and compulsory evacuation were completely given up in large towns.[214] These new proposition were fully supported by John Woodburn, till recently Home Member and now the Lieutenant-Governor of Bengal; Rivaz the new Home Member; Hewett, the Home Secretary, and Surgeon-General Harvey, the Director of the Indian Medical Service. In a way the Bombay government reacted most effectively. The special plague committee was abolished and the municipality was again brought into the picture.[215] The importance of this was that public cooperation which could always be the most effective weapon in an extremely conservative society, was put to use.

The confirmation of its utility could be seen in the fact that Curzon followed it up.

If one attempts to evaluate the plague policy of the Indian Government, one finds many symptoms of muddle and confusion. It was probably due to the fact that it had to work under two limitations. Firstly, the plague policy was not yet evolved and the lessons were learnt the hard way. Secondly, the confusion was worse confounded on account of the unnecessary and persistent interference of the outsiders. It was due to outside influences and imperial considerations that the pilgrims for the *Haj* were stopped which consequently irritated the feelings of the people. Even the Venice Sanitary Convention of 1897 did not prohibit the departure of the pilgrims from the infected areas, if proper precautions were taken.[216]

In so doing the Government went beyond the requirements of the convention. In addition, the Government was ill advised to institute very stringent measures. The excessive use of the searth parties created social and political hardships. Their high-handed attitude neither mitigated plague nor appeased the people. Sandhurst himself said that wholesale searching did not show results which were not out balanced "by disadvantages and hardships, especially those caused by indiscreet or corrupt subordinates. The result was that the entire population was being set against the measures."[217] It was therefore not so surprising that the Plague Commissioners did not favour compulsory segregation or evacuation in their findings.[218]

Fortunately, due to the guarded opposition of Elgin, more unpopular measures of doubtful utility like corpse inspection were avoided. It was equally tragic that the Bombay government was wrongly advised to wrest powers from the municipality. The effective way to deal with epidemics of the type in the given circumstances was to solicit the maximum cooperation from the public. And that is that ultimately happened.

It was only after two years of consistent and patient endeavours on the part of Elgin that a plague policy which laid stress on the isolation of the sick, disinfection of the affected areas and finally in preference to coercion, the compliance of the regulations through persuasion was evolved. It was this policy which won the approval of the Plague Commissioners.[219] The lessons were learnt by Elgin by 1898 and the probable benefit of this experience was reaped by Curzon.

The year 1896-7 was a year of great misfortunes. But India was not overwhelmed by "disruptive forces," as depicted by *The Times*.[220] Nor did the year inaugurate "a repressive regime unparalleled in the annals of India," as asserted by *The Bengalee*.[221] Both these views were journalistic exaggerations.

The most important feature of the period was Elgin's ability to face the crisis and keep his cool. It goes to his credit to steer the ship of the State through the rocks without either grounding it or wrecking it. The situation might have easily gone out of control but for the foresight shown by Elgin. He not only contained the external forces but maintained a united administrative front. Though his policies were by no means liberal, they were decidedly motivated by deliberate caution.

## NOTES

[1] B.M. Malabari, *India in 1897*, Bombay, 1898, p. 3.

[2] Telegram, Viceroy to S.S., 2 October 1896, E.P., vol. 19. See also Report of the Indian Plague Commission, 1901, Para 105.

[3] *Municipal Commissioner's Report*, Para 7. (Hereafter cited as Snow's Report after the name of the chairman.)

[4] From October to December 1895, nearly 250,000 people had fled from Bombay. *Statement of Moral and Material Progress in India*, 1896-7, Parl, Papers, 1898, vol. 63, p. 29.

[5] *Report of the Indian Plague Commission*, op. cit., Paras 600 and 605.

[6] *Report of the Indian Plague Commission*, ibid., Para 27.

[7] *Statement of Moral and Material Progress in India*, 1896-7, Parl, Papers, 1898, vol. 63, p. 180.

[8] *Trade Review of India*, 1896-7, Parl, Papers, (C. 8692), 1898, vol. 64, p. 6.

[9] Cleghorn's Memorandum, Director-General of Indian Medical Service, 16 January 1897, Enc. Indian Govt. to S.S., L. No. 1 (Sen.), 27 January 1897, Revenue Letters from India, vol. 19. (Hereafter cited as Rev. L.I.)

[10] Hamilton to Elgin, 21 January 1897, E.P., vol. 15. See also Telegram, S.S. to Governor of Bombay, 18 January 1897, Enc. Sandhurst to Elgin, 20 January 1897, ibid., vol. 20.

[11] Elgin to Hamilton, 3 February 1897, ibid., vol. 15.

[12] Telegram, Govt. Bombay to Viceroy, 14 February 1897, ibid.

[13] See Elgin to Hamilton, 10 February 1897, *ibid.*, vol. 15.
[14] J. Woodburn's Note, 14 February 1897, Enc. Elgin to Hamilton, 17 February 1897, MSS. Eur. D 509/iv.
[15] MacDonnell to Elgin, 16 February 1897, E.P., vol. 70.
[16] Indian Govt. to Bombay Govt., 6 February 1897, Enc. Indian Govt. to S.S., L. No. 5 (Sen.), 10 February 1897, Rev. L.I., vol. 19.
[17] Indian Govt., to S.S., L. No. 7 (Sen.), 24 February 1897, Para 3, *ibid.*
[18] Elgin to Hamilton, 17 February 1897, E.P., vol. 15.
[19] Two Military Members, Collins and Gen. White and Law Member, Chalmers, dissented from the majority opinion.
[20] Telegram, S.S. to Viceroy, 18 February 1897, E.P., vol. 20.
[21] Hamilton to Elgin, 26 February 1897, *ibid.*, vol. 15. See also Hamilton to Elgin, 19 February, 12 March, 2 April, 1897, *ibid.*
[22] *Report of the Indian Plague Commission, op. cit.*, Para 696.
[23] Elgin to Hamilton, 10 March 1897, E.P., vol. 15.
[24] Telegrams, Hamilton to Sandhurst, 6 January 1897, Enc. Sandhurst to Elgin, 20 June 1897, *ibid.*, vol. 20. See also Hamilton to Elgin, 7/8 January 1897, *ibid.*, vol. 15.
[25] Telegram, Sandhurst to Hamilton, undated, Enc. Sandhurst to Elgin, 20 January 1897, *ibid.*, vol. 70.
[26] See *The Times*, 16 March and 22 March 1897.
See *The Times of India*, 29 January 1897.
See *The Englishman*, 5 February 1897.
See *The Pioneer*, 27 and 28 February and 3 March 1897.
[27] Other members of the Committee were, Mr Snow, the Municipal Commissioner, Surgeon-Major Dimmock of Indian Medical Service and Mr James, an Engineer from the Bombay Corporation, Indian Govt. to S.S., L. No. 9 (San.), 10 March 1897, Para 3, Rev. L.I., vol. 19.
[28] Indian Govt. Notification, 20 February 1897, Enc. Indian Govt. to S.S., L. No. 9 (San.), 10 March 1897, Rev. L.I., vol. 19. See also *Indian Plague Commission Report, op. cit.*, Para 28.
[29] *Report of the Indian Plague Commission*, Para 581.
[30] Quoted in the Memorandum of the Army Sanitary Commission Report of the Municipal Commissioner of Bombay, 1896-97, India Home Proc. (Municipal), 1898, vol. 5646, No. 9.
[31] Sandhurst to Elgin, 17 March 1897, vol. 70.
[32] Plague committee consisted of J. Piele, S. C. Bayley and Charles Crosthwaite.
[33] Elgin to Hamilton, 17 March 1897, *ibid.*, vol. 20.
[34] Indian Govt. to S.S., L. No. 12 (Sen.), 31 March 1897, Para 7, Nov. L.I., vol. 19.
[35] Elgin to Hamilton, 7 April 1897, E.P., vol. 20.
[36] *Ibid.*
[37] Elgin to Hamilton, 4 April 1897 (appendix), *ibid.*
[38] Mackenzie to Elgin, 10 May 1897, *ibid.*, vol. 70.
[39] Elgin to Mackenzie, 17 June 1897, *ibid.*

⁴⁰Elgin to Mackenzie, 31 May 1897, *ibid.*
⁴¹Elgin to Hamilton, 25 May 1897, *ibid.*, vol. 15.
⁴²MacDonnell to Elgin, 4 March 1897, Enc. Elgin to Hamilton, 10 March 1897, MSS. Eur. D 509/iv.
See also Elgin to Hamilton, 24 and 31 March 1897, (appendix), E.P., vol. 15.
⁴³*Hitavadi*, 26 March 1897, Bengal N.N.R., 1897.
⁴⁴12 March 1897, *ibid.*
⁴⁵*Kalaputra*, 18 April 1897, *Sudharak*, 3 May; *Danyan Prakash*, 10 May, *Kesari*, 27 April and 6 May; Mahastra Mitra, 29 April 1897, Bomb. (N.N.R. Report, 1897).
⁴⁶See Poona Memorial to W.C. Rand, 17 April 1897, J.P. Papers 1896 A/97, vol. 456.
⁴⁷Sandhurst to Elgin, 27 June 1897, E.P., vol. 70.
⁴⁸*Ibid.*
⁴⁹*The Times*, 1 July and 3 July 1897.
⁵⁰See Hamilton to Elgin, 14 May and 21 May 1897 (appendix), E.P., vol. 15.
See also "The Musalmans of India and Sultan," *The Contemporary Review*, vol. ixxi, (February 1897).
See also Lepel Griffith, "The Breakdown of the Frontier Policy," *The Nineteenth Century*, vol. xiii, (October 1897).
⁵¹*The Pioneer*, 11 July 1897.
⁵²*The Englishman*, 2 July 1897.
⁵³*The Times of India*, 9 July 1897.
⁵⁴*The St. James Gazette*, 3 July 1897, E.P., vol. 79 (Newspaper cuttings).
See also *The Morning Post*, 3 July 1897, *ibid.*
⁵⁵*The Times*, 2 July 1897.
⁵⁶5 July 1897.
⁵⁷W.W. Hunter was the special correspondent of *The Times* in India.
⁵⁸*The Times*, 19 July 1897.
It is strange but refreshing to see that *The Observer*, 4 July 1897, took a very realistic view and came out against the move to decry the Indian Press. It wrote: "It would be unpardonably silly if the Government were to import some of those continental methods of Press censorship which we are never tired of decrying. . . . The Native Press with their violent and illogical diatribes, may not be a very satisfactory gauge of popular feeling, but it is a rough and probably true index as to what is currently said in still more violent and illogical circles below, and an approximate guide to much underground movements is better than no guide at all." E.P., vol. 79 (Newspaper cuttings).
⁵⁹Hamilton to Elgin, 24 June 1897 (appendix), E.P., vol. 15.
⁶⁰Hamilton to Elgin, 2 July 1897 (appendix), *ibid.*
⁶¹Hamilton to Elgin, 30 July 1897 (appendix), *ibid.*
⁶²Hamilton to Elgin, 19 August 1897 (appendix), *ibid.*, vol. 15.
⁶³Hamilton to Elgin, 12 August 1897 (appendix), *ibid.*

⁶⁴Telegram, S.S. to Viceroy, (Pr. Conf.), 3 July 1897 (appendix), *ibid.*, vol. 20.

⁶⁵Parl. Debates, H. of C., 4 Series, vol. L. p. 863.

⁶⁶Telegram, S.S. to Viceroy (Pr. Conf.), 10 July 1897, (appendix), E.P., vol. 20.

⁶⁷Telegram, Elgin to Hamilton, 4 July 1897 (appendix), *ibid.*

⁶⁸Elgin to MacDonnell, Sandhurst, Lyall, Mackworth Young, 6 July 1897, (appendix); 6 July (appendix); 11 July (appendix) 11 July (appendix) respectively, *ibid.*, vol. 71.

⁶⁹Bombay Govt. to S.S., L. No. 52 (Jud.), Conf., 29 July 1897, Para 3, J. and P. Papers 1657/97, vol. 454.

⁷⁰Sandhurst to Elgin, 27 June 1897, *ibid.*, vol. 70.

⁷¹C.S. Bayley to H.B. Smith, 12 July 1897, J. and P. Papers 1896A/97, vol. 456.

⁷²Mackworth Young to Elgin, 15 July 1897 (appendix), E.P., vol. 71.

⁷³Telegram, Chief Secy. Bengal Govt. to Secy. (Home) Indian Govt., 3 July 1897, India Public (Home) Proc., vol. 5181, October 1897, No. 125.

⁷⁴Telegram, Lt. Governor of Bengal to Viceroy, 6 July 1897, India Public (Home) Proc., vol. 5181, October 1897, No. 133. See also *Calcutta Review*, October 1897, pp. 391-4.

⁷⁵C.C. Stevens to Elgin, 8 July 1897, Enc. Elgin to Hamilton, 14 July 1897, MSS. Eur. D 509/6.

The Lt. Governor reported to Elgin that one Captain Petley made some very inflammatory speeches and on 7 July he took a party of naval officers to Barrackpore without any authority.

⁷⁶W.C. Bolton, Ch. Secy. Bengal to J.P. Hewet, Secy. (Home), Indian Govt., 7 July 1897 (Conf.), J. and P. Papers 1796/97, attached to 1813/97 vol. 456.

⁷⁷Stevens to Elgin, 8 July 1897, *op. cit.*

⁷⁸Elgin to Hamilton, 6 July 1897, E.P., vol. 15.

⁷⁹Elgin to Hamilton, 4 August 1897 (appendix), E.P., vol. 15.

⁸⁰C.S. Bayley to H.B. Smith, 12 August 1897, *ibid.*

⁸¹MacDonnell to Elgin, 16 and 19 July 1897 (appendix), E.P., vol. 71.

⁸²MacDonnell to Elgin, 22 August 1897 (appendix), E.P., vol. 71.

⁸³C.S. Bayley to H.B. Smith, 12 July 1897, J. and P. Papers, 1896A/97, vol. 456.

⁸⁴MacDonnell to Elgin, 22 August 1897 (appendix), *op. cit.*

⁸⁵Lyall to Elgin, 17 July 1897 (appendix), E.P., vol. 71.

⁸⁶Stevens to Elgin, 15 July 1897 (appendix), *ibid.*

Sandhurst to Elgin, 25 July 1897 (appendix), *ibid.*

⁸⁷Macworth Young to Elgin, 15 July (appendix), *ibid.*

⁸⁸Quoted by Elgin, Elgin to Hamilton, 4 August 1897 (appendix), E.P., vol. 71.

⁸⁹Report on the Nature of Vernacular Press of Madra, Chief Secy. Madras to Secy. (Home), Indian Govt., 21 June 1897, J. and P. Papers 1498/97, vol. 452.

## Plague and Sedition

[90]Telegram, Elgin to Hamilton (Pr.), 17 July 1897 (appendix), E.P., vol. 20.
[91]Telegram, Hamilton to Elgin (Pr.), 19 July 1897 (appendix), E.P., vol. 20.
[92]Elgin to Hamilton, 20 July 1897 (appendix), *ibid*.
[93]*Ibid*.
[94]*Ibid*. See also Telegram, Viceroy to S.S., (Pr.), 22 July 1897, E.P., vol. 20.
[95]Telegram, S.S. to Viceroy (Pr.), 23 July 1897 (appendix), *ibid*.
[96]Telegram, S.S. to Sandhurst (Pr.), 23 June 1897, MSS. Eur. D 508/1.
[97]Hamilton to Elgin, 24 June 1897 (appendix), E.P., vol. 15.
[98]The members of the committee were, J. Piele, A.C. Lyall, Charles Crosthwaite, Denis Fitzpatrick and Bayley.
[99]Hamilton to Elgin, 8 July 1897 (appendix), E.P., vol. 15.
[100]*Ibid*.
[101]Hamilton to Elgin, 12 August 1897 (appendix), *ibid*.
[102]Hamilton to Elgin, 19 August 1897 (appendix), *ibid*.
[103]Hamilton to Elgin, 26 August 1897 (appendix),
Hamilton to Elgin, 16 September 1897,
Hamilton to Elgin, 30 September 1897 (appendix), *ibid*.
[104]Hamilton to Elgin, 17 September 1896, *ibid*., vol. 14.
[105]Hamilton to Elgin, 30 October 1896, *ibid*.
[106]*Ibid*.
[107]Hamilton to Elgin, 17 July 1896, *ibid*.
Also Hamilton to Elgin, 11 December 1896, *ibid*.
[108]Hamilton to Elgin, 3 May and 14 August 1897, *ibid*., vol. 15.
See also Hamilton to Elgin, 21 January 1898, *ibid*., vol. 16.
[109]Elgin to Hamilton, 7 September 1896 (appendix), *ibid*., vol. 16.
[110]Elgin to Hamilton, 27 July 1897 (appendix), *ibid*., vol. 15.
[111]Elgin to Woodburn, 20 July 1897 (appendix), *ibid*., vol. 71.
[112]Elgin to Hamilton, 13 July 1897 (appendix), *ibid*., vol. 15.
[113]Elgin to Hamilton 7 October 1896, E.P., vol. 14.
[114]Crosthwaite to Elgin, 12 June 1894, *ibid*., vol. 64.
[115]Elgin to Fowler, 12 June 1894, *ibid*., vol. 12.
See also Indian Govt. to S.S., L. No. 52 (Pub.), Enc. 17 October 1894, Indian Public (Home) Proc., vol. October 1894, Nos. 200-4.
[116]Telegram, Viceroy to S.S., 8 May and 4 June 1894, E.P., vol. 17.
[117]Elgin to Hamilton, 24 March 1897 (appendix), E.P., vol. 17.
[118]Telegram, Queen to Viceroy, 17 September 1894, *ibid*., vol. 125 e.
[119]Telegram, Viceroy to Queen, 18 September 1894, *ibid*.
See for details of riots Proc. of Poona riots, 13 September 1894, Enc. Bombay Govt. to S.S., L. No. 21 (Jud.), 22 December 1894, J.P. Papers 32/95, vol. 389.
[120]E.K.C. Ollivant to J. Piele (Member Indian Council) (Pr.), 3 November 1897; Enc. Hamilton to Elgin, 21 January 1898 (appendix), E.P., vol. 16.
[121]MacDonnell to Elgin, 22 August 1897 (appendix), E.P., vol. 71.
[122]Elgin to Hamilton, 30 December 1897 (appendix), *ibid*.

C.J. Lyall, the Chief Commissioner of Central Provinces expressed this point in detail. "At present I believe that Indian Musalmans—that is, the thinking and educated portion of them—are generally loyal, because they clearly realise that their safety, in presence of the vast Hindu majority, and of the immense growth of the Hindus during last century in power, wealth, education, and influence, is bound up with the existence of British rule."

Lyall to Elgin, 17 July 1897 (appendix), *ibid.*, vol. 71.

[123] Elgin to Hamilton, 27 July 1897 (appendix), *ibid.*, vol. 15.

[124] T.J.C. Plowden to Elgin, 28 July 1898, *ibid.*, vol. 73.

[125] Elgin to Hamilton, 10 February 1898 (appendix), E.P., vol. 16.

[126] Elgin to Hamilton, 30 December 1897 (appendix), *ibid.*, vol. 15. See also Elgin to Hamilton, 21 April 1897, *ibid.*

[127] Elgin to Hamilton, 27 July 1897 (appendix), *ibid.*

[128] Elgin to Hamilton, 25 August 1896, *ibid.*, vol. 14.

[129] B.M. Malabari, The *Indian Problem*, Bombay 1894, p. 12.

[130] See Indian Govt. (Home) to Punjab Govt., 28 March 1896, India Public Proc., vol. 4959, No. 171, 1896.

[131] Punjab Govt. to Indian Govt. (Home), 31 October 1892, *ibid.*, No. 175.

[132] See S.S. to Indian Govt., Despatch No. 1 (Pub.), 9 January 1896, India Public Proc., vol. 4959, No. 170, August 1896.

[133] Note by Denis Fitzpatrick, 10 April 1896, Para 14. India Public Proc., vol. 4959, No. 174, August 1896.

[134] Elgin to Hamilton, 16 June 1896, E.P., vol. 14.

[135] Elgin to Hamilton, 21 July 1896, *ibid.*

[136] Indian Govt., to S.S., L. No. 64 (Pub.), 25 August 1896. India Public Proc., vol. 4959, No. 177, August 1896. See also Proc. No. 178-182.

[137] Elgin's Minute, 24 August 1896, Enc. Elgin to Hamilton, 25 August 1896, MSS. Eur. D 509/2.

[138] *Ibid.*

[139] A. Godley Note, 25 September 1896, J. & P. Papers, 1619/96, vol. 429.

[140] Hamilton's Note, 6 October 1896, *ibid.*

[141] A.C. Lyall, Note, 14 October 1896, *ibid.* See also J. and P. Minute, 21 October 1896, *ibid.* See also India Council Minute Book, vol. 77.

[142] S.S. to Indian Govt. Despatch No. 116 (Pub.), 3 December 1896, Paras 3-5 India Public Proc., vol. 5180, No. 35, February 1897.

[143] Memorial, Indian Association (Lahore), India Public Proc., *ibid.*, No. 14. See also *Report of the Indian National Congress*, 1898, Res. xxi.

[144] The Legislative Council in Punjab came into existence with nine nominated members. The first council consisted of four European officials, one non-official European and four non-officials Indians. India Public Proc., vol. 5181, No. 415, October 1897.

[145] Hamilton to Elgin, 12 August 1897 (appendix), E.P., vol. 15.

## Plague and Sedition

[146] Bombay Govt. to S.S., L. No. 52 (Jud.), 29 July 1897, Para 4, J.P. Papers 1657/97, vol. 454.

[147] *The Kesari*, 15 June 1897.

[148] *Ibid.*, 22 June 1897.

[149] Telegram, Bombay Govt. to Indian Govt., 14 September 1897. India Public Proc., vol. 5413, No. 345, May 1898. See for details, India Public Proc., vol. 5413, Nos. 356-9, May 1898. See also J.P. Papers 2254 and 2255/97, vol. 461. See Report of the Tilak Trial, *Times of India*, 10 September-18 September 1897.

[150] See for details, India Public Proc., vol. 5413, No. 362, May 1898. Also J.P. Papers 2291/97, vol. 462.

[151] For details, India Public Proc., vol. 5413, Nos. 377-80, May 1898.

[152] B.P. Sitaramayya, *The History of the Indian National Congress, 1885-1935*, p. 37.

[153] T.V. Private, Bal Gangadhar Tilak, Ahmedabad, 1958, p. 505.

[154] Sandhurst to Elgin, 12 July 1897 (appendix), E.P., vol. 71.

[155] W.R. Donogh, *The History and Law of Sedition*, Calcutta, 1907, p. 47.

See for the detailed summing up by Justice Strachey, India Public Proc., vol. 5413, No. 359, May 1898. See also J.P. 2576/97, vol. 468.

[156] Elgin to Sandhurst, 50 September 1897 (appendix), E.P., vol. 71.

[157] Telegram, Viceroy to S.S., (Pr.), 4 October 1897 (appendix), *ibid.*, vol. 20.

[158] Indian Govt. to S.S., L. No. 68 (Pub.), 14 October 1897, Paras 2-5. India Public Proc., vol. 5413, No. 334, May 1898.

[159] *Ibid.*, Para 6.

[160] *Ibid.*, Para 7.

[161] *Ibid.*, Para 8.

[162] *Ibid.*, Para 10.

[163] Para 9. This change was strongly favoured by E.C.K. Ollivant and Sandhurst. See Sandhurst to Elgin, 4 October 1897 (appendix), E.P., vol. 71.

[164] Woodburn to Elgin, 3 October 1897 (appendix), E.P., vol. 71.

[165] Elgin to Hamilton, 13 October 1897 (appendix), E.P., vol. 15.

[166] Havelock to Elgin, 15 November 1897, J. and P. Papers 2184/97, vol. 459.

[167] Lyall to Elgin, 19 November 1897, J. and P. Papers 2184/97, vol. 459.

Stevens to Elgin, 4 November 1897 (appendix), E.P., vol. 71. MacDonnell to Elgin, 9 November 1897 (appendix), *ibid.*

[168] Cotton to Elgin, 13 November 1897 (appendix), *ibid.* See also Cotton's Minute, 12 November 1897, J. and P. Papers 2184/97, vol. 459.

[169] Havelock to Elgin, 15 November 1897, *op. cit.*

Mackworth Young to Elgin, 30 November 1897, J. and P. Papers, 2184/97, vol. 459.

[170]Telegram, Viceroy to S.S., (Pr.), 2 December 1897 (appendix), E.P., vol. 20.
[171]*Ibid.*
[172]Elgin to Hamilton, 24 November 1897 (appendix), *ibid.*, vol. 15.
[173]Wilson's Memorandum, 9 November 1897, J. and P. Papers 2184/97, vol. 459.
[174]Godley's Memorandum, 16 November 1897, *ibid.*
[175]Hamilton's Memorandum, 16 November 1897, *ibid.*
[176]Judicial and Public Committee Minute, 24 November 1897, *ibid.*
[177]Godley's Memorandum to Hamilton, 24 November 1897, *ibid.*
[178]Hamilton's Minute, 27 November 1897, *ibid.*
[179]Legal Committee Minute, 4 December 1897, J. and P. Papers, 2184/97, vol. 459.
[180]Telegram, S.S. to Viceroy, (Pr.), 7 December 1897 (appendix), E.P., vol. 20.
[181]Telegram S.S. to Viceroy, (Pr.), 9 December 1897 (appendix), E.P., vol. 20.
[182]Telegram, Viceroy to S.S., (Pr.), 11 December 1897 (appendix), *ibid.*, vol. 20.
[183]Elgin to Hamilton, 16 December 1897 (appendix), E.P., vol. 15.
[184]Telegram, S.S. to Viceroy, (Pr.), 13 December 1897 (appendix), *ibid.*, vol. 20.
[185]See *Proc. of the Council of the Governor-General in India*, 1897, vol. 36.
See also Elgin to Hamilton, 30 December 1897, (appendix), E.P., vol. 15.
See also Bishamber Nath's Note, (Member Legislative Council), 25 December 1897, J. and P. Papers 141/98, attached to J. and P. 529/98, vol. 474.
[186]Assam Govt., to Indian Govt., 31 December 1897, Para 2, J. and P. Papers 195/99 attached to 529/98, *ibid.*
[187]Bengal Govt., to Indian Govt., 18 January 1898, Para 9-11, *ibid.*
Central Provinces Govt. to Indian Govt., 10 January 1898, Para 3 and 7, J. and P. Papers 233/98 attached to 529/98, vol. 474.
[188]*Proc. of the Governor-General Council in India*, 1897, vol. xxxvii, pp. 379-81.
[189]See Naoroji's statement, *The Times*, 29 December 1897.
See R.C. Dutt's letter to the Editor, *Englishman*, 4 January 1898.
See Indian Association to Indian Govt., 21 January 1898, J. and P. Papers, 292/98, attached to 529/98, vol. 474.
See *Report of the Indian National Congress*, 1897, Res. xiii.
See Poona Sarvajanik Sabha to Indian Govt., 2 January 1898, J. and P. Papers 419, attached to 529/98, vol. 474.
[190]Telegram, Viceroy to S.S., (Pr.), 26 January 1898 (appendix), E.P., vol. 21.
[191]W.R. Donagh, *The History and Law of Sedition*, p. 71.
[192]Telegram, Viceroy to S.S., (Pr.), 26 January 1898, *op. cit.*

## Plague and Sedition 185

[193] Telegram, S.S. to Viceroy, (Pr.), 27 January 1898 (appendix), E.P., vol. 21.

[194] See Report of the Select Committee on the Bill to amend Penal Code, Enc. Elgin to Hamilton, 3 February 1898, MSS. Eur. D. 509/ix. See also P. Ananda Charlu's dissenting Note, 31 January 1898, J.P. 529/98, vol. 474.

[195] Elgin to Hamilton, 16 December 1897 (appendix), E.P., vol. 15.

[196] Secy. of the Association to Indian Govt., 10 February 1898, India Leg. Proc., vol. 5480, appendix A31.

[197] H.T. Princep to H.B. Smith, 15 December 1897 (appendix), E.P., vol. 71.

[198] *The Pioneer*, 28 January 1898.

[199] Telegram, Viceroy to S.S., (Pr.), 4 February 1898 (appendix), E.P., vol. 21.

[200] Westland to Elgin, 7 February 1898 (appendix), *ibid.*

[201] See Elgin to Hamilton, 10 February 1898 (appendix), *ibid.*, vol. 16. To Mackenzie's attitude, Elgin had taken strong exception and wrote curtly to him that any of his hostile moves would be "intolerable." Elgin to Mackenzie, 12 February 1898, (appendix), *ibid.*, vol. 72. See also Elgin to Hamilton, 17 February 1898, (appendix), *ibid.*, vol. 16. This brought a prompt apology from the Lt. Governor. Mackenzie to Elgin, 12 February 1898 (appendix), *ibid.*, vol. 72.

[202] Elgin to MacDonnell, 6 February 1898, E.P., vol. 72.

[203] Elgin to Hamilton, 24 February 1898 (appendix), *ibid.*, vol. 16.

[204] Report of the Select Committee on the Bill to amend the Penal Code, Para 24, appendix A49, India Leg. Proc., vol. 5479.

[205] See Indian Govt. to S.S., L. No. 12 (Sanitary), 31 March 1897, Para 2, L.M. 14, (San.), 28 April, Para 3, L. No. 15 (San.), 12 May 1897, Para 3, Rev. L.I., vol. 19.

[206] Sandhurst to Hamilton, 29 August 1897, Enc. Sandhurst to Elgin, 29 August 1897, E.P., vol. 72.

Elgin doubted if corpse inspection would not be very unpopular with the women. He pointed out that even in most advanced countries people had to heed their social and religious customs. He gave the example of Lady Rosebery, a Jew, when she died her body was not touched when funeral ceremony began. He added, "If in England among a highly educated section of society, feeling of the kind is so strong, it would be worse than folly for us to neglect or ignore its existence here." Elgin to Hamilton, 30 December 1897. E.P., vol. 15.

[207] *Report of the Indian Plague Commission*, op. cit., Para 36.

[208] Enc. Indian Govt. to S.S., L. No. 4 (San.), 3 February 1898, Rev. L.I., vol. 21.

[209] Telegram, Govt. Bombay to S.S., 13 March 1898, P.S.L.I., vol. 102.

[210] Telegram, Govt. Bombay to S.S., (Pr.), 9 March 1828, MSS, Eur. D. 508/1.

[211] Campbell Report, pp. 23-27.

See also Indian Govt. to S.S., No. 7 (San.), 14 April 1898, Para 3, Rev. L.I., vol. 21.

[212] MacDonnell to Elgin, 29 April 1898, E.P., vol. 72.

[213] See Hamilton to Elgin, 1 April 1898 (appendix), 7 April (appendix), 6 May 1898 (appendix) and 17 June 1898, *ibid.*

[214] Elgin to Hamilton, 28 April, 26 May, 16 June, 14 July 1898, E.P., vol. 16.

[215] Sandhurst to Elgin, 11 May 1898 (appendix), E.P., vol. 72.

See also Resolution Bombay Govt. 27 May 1898, Enc. No. 9, Indian Govt. to S.S., L. No. 12, 16 June 1898, Rev. L.I., vol. 21.

[216] *Report of the Indian Plague Commission, op. cit.*, Para 696.

[217] Telegram, Governor of Bombay to S.S., 17 March 1898, P.S.L.I., vol. 102/1898.

[218] See *Report of the Indian Commission, op. cit.*, Paras 581, 627 and 637.

[219] See the *Preliminary Report of the Plague Commission*, Enc. Nos. 28-32; Indian Govt. to S.S., L. No. 6 (San.), 9 February 1829, Rev. L.I., vol. 24.

[220] 19 July 1897.

[221] 31 July 1897.

CHAPTER VI

# CONCLUSION

Elgin left Calcutta for London on 6 January 1899. Thus ended a momentous viceroyalty.

At the end of Elgin's tenure there was hardly any forum of Indian public opinion which praised him. To some extent, the reason for this attitude was obvious and possibly justified, because a new and uncertain currency system marked the beginning of the administration; controversial cotton and other exise duties and inadequate and unpopular steps to meet unprecedented natural calamities made it a target for criticism; changes in sedition laws earned it still greater unpopularity. The Indian press censured Elgin for not paying due regard to the wishes of the governed.

The *Indu Prakash* wrote: "Whatever allowance may be made for the serious difficulties Lord Elgin had to contend against, the fact is undeniable that his administration has been not only barren of any good results, but positively productive of harm."[1] The *Amrita Bazar Patrika* deplored a viceroyalty which excited "discontent" and abbetted "repression" and thereby demolished the reputation, British statesmen had built in India for justice and generosity.[2] Some others complained that a "thorough going liberal" had been converted into a "narrow minded Anglo-Indian."[3] Another Bombay weekly described Elgin's rule as "pernicious and mischievous in the extreme."[4] Still another newspaper recorded that "Lord Elgin in India has been a type of the very worst Anglo-Indian" and people would rejoice at his retirement.[5] The same opinion was echoed by the *Bengalee* some time later. It described the period as one "wherein their (the people's) sufferings knew no bounds."[6] "Lord Elgin's administration was," wrote the *Hitavadi*, "from beginning to an end, marked by error, want of intelligence and light mindedness."[7]

Many of these comments lack perspective; they were made in

the heat of the moment. Elgin's administration, in fact, was not so barren of results nor was Elgin a reactionary. On the main issue of finance and currency, Elgin showed a good deal of personal concern for protecting Indian interests. He fully realised the dangers of an unnatural monetary standard and tried his best to establish a gold standard in the country. He was equally alive to the monetary needs of the community. In order to meet the demands of the public and famine relief, he released funds from the monetary reserves (the currency balances) and, by 1898, the fluctuations in the exchange rate ended and the Government treasury was enriched. When Elgin left, the Government showed a surplus, but in the process his administration had to absorb the shocks resulting from the changes that had been made in 1893.

The cotton duty controversy was another important event. Elgin was personally extensively criticised by the Indian public and press for his inability to protect the interest of the Indian textile industry. But the decision in this behalf was forced on Elgin, despite his better judgement under pressure from the Home Government acting under the influence of British textile interests. The decision to impose an excise duty on Indian cloth when there was no question of any competition between Indian and Manchester made goods was, no doubt, an unjust one. The decision asquires added significance when it is recalled that it was dictated by a Liberal Government.

Some of Elgin's most notable achievements in the field of railway expansion were obscured on account of other unfavourable developments. He was the first person to appreciate the value of feeder lines in developing hitherto underdeveloped areas and utilised local capital for their construction. The viceroyalty witnessed the maximum growth of railway lines that had ever taken place in a span of five years. Besides, great experiments were made with the system of mixed economy (private sector and public sector) in the public utility services of India. Elgin was personally responsible for organising the railway establishment and initiated financial and administrative planning in India. His activities in connection with the Indian railways were an outstanding example of his sound administrative ability.

His performance in the most difficult time of famine was also commendable. His non-alarmist and definite views proved fruitful. His food policy, though based on the old principle of free trade, was used in the best possible way in the given circumstances.

Finally, Elgin's association with the changes in the sedition law and the plague rules brought him substantial discredit, despite his role in effectively softening the more stringent measures. Elgin, in fact, showed due regard for the wishes of the public and, as a result, many changes were introduced in the sedition laws before they were finally enacted. Had he been of the same opinion as Hamilton, who could have stopped the reimposition of the Vernacular Press Act? To Elgin must be given due credit for containing racial antipathies which were largely overstated by the Anglo-Indian press and the Secretary of State.

The most important change that emerged out of this stirring period was a hardening of the British attitude towards India. It became quite clear that it was most difficult to reconcile liberalism with autocracy. Justice was alright in the abstract and was upheld, but only as long as vital British political and economic interests did not clash with those of India, as happened in the case of the currency question.

The most important charge levelled against Elgin was that he allowed himself to be guided either by the mandate of the Secretary of State or by the advice of the members of his Executive Council. "The retiring Viceroy," wrote the *Tribune*, "proved an apt pupil in their bureaucracy's hands."[8] Expressing thorough disappointment at Elgin's personal weakness, the *Phoenix* asserted that he should not have entered upon his duties unless he was resolved to do his best and should not have acted as a "puppet or entrusted the keeping of his conscience to others."[9] Maintaining the same beat, the *Paisa Akhbar* stated: "Weakness in a Viceroy of India is a sin and weakness has been the most prominent characteristic of Lord Elgin's administration."[10] Nor did the *India* of London, a Congress journal, spare Elgin. Though it credited Elgin with "excellent intentions" and popular sympathies, it added that "perhaps after the experience of his Government some Indians may prefer a Viceroy who, though his views may be far less in harmony with those of the people of the country, has yet sufficient strength of will to make him the ruller and not the puppet of the high officials at Simla."[11] This stigma continued to be attached to Elgin's reputation even after his death.

The Dictionary of National Biography wrote: "His personal influence on affairs was weakened by a retiring disposition and a self-distrust, from which there sprang a subservience to Whitehall that has perhaps no parallel in Viceregal records."[12]

Was Elgin really a puppet in the hands of his officials? This charge is absolutely unfounded. S. Gopal quotes Curzon to prove that Elgin's period was the "apotheosis of bureaucracy."[13] He further asserted that officials acted as they pleased and goes on to cite a case of a certain executive Councillor who openly defied the Viceroy and could ultimately be controlled only with the help of the Cabinet.[14] Gopal has used this citation completely out of context. The real issue was the imposition of excise duty on Indian cloth and yarn to match the import duty on goods from Manchester. Both Pritchard, the then Public Works Member, and Miller, the then legal Member of the Viceroyl's Council were recalcitrant and threatened to vote against the Government in the Legislative Council. Elgin as a matter of fact, faithfully forwarded their views to the Secretary of State and while doing so, he described their strong feelings against the proposed levy. Nowhere did Elgin demand from Fowler that any action be taken against them. Actually, the significance of the incident is completely contrary to that implied by Gopal. It revealed that the British Government had taken a firm stand in spite of the fact that many in the Indian Government, including Elgin, sympathised with the Indian point of view and had given strong expression to it.

Elgin's attitude towards his colleagues *vis-a-vis* the stand of the Secretary of State was in fact, admirable and statesmanlike. Fowler had acted in an indiscreet and thoroughly dictational way. It lay to Elgin's credit that he did not reopen the wound or add salt to it. He politely warned both Pritchard and Miller of the strong feelings of the Home Government and advised against stretching the point too far. Even a minor outburst from the Viceroy could well have led to the resignation of the Councillors which, in turn, would have proved damaging to the reputation of the Indian Government.[15] When passing judgement on someone, it is not enough merely to quote the opinion of a single prejudiced unsympathetic individual and Gopal has himself sub-

## Conclusion 191

sequently testified to the fact that Curzon was a poor judge of men.[16]

Elgin was, in fact, dominating and assertive, but rarely arrogant. When the Bengal Government opposed the Central Government, Elgin was sufficiently assertive and saw to it that the local government did act contrary to the decided policy. Of course, he did not catch Mackenzie, the Lieutenant-Governor of Bengal, by the ear or punch him on the nose, but in his usual discreet but forthnight way got round him.

Similarly, when Westland and Trevor, two members of the Executive Council, were more inclined to Hamilton's remedy of the "political ill" of the time, he squarely brought them to his side so that the Secretary of State would not get the opportunity of forcing the hands of the Government. It is a tribute to Elgin's administrative ability that he was able to maintain complete discipline in his administration, in spite of the fact that many of his senior officials would have preferred to take a much harder line against Indian demands, than he was willing to allow.

Elgin had a way of getting things done by his subordinates without giving the impression of any undue dominance. An example was the way he handed the issue of the Legislative Council for the Punjab concerning which Elgin had strong feelings. So did Fitzpatrick, the Lieutenant-Governor of the Punjab, but in the opposite direction. Elgin avoided a headlong collision and waited till Fitzpatrick retired; when he made the acceptance of his view by the new Lieutenant-Governor, Mackworth Young, the price of promotion. He thus avoided an unpleasant confrontation like the one Curzon had with Young on the issue of the creation of a separate Province on the North Western frontier.

Elgin did, of course, consult his colleagues on almost all major issues, but this did not imply either weakness or subservience. After discussion on important issues, Elgin usually proceeded, on his own, to recommend, execute or reject policies. The execution of famine policy, particularly food policy, is a pointer in this direction. As regards railways, Elgin more than anyone else was responsible for whatever happened during this period.

Similarly, in dealing with plague, he showed robust commonsense and the policy which finally came to be followed was largely of his working. On technical matters like the currency question, he depended upon the experts though here too, he took keen personal interest. There was certainly nothing wrong in having adopted this attitude. It is characteristic of a sound administrator to interfere as little as possible in the matters where he lacks personal knowledge or understanding.

Yet another of Elgin's distinctive characteristics was his belief in giving credit where it was due and, often, doing this publicly. In a letter to Sandhurst in connection with his plague activities Elgin wrote: "I am a great believer in *Palman qui meruite ferat*. You have fought this fight against plague, and I believe you are about to emerge triumphant, and I should like your name to stand alone in connection with it."[17] Much of the adverse criticism against him resulted either from attaching too much importance to one single issue or in mistaking his unassuming nature for weakness or from a lack of understanding of his administrative policies in their totality.

If, on the one hand, the Indian press assailed Elgin bitterly; the Anglo-Indian and British press praised him lavishly on the other. The *Times of India* called him a "statesman of unpretentious but solid attributes."[18] The *Pioneer* described his all round operations as "highly systematised."[19] *The Times* (London) wrote: "It is but common justice to say that LORD ELGIN has more than justified the wisdom of Mr GLADSTONE's selection. The difficulties with which he has had to contend have been rarely equalled, even in the annals of India. He has manfully confronted them all."[20] These observations were not necessarily impartial either.

The fact of the matter is that Elgin's administration was a period of problem—some old and some new. He had hardly any time to initiate reforms, except in the field of railways. Neither in the field of economics nor in that of politics did Elgin display new or invigorating ideas. The economic aim of his policy was based on the principles of free trade and private enterprise. Even during the famine of 1897 this aim remained the main guiding feature.

The political aim of his policy was to draw the discontented and educated element out into the open and offer them constructive outlets. Yet, in the implementation of this policy, the Government achieved just the opposite. In most part, the response of the

## Conclusion

Government was not active enough or liberal enough to keep pace with the growing political consciousness of the Indian people.

In the field of practical administration, Elgin boldly tackled many problems. He left for Curzon a rich exchequer, an effective famine administration and, at last, a sound plague policy. In this way, he prepared the ground for Curzon's more ambitious plans. Elgin's period was thus a fitting prelude to Curzon's.

### NOTES

[1] 26 December 1898, Bomb. N.N.R., 1899, See also *Kesari*, 27 December 1898, *ibid*.

[2] 3 November 1898, Selections from the Indian Newspapers, Thagi and Dakaiti Department, P.S.L.I., vol. 110.

[3] *Akhbar-i-Am*, 19 October 1898, *ibid*.
See also *Indian Spectator, Gujrati. Champion*, 23 October 1898; *Sudharak*, 24 October; *Indu Prakash*, 24 October; *Kesari*, 25 October 1898, Bomb. N.N.R., 1898.

[4] *Indu Prakash*, 25 October 1898, *ibid*.

[5] *Prabhat*, 9 April 1898, *ibid*.

[6] 7 January 1899.

[7] 6 January 1899, Bengal N.N.R. 1899. See also *Bangawasi*, 6 January 1899, *ibid*.

[8] 1 November 1898, Selections from the Indian Newspapers, Thagi and Dakaiti Department, P.S. L.I., vol. 110.

[9] 26 October 1898, *ibid*.

[10] 26 October 1898, *ibid*.

[11] 28 October 1898, *ibid*.
R.C. Dutt in an article written for the *Indian Mirror* considered that Curzon administration "would be a better change after that of Lord Elgin." Quoted in T.N. Gupta, *Life and Works of Romesh Chandra Datta*, p. 239.

[12] D.N.B., 1912-1928, p. 72.

[13] S. Gopal, *British Policy in India*, 1858-1905, p. 180.

[14] *Ibid*., p. 181.

[15] See Elgin to Miller, 7 November 1894; Elgin to Pritchard, 28 December 1894, E.P., vol. 65.

[16] *British Policy in India*, p. 250.

[17] Elgin to Sandhurst, 18 March 1897, E.P., vol. 70.

[18] 17 October 1898.

[19] 21 October 1898.

[20] 17 October 1898. See also *The Times*, 3 January 1899.

# BIBLIOGRAPHY

### UNPUBLISHED SOURCES

*I. Private Papers*
*A. Elgin Papers.* Correspondence of Lord Elgin relating to the Indian phase of his career. India Office Library (I.O.L.), (MSS. Eur. F. 84), vols. 1-141. (There are also several letters in the possession of the family which have not been deposited with I.O.L. and these letters throw valuable light on Lord Elgin's character and his early life.)
*B. Other Private Papers*
Bruce, Lady E., *Diary, 1894-96.* I.O.L. (Reel No. 430).
*Curzon Collection.* I.O.L. MSS. EUR. F. 111, vols. 158-168, vol. 240, vol. 268.
*Gladstone Papers.* British Museum, ADD. MSS. 44229, 44287, 44290, 44496-8, 44502-3, 44515, 44517, and 44789.
*Hamilton Collection.* I.O.L. MSS. EUR. C. 125-126, vols. 1-3. MSS. EUR. D. 508-510.
*Kilbracken Collection (Arthur Godley),* vols. 1-29. I.O.L. MSS. EUR. F. 102.
*Lansdowne Papers.* I.O.L. MSS. EUR. D. 558, vols. 1-10.
*Ripon Papers.* British Museum, Add. MSS. 43515-6, and 43526.
*Lee-Warner Collection.* I.O.L., MSS. EUR. F. 92.
*Wolverhampton Collection (Sir H.H. Fowler).* I.O L., MSS. EUR. C. 145.

### GOVERNMENT RECORDS

Bengal Native Newspaper Reports 1893-99.
Bills of Exchange drawn on India (Correspondence and Statistics), 1893-1902.
Bombay Native Newspaper Reports, 1893-99.
Finance Departmental Papers. India Office
    1893 vols. 1194, 1216, 1225-6, 1229, 1233-4, 1239-40, 1244
    1894 vols. 1256, 1265, 1271, 1281-2, 1284, 1295, 1302, 1307, 1309-10
    1895 vols. 1366, 1370, 1372, 1376
    1896 vols. 1380, 1382-4
    1897 vols. 1386, 1388-90
    1898 vols. 1393-4

## Bibliography 195

    1899 vols. 1399
Financial Despatches to India (original drafts) 1892-99, vols. 34-41.
Financial Despatches to India (copies) 1892-99, vols. 39-46.
Financial letters received from India
    1892 vol. 173
    1893 vol. 176
    1894 vol. 179
    1895 vol. 182
    1896 vol. 185
    1897 vol. 188
    1898 vol. 191
    1899 vol. 194
Financial Enclosures received from India 1892-99, vols. 174-5, 177-8, 180-1, 183-4, 186-8, 189-90, 192-3, 195-6.
Indian Council Minutes (dissents by the Members of the Council)
    original vol. 5
    copy vol. 2
India Finance and Commerce Proceedings
    1892 vols. 4174-5
    1893 vols. 4392-5
    1894 vols. 4604-7
    1895 vols. 4807-10
    1896 vols. 5025-7, 5029
    1897 vols. 5257-60A
    1898 vols. 5484-88
India Home (Judicial) Proceedings
    1896 vols. 4969-72
    1897 vols. 5194-5
    1898 vols. 5428-30
India Home (Municipal) Proceedings
    1897 vol. 5186
    1898 vol. 5419
    1899 vol. 5646
India Home (Public) Proceedings
    1893 vols. 4341-2
    1894 vols. 4550-1
    1895 vols. 4747-8
    1896 vols. 4958-9
    1897 vols. 5180-1
    1898 vols. 5413-4
    1899 vols. 5638-40
India Legislative Proceedings
    1897 vols. 5253-5
    1898 vols. 5479-82
India Loans Miscellaneous Papers 1857-1898 (not listed at the India Office Library)
India Sanitary Proceedings
    1897 vols. 5188-91

1898 vols. 5421-5
1899 vols. 5648-52
India Separate Revenue (Finance and Commerce) Proceedings
    1894 vol. 4608
    1895 vol. 4811
    1896 vols. 5030-1
    1897 vols. 5261-2
India Statistic and Commerce (Finance and Commerce) Proceedings
    1894 vol. 4606
    1895 vol. 4809
    1896 vol. 5028
    1897 vol. 5260
    1898 vol. 5487
Judicial and Public Departmental Papers India Office
    1894 vols. 367-8, 372, 380-2, 384, 386
    1895 vols. 389-90, 395, 397, 404, 409
    1896 vols. 420, 422, 429
    1897 vols. 440, 449-56, 459, 461-2, 465-66, 468
    1898 vols. 474, 479, 486-7
Madras Native Newspaper Reports 1893-99
Military and Marine letters received from India
    1893-1898 vols. 69-74
Minutes of Council of Secretary of State
    1894-98 vols. 72-81
North Western Provinces and Oudh Native Newspaper Reports 1893-99
Political and Secret letters and Enclosures received from India
    1897 and 1898 vols. 91-110
Public Despatches to India
    1894-98 vols. 14-19
Public and General letters received from India
    1894-98 vols. 19 to 25
Public Works Departmental Papers India Office
    1893 vols. 375, 396
    1894 vols. 402-4, 407, 411-16, 419-27
    1895 vols. 432, 434, 442-4, 446-8, 451
    1896 vols. 455, 458-61, 463, 466, 471, 475
    1897 vols. 480, 487-9, 492-3, 498, 500
    1898 vols. 502-3, 518-19, 522
    1899 vols. 541, 544-5
Public Works Despatches to India
    1892-99 vols. 13-20
Public Works letters received from India
    1892-95 vol. 29
    1895-1901 vol. 30
Punjab Native Newspaper Reports
    1894-99
Railway Despatches to India
    1892-99 vols. 12-19

# Bibliography

Railway and Telegraph letters received from India
   1892-1899 vols. 34-41
Revenue and Agriculture (Famine) Proceedings
   1896 vol. 4982
   1897 vols. 5203-5209
   1897 vols. 5438-5441
Revenue Statistics and Commerce Departmental Papers. India Office
   1894 vols. 324, 359, 393
Revenue and Statistic Despatches to India (copies)
   1892-9 vols. 13-20
Revenue letters received from India
   1892-1900 vols. 13 to 35
Summary of various Departments of Lord Lansdowne
Summary of the various Departments of Lord Elgin

## PUBLISHED SOURCES (OFFICIAL)

*Parliamentary Papers*

| Vol. | Year | No. | Description |
| --- | --- | --- | --- |
| 80 | 1877 | [c. 1870] | Statement of Trade of British India for five years. 1871-72 to 1875-76. |
| 62 | 1880 | [c. 2591] | Report of the Indian Famine Commission—Part I. |
| 62 | 1880 | [c. 2735] | Part II relating to measures of Famine Protection and Prevention. |
| 65 | 1893 | [c. 7060.11] | Appendices to Report of the Indian currency committee. 1893. |
| 60 | 1894 | [c. 7453] | Administrative Report on the Railways in India for 1893-94. |
| 73 | 1895 | [c. 7845] | Administrative Report on the Railways in India for 1894-95. |
| 73 | 1895 | [c. 202] | Papers regarding Cotton Import Duties. |
| 73 | 1895 | [c. 7602] | Indian Tariff Act and Cotton Duties. |
| 62 | 189o | [c. 8136] | Administrative Report on the Railways in India 1895-96. |
| 62 | 1896 | [c. 8259] | Papers relating to Cotton and Excise Duties. |
| 63 | 1897 | [c. 8386] | Papers Relating to Plague. |
| 63 | 1897 | [c. 8511] | Papers Relating to Plague. |
| 63 | 1897 | [c. 8800] | Papers Relating to Plague. |
| 64 | 1897 | [c. 8302] | Papers Regarding Famine Relief. |
| 64 | 1897 | [c. 8388] | Papers Regarding Famine Relief. |
| 64 | 1897 | [c. 8504] | Papers Regarding Famine Relief. |
| 65 | 1897 | [88] | Papers relating to Railways to encourage Private Agencies. |

| | | | |
|---|---|---|---|
| 65 | 1897 | [328] | Statement of Moral and Material Progress in India 1895-96. |
| 65 | 1897 | [c. 8297] | Trade Review of British India 1895-96. |
| 65 | 1897 | [c. 8338] | Trade Tables of British India 1891-92 to 1895-96. |
| 65 | 1897 | [c. 8518] | Administrative Report on Railways in India 1896-97. |
| 62 | 1898 | [c. 8860] | Papers regarding the Famine Relief Operations in India. |
| 62 | 1898 | [c. 8737] | Papers regarding the Famine Relief Operations in India. |
| 62 | 1898 | [c. 8739] | Papers regarding the Famine Relief Operations in India. |
| 62 | 1898 | [c. 8812] | Papers regarding the Famine Relief Operations in India. |
| 62 | 1898 | [c. 8823] | Papers regarding the Famine Relief Operations in India. |
| 63 | 1898 | [c. 8713] | Papers regarding Military Operations undertaken on North Western Frontiers. |
| 63 | 1898 | [c. 8714] | Papers regarding Military Operations undertaken on North Western Frontiers. |
| 63 | 1898 | [c. 8871] | Papers relating to Amendment in the law relating to Sedition. |
| 63 | 1898 | [c. 8800] | Papers relating to Outbreak of Plague in India. |
| 64 | 1898 | [c. 8733] | Tables relating to Trade of British India 1892-3 to 1896-97. |
| 64 | 1898 | [c. 8921] | Administrative Report of the Railways in India 1897-98. |
| 31 | 1899 | [c. 9178] | Report of the Indian Famine Commission 1898. |
| 31 | 1899 | [c. 9390] | Report of the Committee appointed to inquire into the Indian Currency. |
| 33 | 1899 | [c. 9258] | Appendix to the Report by Indian Famine Commission, 1898, vol. vii. |
| 66 Part 1 | 1899 | [211] | Statement of Moral and Material Progress in India 1897-98. |
| 66 | 1899 | [c. 9120] | Review and Tables relating to the trade of British India for five years 1893-94 to 1897-98. |
| 66 | 1899 | [c. 9369] | Administrative Report on Railways 1898-99. |
| 30 | 1900 | [Cd. 139] | Report from Commission on Plague —Minutes of evidences. |

# Bibliography

| 31 | 1900 | [cd. 140] | Report from Commission on Plague —Minutes of evidences. |
| 32 | 1900 | [cd. 141] | Report from Commission on Plague —Minutes of evidences. |
| 72 | 1902 | [cd. 810] | Report of the Indian Plague Commission with summary. |
| 70 | 1902 | [cd. 876] | Report of the Indian Famine Commission 1901. |
| 47 | 1903 | [cd. 1713] | Report of the Administration and Working of Indian Railways [Thomas Robertson Report]. |
| 66 | 1904 | [cd. 1851] | Report of the Indian Agriculture Commission 1901-3. |
| 75 | 1908 | [cd. 4111] | Report of the Committee on Indian Railway Finance and Administration [J.L. Mackay Committee]. |
| 10 | 1921 | [CMD. 1512] | Railway Committee Report [Acworth Committee]. |

*Parliamentary Debates 1894-99*
Proceedings of the Council of Governor-General in India 1892-1899.
Annual Financial Statements of the Government of India 1892-1899.
Monthly Records of the Manchester Chamber of Commerce 1893-99.
Report on the Immigration into Assam and Cachar, 1891-1900.
Report of the Brussels International Monetary Conference 1892.
Report of the Indian Currency Committee 1893.
Papers relating to Currency Question, Simla, 1893.
Reports of Railway Administration 1893-99.
Report of the Bengal Chamber of Commerce 1893-99.
Report of the Bombay Chamber of Commerce 1893-99.
Report of the Indian National Congress 1893-1901.
Report on the Outbreak of Bubonic Plague in Bombay, 1896-97 (by P.C.H. Snow Municipal Commissioner for the City of Bombay).
Report of Bubonic Plague in Bombay by W.F. Gatacre, Chairman Plague Committee, 1896-97.
Report of the Bombay Plague Committee on the Plague in Bombay 1897-98.
Report of the Indian Famine Charitable Relief Fund 1897.
The Plague in India vol. i-iv (Nathan, R.) 1898.
Report of the Royal Commission on the Expenditure of India vols. i-iv, 1900.
Report on Rise of Prices and Wages (K.L. Datta) 1914.
Report of Indian Industrial Commission 1916-18.
Report of the Committee appointed to investigate Revolutionary conspiracies in India 1918.
Report on Indian Constitutional Reforms 1918.
Statistical Abstract of British India 1891-2 to 1903-4.
Statistical Abstract United Kingdom 1891-2 to 1903-4.

NEWSPAPERS

Bangalee
Englishman
Pioneer
Times of India
The Times

ARTICLES, PAMPHLETS, TRACTS

Ahluwalia, M.M., "Press and India's Struggle for freedom 1858-1909," *Journal of Indian History*, vol. xxxviii, part iii, 1960.
Atkinson, Fred., *The Indian Currency Question*, Allahabad, 1894.
Atkinson, F.J., "Average Income of India 1875-1895," *Journal of the Royal Statistical Society*, June 1902.
——, "Silver Prices in India,"*Journal of Royal Statistical Society*, 1894 and 1897.
Baden Powel, "Proposed Law Regarding Alienation of Agricultural Land in the Punjab," *Asiastic Review*, 1900.
Banerjea, S.N., *The Trumpet Voice of India*, London, 1909.
Barbour, D., *The Anglo-Indian and the Rupee*, Bombay, 1892.
——, *The Currency Question from an Indian Point of View*, London, 1894.
Beales, H.L., "The Great Depression in Industry and Trade," *The Economic History Review*, vol. 1, No. 5, 1934.
Bell, Horace, "Recent Railway Policy in India," *Journal of the Society of Arts*, vol. xivi, 1899.
Bell, H., "Railways and Famine," *Journal of the Society of Arts*, vol. xli, 1901.
Bhalchandra Krishna (Sir), *Overcrowding in Bombay*, Bombay, 1904.
Blang, M., "Productivity of Capital in the Lancashire Cotton Industry during the Nineteenth Century," *Economic History Review*, 1960-61.
Bose, A.M., *Backward or Forward*, London, 1899.
Chand Lal, *An Essay on the Decline of Native Industries: Its Causes, Evils and Cure*, Lahore, 1897.
Charlu, A.P., *Six-fold need of Indian Politics*, Madras, 1895.
——, *On Indian Politics*, Madras, 1899.
Cole, W.A., "The Measurement of Economic Growth," *The Economic History Review*, 1958.
Coppock, D.J., "British Industrial Growth during Great Depression (1873-96): A Pessimistic View," *The Economic History Review*, vol. xvii, 1964.
Cotton, H.J.S., *The Problems of India*, London, 1905.
——, *India: A Policy and a Prospect*, London, Undated.
Cunningham, Sir, H.S., "Indian Famines," *East India Association*, vol. 28, 1897.
Dar, P.T. Bishan Narayan, *Signs of the Times*, Lucknow, 1895.
Danvers, Juland, "The Progress of Railways and Trade in India." *Journal of the Society of Arts*, vol. xxxvii, 1889.

Deane, P., "Contemporary Estimates of the National Income" (First half, second half, of the Nineteenth Century), *Economic History Review*, April 1956, April 1957.

Dunn, C.L., "The Economic Value of the Prevention of Disease," *Indian Journal of Economics*, January 1924.

Elliot, C.A., "Recent Famines in India and Reports of the Second Famine Commission," *Asiatic Quarterly Review*, vol. 8, 1899.

———, "On Measures Taken by the Government for the Prevention of Famine," *Journal of the Society of Arts*, vol. 45, 1897.

Forrest, G.W. Sir, *"The Famine in India,"* London, 1897.

Fowler, William, *Indian Currency: An Essay*, London, 1899.

Foxwell, H.S., *A Criticism of Lord Farrer on the Monetary Standard* (Reprinted from The National Revenue for January 1895), London.

Gallaghar, J. and R. Robinson, "The Imperialism of Free Trade," *The Economic History Review*, vol. vi, 1953.

Ghose, S.C., *Indian Railway Finance*, Calcutta, 1912.

Griffin, L., "The Breakdown of Frontier Policy," *The Nineteenth Century*, vol. xlii, October 1897.

Gupta, H.L., "The Economic Impact of West on Indian Industries," *Journal of Indian History*, vol. xxxviii, April 1960.

Handasy, Geo. de Dic, *International Bullion Money*, London, 1894.

Harnety, P., "The Indian Cotton Duties Controversy 1894-6," *English Historical Review*, vol. 77, October 1962.

———, "Nationalism and Imperialism" (The Viceroyalty of Curzon) *Journal of Indian History*, vol. xli, Par. 11, August 1963.

Holderness, T.W., "Indian Famine of 1899," *Journal of the Society of Arts*, vol. 50, 1902.

Hope, Theodore C., "The Rationale of the Railways in India," *Journal of the Society of Arts*, vol. xxxviii, 1890.

*The Indian Services and the depreciation of the Rupee*, London, 1893.

Howard, H.F., *India and the Gold Standard*, London, 1911.

Jamieson, George, *The Silver Question, Injury to British Trade and Manufacture*, London, 1895.

Kellas, J.G., "The Liberal Party in Scotland 1876-1895," *Scottish Historical Review*, vol. xliv, April 1965.

Khan, Ajmal, *Plague*, Delhi, undated.

Lal, Ranchore, *Letters on Currency Questions*, Ahemadabad, 1895.

Lely, Sir F.S.P., "Political Side of Famines in India," *Journal of the Society of Arts*, vol. 55, 1907.

Liston, W.G., "The Plague Military Lecture, 1924," *British Medical Journal*, 1924, vol. 1.

Macdonagh, O., "The Anti-Imperialism of Free Trade," *The Economic History Review*, vol. xiv, 1961-2.

Macleod, H.D., *Indian Currency*, London, 1898.

Malabari, B.M., *The Indian Problem*, Bombay, 1894.

Malabari, Behranji, *India in 1897*, Bombay, 1898.

Marriott, Edward Frere, *The Indian Currency Question*, London, 1899.

Moore, R.J., "Imperialism and Free Trade Policy in India 1853-4," *The Economic History Review*, vol. xviii, 1964.
Musson, A.E., "The Great Depression in Britain 1873-1896," *The Journal of Economic History*, vol. xix, June 1959.
——, "British Industrial Growth 1875-96: A Balanced View," *The Economic History Review*, vol. xvii, 1964.
Naoroji, Dadabhai. *Speech on Financial Relations between U.K. and India*, London, undated.
——, *Statements to Indian Currency Committee 1898*, London, 1898.
Norman, John Henry, *The Currency Problem. Is it False Political Economy*, London, 1895.
Northbrook, E., *North Western Frontier of India*, London, 1898.
Paish, George, "Great Britain's Capital Investments in other Lands," *Journal of Royal Statistical Society*, vol. lxxii, Part 111, 1909.
——, "Great Britain's Capital Investments in Individual Colonial and Foreign Countries," *Journal of Royal Statistical Society* vol. lxxiv, part 11, January 1911.
Parry, J.W., "The Coming of Railways of India and their Prospects," *Journal of the Society of Arts*, vol. 43, 1895.
Phipson, Major Cecil B., *India's Difficulties: Some Ways Out of Them: Indian Poverty and Indian Famines*, London, 1903.
"India under Lord Elgin," *Quarterly Review*, vol. 189, 1899.
"Indian Famine and there Remedies," *Quarterly Review*, vol. 195, 1902.
Rees, "Fighting Famines in India," *Nineteenth Century*, March 1897.
Samarath, V.M., "Famines in India," *Calcutta Review*, 1902.
Sawtell, A., *Indian and the Fiscal Problem*, Lahore, 1903.
Sethur, Deshpande, S.S. Sethur, and K.G. Deshpande [Eds.], *A Full and Authentic Report of the Trial of Bal Gangadhar Tilak*, Bombay, 1897.
Thorburn, S.S., "Agireola Redivivus," *Asiatic Quarterly Review*, 1901.
Wacha, D.E., *Indian Railway Finance*, Madras, 1912.
——, *Indian Military Expenditure*, Madras, 1911.
——, *Indian Currency Commission*, Bombay, 1913.
Wadia, J.A., *The Artificial Currency of the Commerce of India*, Bombay, 1902.
Wallace R., *Lecture on Famines in India*, Edinburgh, 1900.
Walton, J., "Railways Extension in India and its Relation to the Trade of India and the United Kingdom," *Journal of the Society of Arts*, vol. 42, 1894.
Wedderburn, Naoroji, Hume, Bannerjee, *A Call to Arms*, undated.
Wedderburn, "Agricultural Banks for India," *Asiatic Review*, 1898.
Wilson, Charles, "The Entrepreneur in the Industrial Review in Britain," *History*, June 1957.

OTHER WORKS

Acworth, W.M. and W.T. Stephenson, *The Elements of Railway Economics*, London, 1924.

# Bibliography

Adarkar, B.P., *The Indian Tariff Problem*, Allahahad, 1936.
———, *The Indian Monetary Policy*. Allahabad, 1939.
Ahmed Sufia, *Some Aspects of the History of the Muslim Community in Bengal, 1884-1912*, unpublished, Ph.D. Thesis, London, 1960.
Ambedkar, B.R., *The Evolution of Provincial Finance in British India*. London, 1925.
———, *The Problem of the Rupee*, London, 1923.
Anstey, Vera, *Economic Development of India*. London, 1952.
———, *The Trade of Indian Ocean*, London, 1929.
Ashley, P. *Modern Tariff History*, London, 1904.
Ashworth, William, *A Short History of the International Economy 1850-1950*, London, 1954.
Argove, D., *Moderates and Extremists in the Indian National Movement, 1883-1920*, Bombay, 1967.
Bengal, J.C., *History of Indian Association 1876-1951*, Calcutta, 1953.
Balkrishna, *Commercial Relation between India and England*, London 1924.
Balkrishna, R., *Studies in Indian Economic Problems*, London, 1959.
Banerjea, P., *A History of Indian Taxation*, London, 1930.
Banerjea, P.N., *Fiscal Policy in India*, London, 1922.
Banerjea, S.N., *Speeches*, vol. i-v, Calcutta, 1894, 1896.
———, *A Nation in Making*, Calcutta, 1925.
———, *Speeches and Writing*, Madras, undated.
Beran, Paul, *Political Economy of Growth*, New Delhi, 1957.
Barbour, David, *The Theory of Bimetallism*, London, 1895.
Barns, M., *The Indian Press*, London, 1940.
Bayley C.A., *The Local Roots of Indian Politics: Allahabad, 1980-1920*, Oxford, 1975.
Beames, J., *Memoirs of a Bengal Civilian*, London, 1951.
Bell, Horace, *Railway Policy in India*, London 1894.
Bharucha, K.B., *A History of the Cotton Mill Industry in Western India*, Bombay, undated.
Bharucha, S.B., *Speeches on Indian Economics*, Bombay, undated.
Bhatia, B.M., *Famines in India*, Bombay, 1963.
Blunt, Sir Edward, *The Indian Civil Service*, London, 1931.
Bonner, Edna, *The Economic Policy of Government of India, 1898-1905*, unpublished M.A. Thesis, London, 1955.
Bowley, A.L., *Wages in England in the Nineteenth Century*, London, 1900.
Brace, Paul, *Language, Religion and Politics in North India*, Cambridge, 1974.
Broomfield, J.H., *Elite Conflict in a Plural Society: Twentieth Century Bengal*, Berkley, 1968.
Buchanan, D.H., *The Development of Capitalist Enterprise in India*, New York, 1934.
Buckle, G.E. (Ed.), *The Letters of Queen Victoria*, vols. II and III, London, 1931, 1932.
Calvert, H., *The Wealth and Welfare of the Punjab*, London, 1922.

*Combridge History of India*, vol. vi, 1932.
Campbell, George, *Memoirs of my Indian Career*, 2 vols. London, 1893.
Chablani C.L., *Indian Currency, Banking and Exchange*, London, 1932.
Chambers, J.D., *The Workshop of the World: British Economic History from 1820 to 1880*, London, 1961.
Chand, Gyan, *India's Teeming Million*, 1939.
Chandra, Bipan, *The Rise and Growth of Economic Nationalism in India: Economic Policies of Indian Leadership, 1880-1905*, New Delhi, 1966.
Chandravarkar, N.G., *Speeches and Writings*, Bombay, 1911.
Charlu, A., *Speeches in the Supreme Council 1896-8*, Madras, 1903.
Chatterton, A., *Industrial Evolution in India*, Madras, 1912.
Chaudhri, R., *Evolution of Indian Industry*, Calcutta, 1939.
Chesney, Sir George, *Indian Polity*, London, 1904.
Chintamani, C.Y., *Indian Politics since Mutiny*. Allahabad, 1937.
Chirol, Valentine, *Indian Unrest*, London, 1910.
Choksey, R.D., *Economic Life in Bombay 1818-1939*, Bombay, 1963.
Chapham, Sir John, *Great Britain and Free Trade*, Cambridge, 1909.
Clapham, J.H., *Economic Development of France and Germany*, Cambridge, 1921.
Clapham, Sir John, *An Economic History of Modern Britain*, vol. I, London, Cambridge, 1930.
Cole, G.D.H., *Introduction to Economic History 1750-1952*, London, 1953.
(The) *Constitutional Year Book*, London, 1893-99.
Cotton, H.J.S., *Indian and Home Memoires*, London, 1911.
Coupland, R., *India a Resatement*, Oxford, 1945.
Court, W.H.B., *A Concise Economic History of Modern Britain*, Cambridge, 1954.
———, *British Economic History 1870-1914 Commentary and Documents*, London, 1956.
Coyajee, J.C., *The Indian Currency System 1835-1926*, Madras, 1930.
———, *The Indian Fiscal Problem*, Calcutta, 1924.
Cross (Lord), *A Political History 1868-1900*, (Privately Printed), 1903.
Crawford, A., *Our Troubles in Poona and the Deccan*, London, 1897.
Cumming, John, *Modern India*, Oxford, 1932.
Cumming, J. (Ed.), *Political India 1832-1932: A Cooperative Survey of a Century*, Oxford, 1932.
Currie, Maj.-Gen. Fendal, *Below the Surface*, London, 1900.
Curzon, G.N., *British Government in India: The Story of the Viceroy and the Government House*, London, 1925.
Curzon, *Speeches* (vol. i-iv), Calcutta, 1904.
Dadachanji, B.E., *History of Indian Curreny and Exchange*, Bombay, 1928.
Darling, M., *Rusticus Loquitm*, London, 1930.
Darling, M.L., *Punjab Peasant in Prosperity and Debt*, London, 1932.
Dantwala, M.L., *A Hundred Years of Indion Cotton*, Bombay, 1948.
Das, A.K., H.N. Banerjee, *The Impact of Tea Industry in the Life of the Tribals of West Bengal*, Calcutta, 1964.
Das, M.N., *India Under Morley and Minto*, London, 1964.

# Bibliography

Davies, C.C., *The Problems of the North Western Frontier 1890-1908*, Cambridge, 1932.
Desai, A.R., *Social Background of Indian Nationalism*, Bombay, 1954.
Dey, H.L., *Indian Tariff Problem*, London, 1933.
Digby, William, *Prosperous British India*, London, 1901.
Donogh, W.R., *The History and Law of Sedition*, Calcutta, 1917.
Dutt, R.C., *The Economic History of India in the Victorian Age*, London, 1904.
——, *Famine in India*, London, 1900.
Dutt, R.P., *India Today*, London, 1949.
——, *Britain's Crisis of British Empire*, London, 1949.
Dutt, S.C., *Conflicting Tendencies in Indian Economic Thought*, undated.
Elgin, Earl, *Speeches*, Calcutta, 1899.
Elliot, J.C., *Frontier 1839-1947: The Story of the North West Frontier of India*, London, 1968.
Embree, A.T., *India's Search for National Identity*, New York, 1972.
Ensor, R.E.K., *Oxford History of England 1870-1914*, Oxford, 1936.
Forrest, G.W., *The Administration of Lansdowne*, Calcutta, 1894.
Fowler, E.H., *The Life of Lord Wolverhampton*, London, 1912.
Fraser, A.H.L., *Among Indian Rajahs and Ryots*, London, 1911.
Fraser, L., *India Under Curzon and After*, London, 1911.
Frykenburg, R.E. (Ed.), *Land Control and Social Structure in Indian History*, Madison, 1969.
Fuller, B. (Sir), *Some Personal Experience*, London, 1930.
Furnivall, J.S., *Colonial Policy and Practice*, Cambridge, 1948.
Gadgil, D.R., *The Industrial Evolution of India*, Madras, 1933.
Gallaghar, John, Garden Johnson, and A. Seal (Eds.), *Locality, Province and Nation: Essays on Indian Politics 1870-1940*, Cambridge, 1973.
Gandhi, M.P., *The Indian Cotton Textile Industry*, Calcutta, 1930.
Garth, Richard, *Few Plain Truths about India*, London, 1888.
Ghose, H.P., *The Newspaper in India*, Calcutta, 1952.
——, *Press and Press Laws in India*, Calcutta, 1930.
Ghosh, P.C., *The Development of Indian National Congress 1892-1909*, Calcutta, 1960.
Ghosh, Sujata, *The British Indian Association*, Calcutta, undated.
Ghose, S.C., *Organisation of Railways*, Calcutta, 1927.
——, *A Paper on Railway Economics*, Calcutta, 1924.
——, *Lectures on Indian Railway Economy*, Calcutta, 1923.
Gokhale, G.K., *Speeches*, Madras, 1916.
Gopal, R., *Indian Muslims: A Political History 1859-1947*, London, 1959.
——, *Lokamanya Tilak*, Bombay, 1956.
Gopal, S., *The Viceroyalty of Lord Ripon 1880-1884*, London, 1953.
——, *The British Policy in India 1858-1905*, Cambridge, 1965.
Gopala Krishna, P.K., *Development of Economic Ideas in India, 1880-1950*, New Delhi, 1959.
Greenberger, Allen J., *The British Image of India*, London, 1969.
Griffith, P., *The British Impact of India*, London, 1952.

Gordon, L.A., *Bengal: The Nationalist Movement 1876-1940*, New York, 1974.
Gaunzel, J., *Economic Protectionism*, Washington, 1916.
Gujral, L.M., *Internal Administration of Lord Lytton*, Unpublished Ph.D. Thesis, London, 1958.
Gupta, J.N., *Life and Works of Romesh Chandra Dutt*, London, 1911.
Helery, E., *A History of the English People in 1895-1905*, vol. IV, London, 1929.
Hamilton, G.J., *Trade Relations between England and India*, London 1919.
Hamilton, George (Lord), *Parliamentary Reminiscences and Reflections 1889-1906*, London, 1922.
Hanham, H.J., *Elections and Party Management: Politics in the Time of Disraeli and Gladstone*, London, 1959.
Hansen, Alvin, *Guide to Keynes*, New York, 1953.
Hardy, P., *The Muslims of British India*, Cambridge, 1972.
Harris, J., *Much Sounding of Bugles—The Sieg of Chitral 1895*, London, 1975.
Harris, L., *British Policy on the North Western Frontier*, Unpublished, Ph.D. Thesis, London, 1960.
Hayland, John, S., *G.K. Ghokhale*, Calcutta, 1933.
Hennessy, James Pope, *Lord Crewe*, London, 1955.
Hobson, J.A., *Imperialism: A Study*, London, 1954.
Hoffmann, W., *British Industry 1700-1950*, Oxford, 1955.
Holderness, Sir T.W., *People and Problems of India*, London, 1911.
Hutchins, Francis G., *The Illusion of Premanence: British Imperialism*, Princeton, 1967.
Illbert, C., *The Government of India*, Oxford, 1922.
Imlah, A.H., *Economic Elements in the Pax Britanica*, Cambridge, Messachusetts, 1958.
*Imperial Gazetteer of India*, vols. iii and iv, Oxford, 1907.
*Imperial Gazetteer of India* (Provincial Series).
*Indian National Builders* (in three parts), Madras, undated.
Indian National Congress, *Containing full text of all Presidential Addresses, Reprint of all the Congress Resolutions*, Madras, undated.
Iyer, G.S., *Some Economic Aspects of British Rule in India*, Madras, 1903.
Iyer, K.V., *Indian Railway*, London, 1924.
Iyer, Raghwan, *The Glass Curtain between Asia and Europe*, London, 1965.
Jain, L.C, *Monetary Problems of India*, London, 1933.
James, R.R., *Rosebery*, London, 1963.
Jathar, G.B. and S.G. Beri, *Indian Economics*, vol. 1, 7th Edition (Revised), Madras, 1942.
———, *Indian Economics*, vol. II, 9th Edition. Madras, 1952.
Jenk, L.H., *The Migration of British Capital to 1875*, New York, 1927.
Johnson, G., *Provincial Politics and Indian Nationalism: Bombay and the Indian National Congress*, Cambridge, 1973.

Joshi, G.V., *Writing and Speeches*, Poona, 1912.
Kale and G. Ghokhale, *Economic Reforms*, Poona, 1916.
Kale, V.G., *The Study of Indian Economics*, Poona, 1916.
Karandikar, S.L., *Lokamanya Bal Gangadhar Tilak: The Hercules and Prometheus of Modern India*, Poona, 1957.
Karve, D.G., *Poverty and Population of India*, London, 1936.
Keene, H.G., *The Great Anarchy or Darkness before Dawn*. London, 1901.
Kemmerer, E.W., *Money*, London, 1934.
Keynes, J.M., *Indian Currency and Finance*, London, 1924.
Kitson, G. Clark. *The Making of the Victorian England*, London, 1962.
Konwles, L.C.A., *The Economic Development of the British Overseas Empire*, London, 1928.
Kumar, Ravinder, *Western India in the Nineteenth Century: A Study in Social History of Maharashtra*, London, 1968.
Kuznets, S. et al., *Economic Growth: Brazil, India, Japan*, Durham, 1955.
Loveday Alexander, *The History and Economics of Indian Famine*, London, 1914.
Less-Smith, H.B., *India and Tariff Problem*, London, 1909.
Lilley, W.S., *India and its Problems*, London, 1902.
Limaya, P.M., *The History of the Deccan Education Society: 1880-1935*, Poona, 1935.
Lipsett, H.C., *Lord Curzon in India, 1898-1903*, London, 1903.
Lovett, Verney, *A History of Indian Nationalist Movement*, London, 1920.
Low, S. and L.C. Sanders, *The Political History of England 1837-1901*, London, 1907.
Lyall, Alfred, *The Life of the Marquis of Dufferin and Ava*, vols. I and II, London, 1905.
Majumdar, B., *Militant Nationalism in India and its Socio-Religious Background, 1897-1917*, Calcutta, 1968.
Malhotra, D.K., *History and Problems of Indian Currency 1835-1939*, Lahore, 1939.
Malaviya, M.M., *Speeches*, Madras, undated.
Marx and F. Engels, *On Colonialism*, Moscow, undated.
Masani, R.P., *Britain in India*, London, 1960.
―――, *Dadabhai Naoroji: The Grand Old Man of India*, London, 1939.
Mclane, J.R., *Indian Nationalism and Early Congress*, Princeton, 1977.
McMinn, C.W., *Famine Truths, Half Truths*, London, 1902.
Mehta, S.D., *The Cotton Mills of India, 1854-1954*, Bombay, 1955.
Merewether, F.H.S., *Tour Through the Famine Districts of India*, London, 1897.
Millar, C. Khyber, *British India North West Frontier*, London, 1973.
Misra, B.E., *The Indian Middle Class*, London, 1961.
Misra, J.P., *Administration of India Under Lord Lansdowne, 1889-1894*, New Delhi, 1975.
Moon, P.N., *Imperialism and World Politics*, New York, 1927.
Morrison, T., *The Economic Transition in India*, London, 1928.
Morison, J.L., *The Eigth Earl of Elgin*, London, 1928.

Morley, John, *Life of W.E. Gladstone*, vol. III (1880-1898), London, 1903.
Moulton, E.C., *Lord Northbrook's Indian Administration, 1872-1876*, London, 1968.
Murdoch, John, *Famine, Facts and Fallacies*, London, undated.
Naoroji, D., *Poverty and the Un-British Rule in India*, London, 1901.
Nash, V., *The Great Famine*, London, 1900.
Natarajanj, *History of Indian Journalism*, Delhi, 1954.
Nateran, G.A., *Indian Politics*, Madras, 1898.
Newton Lord, *Lansdowne*, London, 1929.
Nicholson, J.S., *Principles of Political Economy*, London, 1906.
O'Donnell, C.J., *The Failure of Lord Curzon: A Study in Imperialism, An Open Letter to the Earl of Rosebery*, London, 1903, published under the pseudonym of "Twenty-eight years in India."
O'Malley, L.S.S., *The Indian Civil Service*, London, 1931.
O'Malley, L.S., *Modern India and the West*, London, 1941.
Panikar, K.M., *Asia and the Western Dominance*, London, 1953.
Parris, H.W., *Government and the Railways*, London, 1965.
Pearse, A.S., *The Cotton Industry of India*, London, 1930.
Philips, C.H., *Evolution of India and Pakistan. Select Documents*, vol. iv, London, 1962.
Pillai, P.P., *Economic Conditions in India*, London, 1925.
Plotnicov, L. and A. Tuden (Eds.), *Essays in Comparative Social Stratification*, Pittsburg, 1970.
Ponniah, J.S., *Principles of Public Finance*, Madras, 1903.
Pradhan, G.P. and A.K. Bhazat, *Lokmanya Tilak*, Bombay, 1958.
Prasad, Amba, *Indian Railways: History in Public Utility Administration*, London, 1960.
Prasad, B., *The Effects of Improved Transport upon the Distribution of Industry and Population with Special Reference to India*, unpublished M.A. Thesis, London, 1954.
Purshotam Das, Thakurdas, *Evolution of the Cotton Trade of Bombay*, Bombay, 1947.
Rai, Lajpat, *Lala Lajpat Rai: The Man in his Word*, Madras, 1907.
Ramanujam, T.V., *The Function of State Railways in Indian National Economy*, Madras, 1944.
Ranade, M.C., *Essay on Indian Economics*, Bombay, 1898.'
Ranchodas, R. and D.K. Thakore, *The Indian Penal Code*, 3rd Edition, Bombay, 1905.
Rau, S. (K)., *The Crisis in India*, Madras, 1918.
Ray, P., *Development in Indian Foreign Trade*, London, 1934.
Ray, P.C., *Indian Famines: Their Causes and Remedies*, Calcutta, 1901.
Redford, A., *Manchester Merchants and Foreign Trade*, vol. ii, Manchester, 1956.
Reed, Sir S. and P.P. Cadell, *India: The New Phase*, London, 1928.
Rees, J.D., *The Real India*, London, 1908.
Rees, Sir J.D., *Modern India*, London, 1910.

## Bibliography

Robinson, R., J. Gallaghar, and A. Dennu, *Africa and the Victorians*, London, 1961.
*Separatism among Indian Muslims: Politics of the United Princes Muslims, 1860-1923*, Cambridge, 1974.
Roll, Eric, *History of Economic Thought*, New York, 1946.
Rostow, W.W., Gayer and Schwartz, *the Growth and Fluctuations of the British Economy 1790-1850*, Oxford, 1953.
*The British Economy in the 19th Century*, Oxford, 1948.
Rothermund, D., *The Phases of Indian Nationalism and other Essays*, Bombay, 1970.
Roy, N.C., *Indian Civil Service*, London, 1935.
Rushforth, F.V., *The India Exchange Problem*, London, 1921.
Saklatvala, S.D., *History of the Mill Owners' Association Bombay*, Bombay, 1931.
Sanyal, N., *Development of Indian Railway*, Calcutta, 1930.
Sastry, N.S.R., *The Statistical Study of India's Industrial Development*, Bombay, undated.
Saul, S.B., *Studies in British Overseas Trade 1870-1914*, London, 1965.
Saxena, V.K., *Indian Reaction of British Policies, 1898-1911*, Delhi, 1978.
Seal, A., *The Emergence of Indian Nationalism: Competition and Collaboration in Late Nineteenth Century*, Cambridge, 1968.
Seeley, Sir John, *The Expansion of England*, London, 1883.
Shah, K.T., *Sixty Years of Indian Finance*, Bombay, 1921.
——*Trade, Tariff and Transport in India*, London, 1923.
——*Federal Finance in India*, Bombay, 1929.
Shah and Khambatta, *Wealth and Taxable Capacity in India*, London, 1924.
Shah, N.J., *History of Indian Tariffs*, Bombay, 1924.
Shay Theodore, *The Legacy of the Lokmanya: The Political Philosophy of Bal Gangadhar Tilak*, Bombay, 1956.
Shirras, G. Findley, *Indian Finance and Banking*, London, 1919.
Singer, Miton and Bernard S. Cohn (Eds.), *Structure and Change in Society*, Chicago, 1968.
Singh, H.L., *Problems and Policies of the British in India*, Bombay, 1963
Singh, S.N., *Secretary of State and His Council 1859-1919*, Delhi, 1962.
Sinha, N.C., *Studies in Indo-British Economy Hundred Years Ago*, Calcutta, 1946.
Sitaramaya, B.P., *History of Indian National Congress 1885-1935*, Madras, 1935.
*Source Materials for a History of the Freedom Movement in India*, vol. 2, Bombay, 1957.
Spear, P., *India: A Modern History*, Michigan, 1961.
Strachey, John, *The End of Empire*, London, 1959.
Strachey, Sir John, *India and its Administrative Progress*, London, 1911.
Swinson, A., *North West Frontier: People and Events, 1839-1943*, London, 1967.
Tahmankar, D.V., *Lokmanya Tilak*, London, 1946.

Taylor, A.J.P., *The Struggle for Mastery in Europe 1848-1918*, London, 1959.
Thomas, P.J., *The Growth of Federal Finance in India 1833-1939*, London, 1939.
Thomson, S.J., *The Silent India*, London, 1913.
Thompson and Garrett, *The Rise and Fulfilment of British Rule in India*, London, 1934.
Thorburns, *His Majesty's Greatest Subject*, London, 1897.
Thorner, D., *Investment in Empire*, Philadelphia, 1950.
Tinker, High, *A New System of Slavery: The Export of Indian Labour Overseas, 1830-1920*, London, 1977.
Towsend, M., *Asia and Europe*, London, 1901.
Tripathi, A., *The Extremist Challenge Between 1890-1910*, Bombay, 1967.
Tripathi, R.D., *Railways in Modern India*, Bombay, 1941.
Tyson, G.W., *The Bengal Chamber of Commerce and Industry 1853-1953*, Calcutta, 1953.
Vakil, C.N., *Tariff Policy in India*, Bombay, 1937.
——— *Economic Outlook in Federal India*, Delhi, 1933.
——— *Financial Developments in Modern India, 1860-1924*, Bombay, 1925.
——— Vakil, C.N. and M.C. Munshi, *Industrial Policy in India*, Bombay, 1934.
——— *Industrial Policy of India*, with special reference to custom tariff, Calcutta, 1934.
Vakil, C.N. and S.K. Muranjan, *Currency and Prices in India*, Bombay, 1927.
Wacha, Dinshaw, *Shells from the Sands of Bombay*, Bombay, 1920.
Wacha, Dinshaw, *Speeches and Writings*, Madras, undated.
Wadia, P.A. and K.T. Merchant, *Our Economic Problem*, Bombay, 1946.
Walround, T., *The Life of Earl af Elgin*, London, 1872.
Wedderburn, *Speeches and Writings*, Madras, 1918.
West, A., *Private Diaries of Sir Algernon West*. London, 1922.
Wolpert, S.A., *A New History of India*, New York, 1977.
———, *Tilak and Gokhale*, California, 1962.
———*Morley and India 1906-1910*, Berkley, 1967.
*Woodburn, Sir John* by his daughter, London, undated.

# INDEX

Achnera, 91
Act of 1835, 1
Act of 1892, 165
Act of 1893, 8
Acworth Committee, 79, 87, 96
Afghan war, 70
Africa, 40
Afridis, 18
Afzal Khan, 166
Agra, 109
Aligarh, 124
Allahabad, 22, 108, 124, 130
Allan, Arthur, 73
Amalner, 94
America, 47, 116
*Ams-i-Hind* (Urdu), 130
Arbuthnot, Sir, 37
Assam, 93, 95, 155
Assam-Bengal Railway, 72, 77, 80, 95-96
Assam-Bihar Railway, 90
Ayerst, C.E., 152
Azimgarh, 92, 109

Bahramghat, 91
Balaghat, 126
Ballia, 92
Banares, 92
Banda, 108, 124
Banerjee, S.N., 125, 167
*Bangawasi, The*, 37, 110, 115
Bank of England, 13
Barbour, David, 2-4, 8
Bareily, 91
Baroda, 90
Barrackpore, 155
Beach, 19
Benares, 153

Bengal, 70, 108-109, 116, 120-21, 127, 131
Bengal Government, 116-117; appeal rejected, 118
Bengal and North Western Railway, 92
Bengal Central Railway, 70, 77
Bengal Chamber of Commerce, 73
Bengal Nagpur Railway, 94
*Bengalee, The*, 125, 167
Berar, 155
Bayley, C.S., 154, 155
Bezwada, 94
Bhadrachalam, 126
Bharucha, Shapurji, 22
Bhatia, B.M., 122
Bhatinda, 89
Bhatni, 92
Bihar, 110, 117
Bijapur, 124
Birtwistle, Thomas, 60
Bisset, Lt. Col., 72, 85
*Blue Book*, 56
Bogra, 93
Bombay, 26, 68, 73, 90, 94, 95, 108-109, 115, 120, 124, 126, 145, 147, 152; Chamber of Commerce, 21, 55, 57, 75, 94; Collector of Customs, 39; export of cotton goods, 41; plague administration, 148; port closed, 147
*Bombay Gazette, The*, 115
Bombay Millowners' Association, 55
Bose, B.K., 134
Bourdillion, 116
Brackenbury, George, 37, 45, 49
Bruce, Duff, 72, 73

Brussels Conference, 3
Bullandshahar, 124
Bundelkhand famine, 128
Bunner, 18
Burma, 34, 47-48, 109, 127, 155, 164

Calcutta, 73, 89, 94-95, 110, 114, 127, 147, 152, 158
Calcutta Bar, 173
Campbell, Sir George, 106
Carnatic, 120
Cawnpore, 91-92, 115
Central India Railway, 90
Central Provinces, 94, 108, 111-112, 124, 126, 132, 134, 155
Chalmers, Lord, 171-173
*Charu Mihir, The*, 114
Chattisgarh, 94
Chenab, 89
China, 25
Chirol, Valentine, 59
Chitnavis, Gangadhar Rao Madhava, 36
Chitpur, 152
Chitpur riots, 154
Chitral crisis, 85
Cleghorn, 146-147, 151
Cole, G.D.H., 58
Collen, 150
Colvin, C.S., 73, 84, 92
Conservative, 35, 60; back to power, 49
Coorge, 109
Cotton, 169, 171
Cotton Duties Act, 57-58
Cotton Duties Bill, 45
Courtney, L., 5
Criminal Law, 156
Criminal Procedure Code, 167-169, 171-172, 174
Cromer, Lord, 36
Cross, Lord, 7, 49, 90
Crosthwaite, C.H.T., 78-79, 91, 119, 161
Currency Committee, 5-6
Currency policy; 9-18
Currency question, 18

Currency Reserves, 13
Currie, 6
Cuttack, 94

Daccan, 94, 120, 132
Dhar, Bishnu Narayan, 161
Dalhousie, Lord, 68, 95, 97
Damoh, 132
Darhanga, 124
Delhi-Kalka Railway, 77
Delhi-Samasata Railway, 89
Dhanti, 94
Drain theory, 135
Dutt, R.C., 8, 135

East India Company, 1, 43, 106; board of control, 43
East India Railway, 17, 92
*Economist, The*, 22
Elgin, Lord, 1, 12, 23, 68, 96, 108, 111, 135; currency policy, 9, 11-14, 16-18, 20-22; Viceroyality of, 11, 44, 59, 68, 96; bimetallism, 17; gold standard, 18; comes to India, 34; on import duty, 34; pleads with Fowler, 35; cotton duties, 37-39, 43, 48-52; subservient to White Hall, 45, 165; railway expansion, 68, 72-88, 96-97; railway conference, 81, 97; famine policy, 109, 111, 117, 120-121, 125, 127-136; policy criticised, 110-111, 114-116, 119, 122-125, 130; policy of non-intervention, 117, 122, 126-127; plague measures, 145, 151, 176; native press, 155, 160-161; Hindu-Muslim issue, 161-162; Indian Penal Code amendment of, 168, 173; sedition law, 174
England, 4, 17, 60, 72; economic interests of, 33, 59; import of goods from, 42; exporters in, 54; industrial monopoly, 58; railways in, 78, 86; industrial revolution in, 58
*Englishman, The*, 152

# Index

Europe, 4, 9
Evans, G., 45, 173
Exchange Banks, 15
Exchange Compensation Allowance, 8

Famine Commission, 70, 107, 115, 123, 130, 132-133
Famine Insurance Grant, 39
Famine policy, 145
Filgate, Col., 77
Finlay, J., 12-13
Fitzpatrick, 164
Fowler, Sir Henry, 9, 36, 38; Commission, 19, 22-24; cotton duties, 43-44, 47; defends excise duty, 47-48; Lancashire deputation, 48-49; writes to Elgin, 48; expansion of railway, 72, 74, 76, 85, 92
France, 16-18

Ganjan, 132
Gatae, 149
*Gazette of India*, 117
Gazipur, 92
Giffen, R., 22
Gladstone, 36, 160
Godavari, 124, 126
Godley, Arthur, 35, 38, 43, 49-51, 92, 119, 165, 170
Gogra Ganges Doab, 91-92
Gokhale, 24
Goschen, G.J., 47
Great Indian Peninsula Railway, 69
Greeco-Turkish war, 152
Griffith, 45

Haj, 176; pilgrimage, 147-148; muslim reaction, 151, 155
Hajipur, 92
Hamilton, Lord George, 11, 13-14, 22, 92; interest in bimetallism, 16; on gold standard, 15, 19-20; influence on Elgin, 17; on cotton duty, 47, 49-52; endorses guarantee policy, 77; tribute to Elgin, 82; famine policy, 111, 113-114, 118-119; expansion of railways, 75, 80, 83; plague and sedition, 147-149, 153, 157, 158, 162; native press, 157, 173; Indian Penal Code amendment of, 168, 173

Hamirpur, 108
Hanham, H.J., 60
Hardie, R., 92, 119, 121
Havelock, 132, 169
*Hindustan (Hindi)*, 130
Hindu Muslim riots, 161
Himmat Khan, 154
Hindus, 149, 153, 160, 162, 167
Hissar, 124
*Hitavadi, The*, 151
Holderness, T.W., 123
Hong Kong, 149
Herschell, Lord, 4; Committee, 5-6, 8, 24; appointment, 4; report, 5, 10; import duty, imposition of, 34
*Hitavedi, The*, 111
Hoffman, 58
Home Charges, 2, 7, 9, 14, 26
Howrah, 94
Hydaman, 114

Ibbetson, Denzil, 136
Id festival, 162
Incheape, Lord, 3
India, 11, 17, 21, 47, 72, 74, 80; gold shipment to, 19; competition with Lancashire, 42
Indian Charitable Fund, 131
Indian Currency Association, 3, 10, 22
Indian export trade, 10
Indian Medical Service, 146, 175
Indian Millowners' Association, 39, 55, 57
Indian National Congress, 8, 21, 22, 26, 114, 116, 125, 163, 167
Indian Penal Code, 166, 169, 171-172, 174
*Indian Spectator, The*, 114
India Office, 35, 42, 73, 76, 86
Indus, 89

International Monetary Conference, 3
Jalaun, 108
Jalgaon, 94
Jamalpur, 93
James, Sir Henry, 47, 49
Jammu, 89
Japan, 25, 26, 40-41
Jhansi, 108
Jindh, 89
Jubbulpur, 124, 132
Jullundur, 124

Kalinganj, 93
Kalyan, 68
Karachi, 89-90, 95, 146, 150
Kathiawar Railway, 90, 92
Katri, 84
*Kesari*, 166
Khanewal, 88-89
Khyber, 96; pass, 18
Kimberley, 3, 7, 10, 34-35, 39
Knox, John, 47
Kosi, 92
Kotri, 89
Kumaon, 70

Lahore, 152
Laing, Samuel, 46
Lancashire, 35, 39, 47-48; deputation to Fowler, 47-50; cotton duty question, 49-58
Lansdowne, Lord, 1, 3-4, 7-8; Council, 2; correspondence of, 6
Law, Jay, Govind, 22
Lawrence, 69
Liberal, 35, 49, 60
Lombard Street, 3, 13
London, 9, 13, 19-20, 60, 74, 80; Chamber of Commerce, 72-73
Lord, George, 51
Lawson, 149-151
Lucknow, 91
Lucknow and Bareily Railway, 90
Lyall, A.G., 37, 92, 112, 165
Lyall, C.J., 133, 156
Lyall, J.B., 134, 164
Lyallpur, 89-90

Lytton, Lord, 33-34, 46, 115, 135; Press Act, 151-157

McDonagh, 60
MacDonnell, A.P., 22-24, 26, 111-113, 117, 125, 130, 147, 154-156, 162, 169, 175
Mackay, J.L., 3; report, 79; Committee, 86
Mackenzie, 108, 110, 113, 119, 150, 173
Madras, 94-95, 109, 120, 147, 155, 157
Maharaja of Dharbanga, 36
*Mahratha*, 8
Malabari, B.M., 145
Mandla, 126
Manchester, 33-35, 37-39, 41, 43; Chamber of Commerce, 6, 43; monopoly, 39; exports to China, 40; excise duty, 47; Cotton duty question, 49, 52, 56, 59
Malabar, 124
Mandalay Kunlon railway, 95-96
Marriot, E.F., 20
Mary Queen of Scots, 47
Mathura-Nagda railway, 85
Mehta, Phirozeshah, 45, 163
Mhow, 109
Midnapur, 94
Mill, J.S., 36
Miller, 43
Mohmands, 18
Monghair, 124
Mowbray, R.G.C., 47
Multan, 89
Muslims, 149, 153, 160, 162
Mutiny, 153
Muzaffarnagar, 109
Mymensingh, 93
Mysore, 109, 152

Nagpur, 109, 124, 134
Nandurbar, 94
Naoroji, Dadabhai, 8, 21-23, 25, 114, 135
Nepal, 93-94
Nizam of Hyderabad, 163

*Index* 215

Northbrook, Lord, 33, 106, 110, 115, 135; on cotton duty, 51-52; famine policy of, 126-127
North Western Frontier, 18, 135
North Western Provinces and Oudh, 22, 108-109, 111, 113, 120-121, 127-128, 130-131, 147, 151, 161-162
North West Railway, 88-89

O'Callaghan, 85, 91
O'Conor, J.E., 9, 22-24, 117
Oldham, 60
Ollivant, K.C., 154, 162
Oudh, 22, 90, 127
Oudh and Rohilkhand State Railway, 91

Panch Mahal, 124
Pen-Islam movement, 152, 155
Parsi, 167
Partabgunj, 93
Patna, 92, 116, 124, 127
Paul, Sir C., 173
Persia, 116
Peshawar, 18, 154
Piele, J., 60
*Pioneer, The*, 152, 156, 173
Plague, 145; riots, 150, 152; rules, 156; measures, 162; Commissioner, 176
Playfair, 36, 45
Plowden, T.J.C., 163
Poona, 124, 126, 150, 152-154, 159; Sarvajanak, Sabha, 116; riots, 156, 166
Press Act, 154
Press Legislation, 171
Princep, H.T., 173
Privy Council, 166-167
Pritchard, Charles, 36, 43, 74, 85, 91
Punjab, 37, 89, 109, 120, 124, 152, 164

Quetta, 89

Rachna Doab, 89, 95

Raipur, 94, 124
Rajjim, 94
Rajputana, 90, 92
Rajputana Malwa Railway, 90
Ram Charan Dass, 22
Rand, W.C., 152, 154, 158, 166
Reade, 149
Reay, Lord, 86
Ripon, Lord, 34, 110, 160
Rivaz, 173, 175
Robertson, Thomas, 79
Rohilkhand, 70, 90
Rohilkhand-Kumaon Railway, 90-91
Rohri, 90
Rohri-Kotri line, 89, 95
Rohtak, 89
Ross, Captain, 152
Roy, Mohiney Mohan, 45
Ruksaul, 93-94
Rungpore, 93
Russia, 116

*St. James Gazette*, 152
Salisbury, Lord, 18, 33, 49, 148
Sandhurst, 148, 150, 154, 164, 174
Samasata, 89
Sambalpur, 124
Sauger, 94, 132
Sauger-Katni railway, 109
Sayani, 116
Scotland, 60
Sedition, 157, 166; laws, 154; trials, 167
Segowali, 93
Shahabad, 127
Shakurpur, 124
Shivaji, 166
Simla, 157
Sini, 94
Smith, Babington, 16, 111
Soron, 91
Southern Mahretha railways, 70, 77
South Punjab Railway, 75, 89
Stevens, 36, 45, 155, 169
Strachey, H., 79
Strachey, J., 92
Subhankhali, 93

Sultanpur, 93
Surat, 94
Swat tribes, 18

Tariff Act, 57
Tariff Bill, 36-37, 45
Tagore, Jotendra Mohan, 154-155
Tilak, B.G., 167
*Times, The*, 21, 47, 113, 152-153
*Times of India, The*, 152
Tirhoot State Railway, 70, 77, 90, 93
Tochi, 18, 154
Tohana, 89
Trevor, A.C., 86, 172
Turkey, 155

United States, 16-18
Upper Burma, 8

Vernacular, Press Act, 156, 158
Viceroy, 8, 43-45, 48; proposal to Kimberley, 34; Legislative Council, 44-45; position of, 44; Executive Council, 84
Victoria, Queen, 43-44, 119, 152, 161

Vishram, Fazul Bhai, 45
Vizagapatam, 132
*Voice of India, The*, 114

Wacha, D.E., 8, 21, 135
Wales, 60
Waterfield, 84
Wazirabad, 88-89
Waziris revolt, 18
Wedderburn, 114
Weodhurn, John, 147
Western Railway Company, 92
Western State Railway, 89
Westland, J., 12-17, 21, 26, 37, 45-46, 74, 77, 91, 160, 172; on gold standard, 20; visits Bombay, 39; on import duty, 42; cotton duties, 49-57; statement in *Blue Book*, 53; Tariff Bill, 56; guarantee policy, 77-78; railway expenditure, 83, 84; apposes Bengal Government, 117
Wilson, 36, 170
Woodburn, John, 111-113, 164, 168, 169, 175

Young, Mackworth, 154, 156, 164, 169, 175

**LIBRARY OF DAVIDSON COLLEGE**